Mary Ellen's Giant Book of Helpful Hints

Three Books in One

Mary Ellen's Giant Book of Helpful Hints

Three Books in One

Mary Ellen's Best of Helpful Hints
by Mary Ellen Pinkham and Pearl Higginbotham

**Mary Ellen's Best of Helpful Hints
Book II**
by Mary Ellen Pinkham

**Mary Ellen's
Best of Helpful Kitchen Hints**
by Mary Ellen Pinkham

Illustrated by Lynn Johnston

WINGS BOOKS
New York

This omnibus was originally published in separate volumes under the titles:

Mary Ellen's Best of Helpful Hints, copyright © 1976 by Mary Ellen Enterprises; revised edition copyright © 1979 by Pearl Higginbotham and Mary Ellen Pinkham

Mary Ellen's Best of Helpful Hints Book II, copyright © 1981 by Mary Ellen Enterprises

Mary Ellen's Best of Helpful Kitchen Hints, copyright © 1980 by Mary Ellen Enterprises

This 1994 edition is published by Wings Books, a division of Random House Value Publishing, Inc., 201 East 50th Street, New York, New York, 10022, by arrangement with the author.

Wings Books and colophon are trademarks of Random House Value Publishing, Inc.

Random House
New York • Toronto • London • Sydney • Auckland
http://www.randomhouse.com/

Printed and bound in the United States of America

Library of Congress Cataloging-in-Publication Data

Pinkham, Mary Ellen.
    [Giant book of helpful hints]
    Mary Ellen's giant book of helpful hints ; three books in one.
        p.   cm.
    Includes index.
    Contents: [1]. Mary Ellen's best of helpful hints—[2]. Mary
Ellen's best of helpful hints book II—[3]. Mary Ellen's best of
helpful kitchen hints.
    ISBN 0-517-10179-3
1. Home economics.   2. Cookery.   I. Pinkham, Mary Ellen. Best of helpful hints.
1979 II. Pinkham, Mary Ellen. Best of helpful hints. Book 2. 1981   III. Pinkham,
Mary Ellen. Best of helpful kitchen hints. 1980.   IV. Title
TX158.P583   1994
640—dc20   93–38935
                                                                                  CIP

10 9 8 7 6 5

Contents

Mary Ellen's Best of Helpful Hints

by
Mary Ellen Pinkham
and
Pearl Higginbotham

Dedication

*This book is dedicated to our many
friends who made this collection
of helpful hints possible.*

Acknowledgements

The authors wish to express their appreciation
to Courage Center Auxiliary, Southwest Lioness Club,
Sheila "Mouse" Doar, Irene Rice, Wilbur Toll,
June Mattson, Metro Marketing, Gen Bolger,
Bruce Lansky and Associates.

You've all played a big part in making
The Best of Helpful Hints
a bestseller.

Contents

Introduction

If you've heard a lot of "helpful hints" but can't remember them when you've got red wine all over your best tablecloth or stains on the new carpet, then this book was designed for you. We've organized them into convenient categories for quick reference when you really need them.

Our hints are easy to use and employ items usually found in most kitchen cupboards or on workshop shelves. Others use items readily available from your neighborhood drug or hardware store. Few require expensive commercial cleaning products.

That's not to imply, of course, that our hints are restricted to cleaning. Valuable tips on plant care, beauty aids, childraising, cooking and many more are included. In short, anything to make your life a bit easier and a bit more fun.

We've even supplied a few blank pages at the end so you can write down the next helpful hint that sounds good to you and add to what might well be your most useful and most used reference book.

The Best
of Hints for
the Kitchen

Oops!
When Something
Goes Wrong

Too salty
- For soup and stew, add cut raw potatoes and discard once they have cooked and absorbed the salt.
- Another remedy for salty soup and stew is to add a teaspoon each of cider vinegar and sugar.
- Or, simply add sugar.

Too sweet
- Add salt.
- If it's a main dish or vegetable, add a teaspoon of cider vinegar.

Pale gravy
- Color with a few drops of Kitchen Bouquet (available at grocery stores).
- To avoid the problem in the first place, brown the flour well before adding the liquid. This also helps prevent lumpy gravy.
- A different way of browning flour is to put some flour into a custard cup and place beside meat in the oven. Once the meat is done the flour will be nice and brown, ready to make a rich, brown gravy.

Thin gravy
- Mix water and flour or cornstarch into a smooth paste. Add gradually, stirring constantly, and bring to a boil.
- Try instant potato flakes instead of flour.

Gravy—smooth as silk

- Keep a jar with a mixture of equal parts of flour and cornstarch. Put 3 or 4 tablespoons of this mixture in another jar and add some water. Shake, and in a few minutes you will have a smooth paste for gravy.

Greasy gravy

- Add a small amount of baking soda if it is quite greasy.
- See Removing the Excess Fat, Kitchen Hints.

Wilted vegetables

- If fresh vegetables are wilted or blemished, pick off the brown edges. Sprinkle with cool water, wrap in towel and refrigerate for an hour or so.
- Perk up soggy lettuce by adding lemon juice to a bowl of cold water and soak for an hour in the refrigerator.
- Douse quickly in hot and then ice water with a little apple cider vinegar added.
- Lettuce and celery will crisp up fast if you place it in a pan of cold water and add a few raw sliced potatoes.

Cream that will not whip

- Chill cream, bowl and beater well.
- Set bowl of cream into a bowl of ice while you're whipping.
- Add the white of an egg. Chill and then whip.
- If the cream still does not stiffen, gradually whip in 3 or 4 drops of lemon juice.
- Cream whipped ahead of time will not separate if you add a touch of unflavored gelatin (¼ teaspoon per cup of cream).
- To eliminate a lot of mess when whipping cream with an electric beater, try this: Cut 2 small holes in the middle of a piece of waxed paper, then slip the stems of the beaters through the holes and attach the beaters to the machine. Simply place paper and beaters over the bowl and whip away.

Soggy mashed potatoes

- Overcooked potatoes can become soggy when the milk is added. Sprinkle with dry powdered milk for the fluffiest mashed potatoes ever.

Soggy potato chips, cereal and crackers
- If potato chips lose their freshness, place under the broiler for a few moments. Care must be taken not to brown them.
- You can crisp soggy cereal and crackers by putting them on a cookie sheet and heating for a few minutes in the oven.

Brown sugar "hard as a rock"
- If you need it in a hurry, simply grate the amount called for with a hand grater.
- Soften by placing a slice of soft bread in the package and closing tightly. In a couple hours the brown sugar will be soft again.
- Put brown sugar and a cup of water (do not add to the sugar, set it alongside of it) in a covered pan. Place in the oven (low heat) for a while.
- Or, buy liquid brown sugar.

Frozen bread loaves and rolls
- Place in brown paper bag and put in 325-degree oven for 5 minutes to thaw completely.

To keep the salt shaking
- Wrap a small piece of aluminum foil tightly around the shaker. The foil is moisture proof and it will keep dampness out of the salt.
- To prevent clogging, keep 5 to 10 grains of rice inside your shaker.

Hurry Ups
getting it done in the
shortest time
possible

Baked potatoes in a hurry
- Boil them in salted water for about 10 minutes before popping into a very hot oven.
- Cut a thin slice from each end before popping into the oven.
- Insert a nail to shorten the baking time by 15 minutes.

Chopping onions without tears
- You'll shed less tears if you cut the root end of the onion off last.
- Freeze or refrigerate before chopping.
- Peel under cold running water.
- Or, periodically rinse hands under cold water while chopping.

Peeling thin-skinned fruit
- Refrigerate tomatoes. Hold tomato firmly and scrape with a paring knife from the bottom to the top several times. Prick the skin with the point of the knife. The peeling will remove easily.
- Place thin-skinned fruits into a bowl, cover with boiling water and let set for 1 minute. Peel with a paring knife.
- Or, spear the fruit on a fork and hold over a gas flame until the skin cracks, then peel.

Ripe ideas
- Instead of using a fruit ripening bowl, place green fruits in a perforated plastic bag. The holes allow air movement, yet retain the odorless ethylene gas which fruits produce to promote ripening.
- Exposure to direct sunlight softens tomatoes instead of ripening them. Leave the tomatoes, stem-up, in any spot where they will be out of direct sunlight.
- Ripen green bananas or green tomatoes by wrapping them in a wet dish towel and placing them in a paper sack.
- Bury avocados in a bowl of flour.

Removing the excess fat

- If time allows, the best method is refrigeration until the fat hardens on the top.
- Eliminate fat from soup and stew by dropping ice cubes into the pot. As you stir, the fat will cling to the cubes. Discard the cubes before they melt. Or, wrap ice cubes in a piece of cheesecloth or paper towel and skim over the top.
- Lettuce leaves absorb fat also. Place a few into the pot and watch the fat cling to them.
- If you prop up one leg of your electric fry pan (set it on a knife handle) you can make relatively grease free hamburgers or bacon by frying on the elevated side of the pan.
- When broiling meats on a rack, place a piece of bread in the broiler pan to soak up the dripping fat. This not only eliminates smoking fat, but reduces the chances of the fat catching fire.

Eliminating the spattering and sticking

- When pan frying or sauteing, always heat your pan before adding the butter or oil. Not even eggs stick with this method.

- Sprinkle a little salt into the frying pan to prevent spattering.
- Vinegar brought to a boil in a new frying pan will prevent foods from sticking.
- When frying, turn a metal colander upside down over the skillet. This allows steam to escape, but keeps the fat from spattering.
- Meat loaf will not stick if you place a slice of bacon on the bottom of the pan.
- If muffins are sticking to the tin pan, place the hot pan on a wet towel. They will slide right out.

Non-smoke broiling
- Add a cup of water to the bottom portion of the broiling pan before sliding into the oven. The water absorbs smoke and grease.

Vanishing unpleasant cooking odors
- While cooking vegetables that give off unpleasant odors, simmer a small pan of vinegar on top of the stove.
- Or, add vinegar to the cooking water.
- Add a few teaspoons of sugar and cinnamon to an empty pie tin and slowly burn over the stove. Your family will think you have been baking all day.

Tenderizing meat
- *Boiled meat:* Add a tablespoon of vinegar to the cooking water.
- *Tough meat or game:* Make a marinade of equal parts cooking vinegar and heated bouillon. Marinade for two hours.
- *Steak:* Simply rub in a mixture of cooking vinegar and oil. Allow to stand for 2 hours.
- And if you want to stew an old hen, soak it in vinegar for several hours before cooking. It will taste like a spring chicken!

Don't "clam up"
- Clams and oysters will be simple to open if washed with cold water, then placed in a plastic bag and put in the freezer for an hour.

Preventing boil-overs
- Add a lump of butter or a few teaspoons of cooking oil to the water. Rice, noodles or spaghetti will not boil over or stick together.

Preventing skin on sauces and jellies
- Spread a thin layer of melted butter or cream over jellies, puddings and other sauces right after cooking. Stir and all the skin and foam will disappear.

Preparing cut fruit ahead of time
- Toss the freshly cut fruit in lemon juice and it will not darken. The juice of half a lemon is enough for a quart or two of cut fruits.
- Or, cover with 1 cup syrup made of equal parts of water and sugar cooked until syrupy.

Softening butter
- Grating a stick of butter softens it quickly.
- Soften for spreading by inverting a small heated pan over the butter dish for a while.

Measuring sticky liquids
- Before measuring honey or other syrup, oil the cup with cooking oil and rinse in hot water.

Instant white sauce
- Blend together 1 cup soft butter and 1 cup flour. Spread in an ice cube tray, chill well, cut into 16 cubes before storing in a plastic bag in the freezer. For medium-thick sauce, drop 1 cube into 1 cup of milk and heat slowly, stirring as it thickens.

Getting the catsup out of the bottle
- Insert a drinking straw, push it to the bottom of the bottle, and then remove. Enough air will be admitted to start an even flow.

Unmolding gelatin
- Rinse the mold pan in cold water and then coat with salad oil. Your mold will drop out easily and will have an appealing luster.

Hamburgers in a hurry
- Poke a hole in their centers when shaping. The center will cook quickly and when the hamburgers are done, the holes are gone.

Shrinkless sausage
- Sausages will shrink less and not break at all if they are boiled about 8 minutes before being fried.
- Or, you can roll them lightly in flour before frying.

Removing the corn silk
- Dampen a paper towel or terry cloth and brush downward on the cob of corn. Every strand should come off.

Cutting sticky foods
- Before chopping, flour the pieces in a paper bag.
- Or, dip your shears or knife in hot water while cutting.

What a ham!
- Ridding the ham of the rind: Slit the rind lengthwise on the underside before placing it in the roasting pan. As the ham bakes, the rind will pull away and can be removed easily without lifting the ham.

A good cup of coffee
- One pinch of salt in the basket will remove some of the acid taste. For clear coffee, put egg shells in after perking. And remember, always start with cold water.

Your own mini "Mr. Coffee"
- Put a teaspoon of "drip" coffee into a small strainer (2½ inch diameter) and place in a cup. Pour boiling water over grounds until cup is full. Let steep to desired strength. It's not a bad idea to place mini coffee filters (make your own) in the strainer before adding coffee.

Two "flavorite" hints
- A different flavoring for tea: Instead of using sugar, dissolve old-fashioned lemon drops or hard mint candy in your tea. They melt quickly and keep the tea clean and brisk.
- Iced tea: Add a small amount of very hot water to instant tea before adding cold water. The crystals will dissolve completely for better flavor.

Some "nutty ideas" for shelling

Shelling Brazil nuts
- Bake at 350 degrees for 15 minutes, or freeze. Crack and shell.

Shelling chestnuts
- Cut a slit in the flat side of each nut; cover with water; boil for 10 minutes. Use a paring knife to peel off shell, then membrane.

Shelling walnuts
- If it's important to get the walnut meat out whole, soak overnight in salt water before cracking gently.

Opening coconuts

● Puncture the eyes with an ice pick and drain out the coconut milk. Place the coconut in a shallow pan and bake at 350 degrees for 45 minutes to 1 hour, until the shell begins to crack. Cool it enough to handle, then tap it smartly with a hammer. The shell will almost spring apart. Pry out the meat with a knife.

Shredding coconuts

● Peel off brown skin with a swivel-bladed peeler or paring knife. Place pieces of coconut in blender with some of the coconut milk (or the liquid called for in the recipe). Process until fine; pour out and continue with the remaining coconut. This short-shredded coconut is suitable for use in pie fillings, batters and fruit desserts.

How to prepare a hard-boiled egg

- Don't laugh, there is more to it than you think. Place eggs in a pan, cover with cold water and pour in some vinegar or salt. The vinegar will keep the eggs from oozing out if the shells crack while cooking. Bring to a boil and remove from heat. Let set in covered pan for 15 minutes. Drain off hot water. Now shake the pan back and forth, causing the eggs to crack against the side. Cool with cold water and peel.

Here are some more "eggscellent" hints

- To determine whether an egg is fresh without breaking the shell, immerse the egg in a pan of cool salted water. If it sinks to the bottom, it is fresh. If it rises to the surface, throw it away.
- Fresh eggs are rough and chalky in appearance. Old eggs are smooth and shiny.
- To determine whether an egg is hard-boiled, spin it. If it spins round and round, it is hard-boiled. If it wobbles and will not spin, it is raw.
- Pierce the end of an egg with a pin, and it will not break when placed in boiling water.
- A few drops of vinegar will keep poached eggs from running all over the pan.

- Eggs beat up fluffier when not too cold. They should be at cool room temperature for best results.
- By adding vinegar to the water, you can boil cracked eggs without having the white run out of the shell.
- When eggs are stuck to the carton, just wet the box and the eggs can be easily removed without cracking the shells.
- Beaten egg whites will be more stable if you add 1 teaspoon cream of tartar to each cup of egg whites (7 or 8 eggs).
- A small funnel is handy for separating egg whites from yolks. Open the egg over the funnel and the white will run through and the yolk will remain.
- For baking, it's best to use medium to large eggs. Extra large eggs may cause cakes to fall when cooled.
- Brown and white shelled eggs are of the same quality.
- Egg shells can be removed easily from hot hard boiled eggs if they are quickly rinsed in cold water first.
- To keep egg yolks fresh for several days cover them with cold water and store in the refrigerator.
- Egg whites can be kept frozen up to 1 year. Add them to a plastic container as you "collect them" for use in meringues, angelfood cake...1 cup equals 7 or 8 egg whites. You can also refreeze defrosted egg whites.
- For fluffier omelets, add a pinch of cornstarch before beating.

Cleanups—
for "all around" the
kitchen

Appliances

- To rid yellowing from white appliances try this: Mix together: ½ cup bleach, ¼ cup baking soda and 4 cups warm water. Apply with a sponge and let set for 10 minutes. Rinse and dry thoroughly.
- Instead of using commercial waxes, shine with rubbing alcohol.
- For quick clean-ups, rub with equal parts water and household ammonia.
- Or, try club soda. It cleans and polishes at the same time.

Blender

- Fill part way with hot water and add a drop of detergent. Cover and turn it on for a few seconds. Rinse and drain dry.

Breadboards

- To rid cutting board of onion, garlic or fish smell, cut a lime or lemon in two and rub the surface with the cut side of the fruit.
- Or, make a paste of baking soda and water and apply generously. Rinse.

Broiler pan

- Sprinkle the hot pan heavily with dry laundry detergent. Cover with a dampened paper towel and let the burned food set for a while. The pan should require little scouring.

Can opener

- Loosen grime by brushing with an old toothbrush. To thoroughly clean blades, run a paper towel through the cutting process.

Cast iron skillets

- Clean the *outside* of the pan with commercial oven cleaner. Let set for 2 hours and the accumulated black stains can be removed with vinegar and water.

- After cleaning pan, take a piece of waxed paper and while skillet is still warm, wipe around the inside to prevent rusting.
- Or, when clean rub a small amount of oil on the inside of the pan to keep it seasoned.
- Did you know? Cooking in cast iron definitely boosts iron intake. Soup simmered for a few hours in an iron pot has almost thirty times more iron than soup cooked in another pan.

Copper pots

- Fill a spray bottle with vinegar and add 3 tablespoons of salt. Spray solution liberally on copper pot. Let set for a while, then simply rub clean.
- Dip lemon halves in salt and rub.
- Or, rub with Worcestershire sauce or catsup. The tarnish will disappear.

Burnt and scorched pans

- Sprinkle burnt pots liberally with baking soda, adding just enough water to moisten. Let stand for several hours. You can generally lift the burned portion right out of the pan.
- Stubborn stains on non-stick cookware can be removed by boiling 2 tablespoons of baking soda, ½ cup vinegar and 1 cup water for 10 minutes. Re-season pan with salad oil.
- Always place a jar lid or marbles in the bottom part of your double boiler. The rattling sound will signal if the water has boiled away.
- See Broiler pan, Kitchen Hints.

Dishes

- Save time and money by using the cheapest brand of dishwashing detergent available, but add a few tablespoons of vinegar to the dishwater. The vinegar will cut the grease and leave your dishes sparkling clean.
- Before washing fine china and crystal, place a towel on the bottom of the sink to act as a cushion.
- To remove coffee or tea stains and cigarette burns from fine china, rub with a damp cloth dipped in baking soda.
- To quickly remove food that is stuck to a casserole dish, fill with boiling water and add 2 tablespoons of baking soda or salt.

Dishwasher film

- Fill dishwasher with all your dirty dishes. However, never put any silver, aluminum or brass in the washer when this method is used or you will have a mess. Put a bowl in the bottom of the dishwasher. Pour 1 cup of household bleach into the bowl. Run through washing cycle but do not dry. This is important. Fill bowl again with 1 cup white vinegar and let the dishwasher go through entire cycle. This will remove all film not only from your glasses but from your dishwasher too.

Drains

- When a drain is clogged with grease, pour a cup of salt and a cup of baking soda into the drain followed by a kettle of boiling water. The grease will usually dissolve immediately and open the drain.
- Coffee grounds are a no-no. They do a nice job of clogging, especially if they get mixed with grease.

Garbage disposal

- Grind a half lemon or orange rinds in the disposal to remove any unpleasant odor.

Glassware

- Never put a delicate glass in hot water bottom side first; it will crack from sudden expansion. The most delicate glassware will be safe if it is slipped in edgewise.
- Vinegar is a must when washing crystal. Rinse in 1 part vinegar to 3 parts warm water. Air dry.

- When one glass is stuck inside another, do not force them apart. Fill the top glass with cold water and dip the lower one in hot water. They will come apart without breaking.
- A small nick in the rim of a glass can be smoothed out by using an emery board.
- Scratches on glassware will disappear if polished with tooth-paste.

Grater
- For a fast and simple clean-up, rub salad oil on the grater before using.
- Use a toothbrush to brush lemon rind, cheese, onion or whatever out of the grater before washing it.

Meat grinder
- Before washing, run a piece of bread through it.

Oven
- Following a spill, sprinkle with salt immediately. When oven is cool brush off burnt food and wipe with a damp sponge.
- Sprinkle bottom of oven with automatic dishwasher soap and cover with wet paper towels. Let stand for a few hours.
- A quick way to clean oven parts is to place a bath towel in the bathtub and pile all removable parts from the oven onto it. Draw enough hot water to just cover the parts and sprinkle a cup of dishwasher soap over it. While you are cleaning the inside of the oven, the rest will be cleaning itself.
- An inexpensive oven cleaner: Set oven on warm for about 20 minutes, then turn off. Place a small dish of full strength ammonia on the top shelf. Put a large pan of boiling water on the bottom shelf and let it set overnight. In the morning, open oven and let it air a while before washing off with soap and water. Even the hard baked-on grease will wash off easily.

Plastic cups, dishes and containers
- Coffee or tea stains can be scoured out with baking soda.
- Or, fill the stained cup with hot water and drop in a few denture cleanser tablets. Let soak for 1 hour.
- To rid foul odors from plastic containers, place crumpled-up newspaper (black and white only) into the container. Cover tightly and leave overnight.

Refrigerator

- To help eliminate odors fill a small bowl with charcoal (the kind used for potted plants) and place it on a shelf in the refrigerator. It absorbs odors rapidly.
- An open box of baking soda will absorb food odors for at least a month or two.
- A little vanilla poured on a piece of cotton and placed in the refrigerator will eliminate odors.
- To prevent mildew from forming, wipe with vinegar. The acid effectively kills the mildew fungus.
- Use a glycerine-soaked cloth to wipe sides and shelves. Future spills wipe up easier. And after the freezer has been defrosted, coat the inside coils with glycerine. The next time you defrost, the ice will loosen quickly and drop off in sheets.

Sinks

- For a sparkling white sink, place paper towels across the bottom of your sink and saturate with household bleach. Let set for ½ hour or so.
- Rub stainless steel sinks with lighter fluid if rust marks appear. After the rust disappears, wipe with your regular kitchen cleaner.
- Use a cloth dampened with rubbing alcohol to remove water spots from stainless steel.
- Spots on stainless steel can also be removed with white vinegar.
- Club soda will shine up stainless steel in a jiffy.
- See Bathroom cleaners, Bathroom Hints

Sponge

- To renew and freshen, soak overnight in salt or baking soda water.
- Wash in dishwasher.

Teakettle

- To remove lime deposits, fill with equal parts vinegar and water. Bring to a boil and allow to stand overnight.

Thermos bottle

- Put a few tablespoons of baking soda in bottle and fill with warm water.

- Or, drop in a few denture cleanser tablets and let soak for an hour or so.

Tin pie pans
- Remove rust by dipping a raw potato in cleaning powder and scouring.

Keeping Food Fresh
and other kitchen goodies

Bacon and sausage
- To prevent bacon from curling, dip the strips in cold water before frying.
- Bacon will lie flat in the pan if you prick it thoroughly with a fork as it fries.
- Keep bacon slices from sticking together; roll the package into a tube shape and secure with rubber bands.
- A quick way to separate frozen bacon: Heat a spatula over the stove burner, then slide it under each slice to separate it from the others.
- Have you ever tried to get roll sausage out of a package, only to find that half of it is stuck to the surrounding paper? Try running cold water over the paper before you remove the contents. Or, let it set in cold ice water for awhile.

Bananas
- Toss freshly peeled bananas in lemon juice and they will not darken.
- Freeze bananas that are on the verge of going bad. They also make delicious popsicles.
- If they've darkened, peel and beat slightly. Put into a plastic container and freeze until it's time to bake bread or cake.

Bread
- A rib of celery in your bread bag will keep the bread fresh for a longer time.
- Freshen dried bread by wrapping in a damp towel and placing it in the refrigerator for 24 hours. Remove towel and heat in oven for a few minutes.

Broccoli

- Broccoli stems can be cooked in the same length of time as the flowers if you make X incisions from top to bottom through stems.

Brown sugar

- Store in plastic bag. Wrap tightly. Place in coffee can with snap-on lid.

Butter

- A butter stretcher: To make 2 pounds of butter, slowly beat in 2 cups of evaporated milk (a little at a time) to 1 pound of butter. Pour into pan and chill.

Cake

- Place ½ apple in the cake box.
- Or, a slice of fresh bread fastened with toothpicks to the cut edge of a cake will keep the cake from drying out and getting stale.

Cheese

- To keep cheese from drying out, wrap in a cloth dampened with vinegar.

Cookies

- Place crushed tissue paper on the bottom of your cookie jar.

Corn

- To keep sweet corn yellow add 1 teaspoon lemon juice to the cooking water, a minute before you remove it from the stove.
- Salted cooking water only toughens corn.

Cottage cheese

- Store carton upside down. It will keep twice as long.

Crackers
- Can be kept crisp in the most humid weather by storing in the refrigerator. Be sure they are wrapped securely.

Cranberries
- Cranberries will grind very neatly when frozen. Wash the berries, pat dry and freeze in plastic bag until ready for use.

Fish and shrimp
- Thaw fish in milk. The milk draws out the frozen taste and provides a fresh-caught flavor.
- Or, try soaking fish in vinegar and water before cooking it for a sweet tender taste.
- The fishy smell can be removed from your hands by washing with vinegar and water or salt and water.
- To get rid of the "canned taste" in canned shrimp, soak them in a little sherry and 2 tablespoons of vinegar for about 15 minutes.

Garlic
- Garlic cloves can be kept in the freezer. When ready to use, peel and chop before thawing.
- Or, garlic cloves will never dry out if you store them in a bottle of cooking oil. After the garlic is used up, you can use the garlic-flavored oil for salad dressing.

Honey
- Put honey in small plastic freezer containers to prevent sugaring. It also thaws out in a short time.
- If it has sugared, simply place the jar in a boiling pot of water.

Ice cream
- Ice cream that has been opened and returned to the freezer sometimes forms a waxlike film on the top. To prevent this, after part of the ice cream has been removed press a piece of waxed paper against the surface and reseal the carton.

Lemons

- Store whole lemons in a tightly sealed jar of water in the refrigerator. They will yield much more juice than when first purchased.
- After you've squeezed a lemon for its juice, wrap and freeze the rind. When a recipe calls for lemon rind, you will not have to grate a fresh lemon.
- Submerging a lemon in hot water for 15 minutes before squeezing will yield almost twice the amount of juice.
- Or, warm them in your oven for a few minutes before squeezing.

Lettuce and celery

- They keep longer if you store them in the refrigerator in paper bags instead of cellophane ones. Do not remove the outside leaves of either until ready to use.
- Lettuce will not rust as quickly if you place a paper towel or napkin in the storage container.
- Line the bottom of the vegetable compartment with paper toweling. This absorbs the excess moisture and keeps all vegetables and fruits fresher for a longer period of time.
- Or, put a few dry sponges in the vegetable compartment to absorb moisture.

Marshmallows

- They will not dry out if stored in the freezer. Simply cut with scissors when ready to use.

Meat

- When browning any piece of meat, the job will be done more quickly and effectively if the meat is perfectly dry and the fat is very hot.

Olive oil

- You can lengthen the life of olive oil by adding a cube of sugar to the bottle.

Onions

- Once an onion has been cut in half, rub the left-over side with butter and it will keep fresh longer.

Parsley
- Keep fresh and crisp by storing in a wide-mouth jar with a tight lid.
- Parsley can also be frozen.

Too many peeled potatoes
- Cover them with cold water to which a few drops of vinegar have been added. Keep refrigerated and they will last for 3 or 4 days.

Popcorn
- It should always be kept in the freezer. Not only will it stay fresh, but freezing helps eliminate "old maids".
- "Old maids" can also be eliminated by running ice cold water over the kernels before throwing into the popper.

Potatoes
- A leftover baked potato can be rebaked if you dip it in water and bake in a 350-degree oven for about 20 minutes.

Poultry
- After flouring chicken, chill for 1 hour. The coating adheres better during frying.
- For golden brown chicken every time, put a few drops of yellow food coloring in the shortening before it has heated.
- Wear rubber gloves to transfer a turkey from roasting pan to platter.
- Truss the bird with dental floss when grilling. Dental floss does not burn and is very strong.

Salad
- To remove the core from a head of lettuce, hit the core end once against the countertop sharply. The core will then twist out. This method prevents unsightly brown spots which result when you cut into the core end.

- If salad greens are wet and you need them right away, place in a pillow case and spin dry in your washing machine for a few seconds. This hint is especially good to know if you are serving salad to a large crowd.

Salt
- Since most recipes call for both salt and pepper, keep a large shaker filled with a mixture of both. ¾ salt and ¼ pepper is a good combination.

- When to add salt:
      Soups and stews: Add early
      Meats: Sprinkle just before taking off the stove.
      Vegetables: Cook in salted water.

Soup
- Before opening a can of soup, shake well and open it at the bottom end instead of the top. The soup will slide out nicely.

Vegetables
- To restore a fresh flavor to frozen vegetables, pour boiling hot water over them, rinsing away all traces of the frozen water.
- Try cooking in broth for a nice flavor.

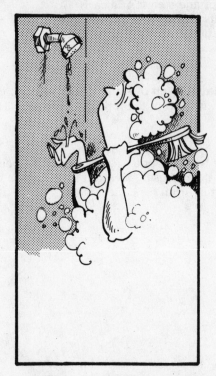

The Best of Hints for the Bathroom

Cleaning the bathtub

- For an extremely stained tub, use a mixture of peroxide and cream of tartar. Make a paste and scrub vigorously with a small brush. Rinse thoroughly.
- If stains persist, spread the above mixture over stains and apply a drop or two of household ammonia. Allow to set for two hours before scrubbing.
- Very old porcelain stains: Shave a bar of naphtha soap into a bucket of hot water and add ½ cup of mineral spirits. Stir to dissolve the soap, then brush on stain vigorously.

More tub and sink cleaners

- Light stains can often be removed by simply rubbing with a cut lemon.
- For dark stains, and especially rust, rub with a paste of borax and lemon juice.
- To brighten up a bathtub which has yellowed, rub with a solution of salt and turpentine.

A sure way to remove bathtub decals

- Soak decals in mineral spirits, then scrape away. Spray down with Fantastik spray cleanser and rub with the abrasive side of a sponge. Now, wax the entire tub, tiles and faucets with Turtle Wax. It will shine like new. Turtle Wax is an excellent cleaner and refinisher.
- Rub in Turtle Wax well with a soft cloth and let stand for a few minutes. Do not let it dry. Polish with a clean cloth or buff with an electric buffer. Your bathroom will gleam.

Clogged shower heads

- If your shower head is clogged, try boiling it in ½ cup vinegar and 1 quart water for 15 minutes.
- For plastic shower heads, soak in equal amounts of hot vinegar and water.

Ceramic tile
- Before you start cleaning the walls or tiles, run your shower a while with the hottest tap water available. Dirt loosened by steam will come off faster.
- For light jobs, wash with a solution of ½ cup ammonia, ½ cup white vinegar, ¼ cup washing soda and 1 gallon warm water.
- For extensive stains, make a paste of baking soda and bleach, then scrub with a small brush. Rinse thoroughly.
- Or, try a product by the name of Crome & Tile Cleaner by Santeen Products (available at hardware stores). It does a fantastic job of cleaning the recessed spaces between tiles.

Heavy shower stall film
- Rub lightly with a plain piece of dry fine steel wool (not the soap filled variety). Try a patch first to be sure it isn't scratching your tile. If it is, you should use a finer piece of steel wool. As you scour the tile, you will see the scum coming right off. Wash down after the job is completed.

Washing shower curtains
- Fill the washing machine with warm water and add 2 large bath towels. Add ½ cup each of detergent and baking soda. Run through entire wash cycle. However, add 1 cup vinegar to the rinse water. Do not spin dry or wash vinegar out. This method will not work without the bath towels. Hang immediately. Wrinkles will disappear after curtain has thoroughly dried.

Removing mildew from shower curtains
- To prevent mildew, soak in a solution of salt water before hanging them for use.
- Use baking soda to remove mildew from small areas.
- For stubborn stains on light colored curtains, wash in above manner, followed by a rub-down with lemon juice.

Two excellent fixture cleaners
- To save time and money while providing the best shine possible to bathroom fixtures, use an old cloth which has been dunked in kerosene. Kerosene removes scum quickly and the odor will only remain for a while.

- Spray fixtures liberally with Spray & Wash laundry soil and stain remover. Rub with cloth for an excellent shine.

Toilet rings
- Flush toilet to wet sides. Apply paste of borax and lemon juice. Let set for 2 hours and then scrub thoroughly.
- Or, rub with a fine grade of sandpaper. If the rings are years old, try wet sandpaper (available at hardware stores).

Glass shower doors
- For a quick shine, rub with a sponge dampened in white vinegar.

What to do with your basic drip
- If the drip occurs during the night and you can't sleep, simply wrap a cloth around the opening of the faucet.
- Or, tie a string to the faucet, long enough to reach the drain. Water will run down the string noiselessly until you have time to fix it.

Sweet smells in the bathroom
- For a nice aroma, place a fabric softener sheet in the wastepaper basket.
- Or, add a touch of fragrance by dabbing your favorite perfume on a lightbulb. When the light is on, the heat releases the aroma.

The Best
of Hints for
Beauty

"Face It"
. . . these are going
to be great hints!

The greatest moisturizer
- Wash face thoroughly. While face is still wet rub in a tiny amount of petroleum jelly. Continue wetting face until the jelly is spread evenly and does not appear greasy. Many expensive health spas use this treatment, but they never reveal their secret. You will be surprised at how soft and smooth your face feels. Remember, it will not stay greasy if you keep adding water a little at a time.

Teach your skin not to be "taut"
- Pour some apple cider vinegar into a basin of warm water and splash your face thoroughly. Let dry without using a towel. If used once a day, this will restore the natural ph-balance or acid mantle to your skin. Acne sufferers should try this also, but be sure to start with a perfectly clean face.
- Instead of splashing the solution on, spray it on your face. The spray bottle is always handy and you'll never forget.

Mineral water splash...fresher makeup
- After your face is thoroughly clean, spray with cold mineral water.
- After you have applied your makeup, spray your face with mineral water or soak tissue in mineral water and lightly dab it all over your face. Your makeup will stay fresh longer than usual.

The fastest way to dry up a blemish
- Dab it with lemon juice a few times a day.

The best deep pore cleanser around
- Bring a quart of water to a boil and take it to a table. Add the juice or peel of half a lemon and a handful of any herbs (rosemary, basil, thyme, mint...). Cover your hair with a shower cap and drape another towel over your head and the pot, holding your face about 12 inches above the water. With closed eyes, let your face steam for 15 minutes. Afterward, rinse with very cold water to close pores.
  Note: Do not use more than once a week or you will deplete your skin of too many natural oils.

A cheap but terrific facial scrub
- Make a paste of oatmeal and water. Apply to face and allow to dry until it feels tight. Rub off with your fingers, using lots of back and forth motion. This scrub sloughs off dead skin, gets rid of blackheads.

Sweeten your complexion with sugar
- Mix a teaspoon of sugar with soap lather and use the same as cleansing grains.

Treat yourself to a hot oil treatment
- For a professional hot oil treatment, saturate hair with olive, sesame or corn oil. Run the hottest water possible over 2 towels in your washing machine. After towels are wet, turn machine to spin cycle. Wrap head in plastic or aluminum foil before applying hot towels. Wait 20 minutes for best results. By using this method, your towels will be hot without the mess of dripping water.

Setting lotion
- A teaspoon of sugar or gelatin dissolved in a cup of warm water makes a handy setting lotion.
- Or, for an extra firm set, use your favorite flavor of Jello. That's right, fully prepared and ready to eat. Use as you would any jellied type of setting lotion.
- Also, try witch hazel or stale beer.

Hair conditioner
- Mayonnaise gives dry hair a good conditioning. Apply ½ cup mayonnaise to dry, unwashed hair. Cover with a plastic bag and wait for 15 minutes. Rinse a few times before shampooing thoroughly.

Final rinse
- For blondes, rinse hair with water containing a few table-spoons of lemon juice. For brunettes and redheads, rinse with water containing several tablespoons of apple cider vinegar. Both will remove soapy film and give the hair a beautiful shine.
- Brunettes and redheads can also rinse their hair with coffee. Do not rinse it out. You will be amazed at how rich and shiny your hair will appear.

Homemade dry shampoo
- If regular shampooing is impossible, make your own dry shampoo by mixing together 1 tablespoon salt and ½ cup cornmeal. Transfer to a large holed salt shaker, sprinkle it on oily hair lightly and brush out dirt and grime.
- Baby powder or cornstarch can also be used as dry shampoos.

A quick hair set
- Instead of using electric rollers every day, try the following tip: Roll hair completely dry and cover with a warm damp towel for a few minutes. Allow hair to dry for a perfect quick set.

Terrific eye cream
- Before retiring, apply castor oil around your eyes. Make sure it is the odorless form. Plastic surgeons use it on their patients following surgery.

Manicure
- Mix 1 cup warm water and juice of ½ lemon. Soak fingertips 5 minutes. Rinse and pat dry, pushing back cuticles. Rub lemon peel against nail, back and forth vigorously. Finish by buffing with a soft cloth.

Quick drying nail polish
- For faster drying nail polish, set hands in a bowl of very cold water when nails are partially dry.
- Or, stick your hands in the freezer.

Non-stick nail polish bottle
- Treat a new bottle of nail polish by rubbing petroleum jelly inside the cover and on the grooves of the bottle. You will never have any trouble opening it, even after months.

You'll never have to throw away nail polish again
- Your nail polish will always be smooth and easy to apply if you store it in the refrigerator. Frosted nail polish will not separate either.
- However, if it has hardened or gotten to the gummy stage, place the bottle in a pan of boiling water. In no time the polish will be good as new.

Longer lasting perfume
- Oily skin holds perfume scents longer than dry skin. So, before applying perfume, rub a very thin layer of Vaseline on your skin and you will smell delicious for hours.

Cucumber for tired eyes
- Place fresh cold cucumbers on your eyelids to rid them of redness and puffiness.

Make your own deodorant—two different ways
- Mix 2 tablespoons alum (available at drug stores) into 1 pint warm water. Stir well. Add a small amount of your favorite cologne or after-shave lotion. Transfer to spray bottle.
- Or, mix 2 teaspoons of baking soda, 2 teaspoons of petroleum jelly and 2 teaspoons of talcum powder. Heat in a double boiler over low heat and stir until smooth cream forms. Put cream in a small container with a tight lid and use as you would regular cream deodorant.

A "berry" good treatment for teeth
- Dip a toothbrush in a mashed strawberry and brush vigorously to remove yellowing and stains.

- Or, brush with plain baking soda until you see the difference.

Mending broken lipstick
- Heat the broken ends over a match until they melt enough to adhere when pressed together. Cool in refrigerator.

Sunburn relievers
- To cool down affected areas, rub with apple cider vinegar.
- Pat with a wet tea bag
- Or, apply a paste of baking soda and water.

The Best of Hints for the Car

Some Hints You "Auto" Try

Washing your car

- Instead of washing your car with soap and water, try washing with a bucket of water and 1 cup kerosene followed by a good wiping with soft cloths. The best part of it is that no matter how dirty your car is it will not need wetting down before starting, nor rinsing once you have finished. When it rains the car will actually bead off water. It helps prevent rust. Use no wax with this method.

Quick cleaning windows

- Baking soda quickly cleans spatters and traffic grime from windshields, headlights, chrome and enamel. Wipe with soda sprinkled onto a damp sponge. Rinse.
- Use plastic net bags (the kind onions come in) to wash windshields when insects have accumulated. Simply tie a few bags into one bag and rub away.

Removing bumper stickers

- Use nail polish remover or lighter fluid. Gently scrape away with a razor blade or knife.

Removing rust spots

- Briskly scrub the rust spots on your bumpers with a piece of foil which has been crumpled or use fine steel wool.
- Use a soap filled steel wool pad.
- Kerosene helps too.

Scratches

- Take a matching color crayon and work into the scratch well.

Tar removers

- Soak tar spots with raw linseed oil. Allow to stand until soft. Then, wipe with a soft cloth which has been dampened with the oil.

- Guess what? Peanut butter has also been known to remove tar.

To remove price tag sheets
- Sponge hot vinegar onto the price sheets liberally. Scrape gently. Continue applying vinegar until sheet is gone.
- Lemon extract works also.
- Or, apply salad oil. Let set for a while and scrape away.

Two parking hints
- On cold days and evenings, back your car into the garage. If needed, your car will be in good position for using jumper cables.
- If you have bumped the front fender of your car into the back wall of your garage, try this: Suspend a small rubber ball on a string from the ceiling of the garage so that when the ball strikes your windshield you will know the car is far enough in to close the garage door.

Ways to identify your car or bike
- Drop a business card or file card with your name and address down the window slot. Just in case you have to prove the car is yours some day.
- To identify a stolen bicycle, even though the serial number may have been filed off, roll the file card around a pencil, remove the bicycle's seatpost and drop the card into the bicycle frame. It can easily be removed as proof of ownership.

Cigarette ashes
- Ashes that continue to burn in the car ashtray are a nuisance. Prevent this by placing an inch of baking soda (or gravel) in the bottom of the tray.

Battery corrosion—proofer
- Scrub battery terminals and holder with a strong solution of baking soda water. Then, smear with petroleum jelly.

Preventing doors and trunk from freezing
- Wipe or spray the rubber gaskets with a heavy coating of vegetable oil. The oil will seal out water, but will not harm the gasket. This is especially good before having your car washed in the winter.

Opening a frozen lock
- Heat the key with a cigarette lighter or match. Never force the key. Turn very gently.

Would you believe, a hair dryer will start your car?
- Before you call the car starting service on cold mornings, remember this: your car will probably start if you blow hot air on the carburetor from a hair dryer. It works... it honestly does.

Salt remover for carpeting
- Combine equal amounts of vinegar and water to remove salt residue left behind from winter.

To eliminate windshield freeze-ups when parked outdoors
- Place your rubber floor mats over the windshields. Secure the mat with windshield wipers. You will save yourself the chore of scraping.

Make your own washer solvent that won't freeze
- Combine 1 quart rubbing alcohol, 1 cup water, 2 tablespoons liquid detergent. This formula is guaranteed not to freeze down to 35 degrees below zero.

Before you get stuck
- Place a bag of kitty litter in your car trunk, just in case you get stuck in the ice or snow. It provides excellent traction.

If you are stuck
- And there is no kitty litter, sand or shovel available, remove the rubber mats from your car and place them in front of the rear wheels. You just might get out all by yourself.

Did you know
- Some experts say that the 1973 models in general are "the world's biggest gas burners"?

The Best of Hints for the Carpet

The first step is the most important!

- The first and most important step for preventing a spill turning into a stain is blotting up as much moisture as you possibly can. Scrape up any solids and blot with lots of clean towels. Begin at the outer edge of the stain and blot toward the center. Do not rub because this will only spread the stain. And do not apply a spot remover until you have done a thorough job of blotting.

Stains be gone

- *For fresh stains:* Plain club soda is an instant spot remover and it is fantastic. Pour a little on the spot, let it set for a few seconds and sponge up thoroughly.
- *For older stains:* Combine 2 tablespoons detergent, 3 tablespoons vinegar and 1 quart of warm water. Work into stain and blot as dry as possible.
- *Tide is the best stain remover for stubborn spots:* Make a sudsy solution of Tide laundry detergent and warm water. Brush the suds into the stain vertically and horizontally with a soft brush. Blot up excess. If the stain persists, repeat process. This works 9¾ times out of 10.

The last step is important too!
- After you've completed one of the above methods, cover the spot with a clean towel and place a heavy book on top of it. When the towel becomes damp replace it with a dry one.

An instant spot remover
- Try shaving cream. Foam is a good spot remover and it is ready instantly. Wash up with water or club soda.

Repairing a burn
- Remove some fuzz from the carpet, either by shaving or pulling out with a tweezer. Roll into the shape of the burn. Apply a good cement glue to the backing of the rug and press the fuzz down into the burned spot. Cover with a piece of cleansing tissue and place a heavy book on top. This will cause the glue to dry very slowly and you will get the best results.

Flattened carpet
- If heavy furniture has flattened the pile of your rugs, raise it with a steam iron. Build up good steam and hold your iron over the damaged spot. Do not touch the carpet with the iron. Brush briskly.

Removing candle wax drippings
- Place a blotter or brown paper bag over the spot and put a hot iron over the blotter. After a few minutes, the wax will be absorbed into the blotter. Repeat if necessary.

Repairing braided rugs
- Braided rugs often rip apart. Instead of sewing them use clear fabric glue to repair. It's that fast and easy.

Spot remover for indoor-outdoor carpeting
- Spray spots liberally with a pre-wash commercial spray. Let it set several minutes, then hose down and watch the spots disappear.

A carpet brightener
- Sprinkle a generous amount of cornstarch on your carpet. Let stand for an hour before vacuuming. You will be amazed at the results.

Before you shampoo

- To prevent rust marks from forming on a wet carpet, put little plastic bags or small glass jars on each furniture leg. This also eliminates the dreadful job of moving furniture from one end of the room to the other.

Who tracked the mud in?

- Sprinkle cornstarch on damp mud spots. Give the cornstarch at least 15 minutes to soak up the mud, then vacuum up and away.

Sooty footmarks

- Try an artgum eraser on light colored carpets.
- Or, sprinkle soiled areas with salt. Wait ½ hour and then vacuum.

Opposites attract

- Ever wanted to be a genius? Then, next time red wine spills on your carpet, remove it with white wine.

Removing chewing gum

- Press ice cubes against the gum until it becomes brittle and breaks off. Then use a spot remover to vanish last traces.

Glue

- Glue can be loosened by saturating the spot with a cloth soaked in vinegar.

Ballpoint ink marks

- Saturate the spot with hairspray. Allow to dry. Brush lightly with a solution of water and vinegar.

The Best
of Hints for
Children

Tips for the newborn

- To allow mother a few extra hours' sleep, use the same perfume freely while at the hospital and when you get home. Later dab your perfume on baby's crib sheets or pillow. He will smell the mama smell and feel safe and content.
- If baby bubbles a bit after feeding and must have his shirt changed frequently to keep him smelling sweet, try this: moisten a cloth with water, dip it in baking soda and dab at the dribbled shirt. The odor will disappear.
- Keep a heating pad (or hot water bottle) beside baby's crib and when he is up for his night feedings, turn the pad on warm and place on the crib mattress. When you put baby back down, his bed will be nice and warm and he will settle down more quickly. Be sure to remove the heating pad.

Making a traveling bed for baby

- If you are traveling with a small baby and do not want to haul a crib, simply use a small, inflatable plastic pool and blow up. Cover with a sheet and secure the ends underneath.

Make your own baby food

- Puree fresh vegetables, place in ice cube trays, and freeze for use at a later date.

Baby bottles

- Place a few agate marbles in the sterilizer or a sauce pan when cleaning bottles. The marbles will gather all the corrosion.
- Save a couple of empty soft drink cartons and use them to hold baby bottles in the refrigerator. The bottles can be easily removed for access to anything stored behind.

A few hints for the sick or hurt child

- If your child has trouble swallowing a pill, place it in a teaspoon of applesauce and see how easily it goes down.
- A penny sucker makes an excellent tongue depressor when checking for a sore throat.
- To remove a splinter from a child's finger, soak the injured part in any cooking oil for a few minutes. The splinter can be easily removed. Also, applying an ice cube to the finger for several minutes will numb the area and allow the splinter to be removed painlessly. Then you can kiss it and make it all better.

- To eliminate the "ouch" when removing adhesive tape from your child's skin, just saturate a piece of cotton with baby oil and rub over the tape. It will come right off without hurting the skin.

Safety tips
- Even adults sometimes walk into closed, sliding glass doors. To help youngsters avoid this hazard, place a piece of colored tape on the glass at eye level to alert the child when the door is closed.
- When your child reaches the creeping stage, tape light cords tightly around a table leg. This will prevent him from pulling lamps onto the floor. If you use transparent tape it will not mar the furniture.
- To protect your child from mashed fingers, place a cork at each end of the keyboard on the piano. Now, if the lid drops, his fingers are saved.
- If your toddler tries to sneak outside when you are not looking, try the old "doorbell" trick. Tie a small bell to the door. You will always be able to hear when the door is being opened.

Baby's first pair of shoes
- For baby's first pair of hard-soled shoes, walking on a hard surface is like walking on ice for an adult. If you glue a very thin strip of foam rubber to the soles of the shoes, the baby will gain confidence when he is walking. When foam rubber is worn, scrape off the remains with a razor blade and apply a new piece.

Teaching how to put shoes on
- To teach a child how to put the right shoe on the right foot, mark or tape the inside of the right shoe only.

Polishing baby shoes
- If the shoes are scuffed badly and do not seem to take the polish, rub them with a piece of raw potato or rubbing alcohol before polishing.
- After polishing, spray with hairspray to prevent polish from coming off so easily.
- Or, apply clear fingernail polish to the spots which scuff most frequently.

Tongue tied
- To prevent the tongues of your child's shoes from sliding out of place, cut two small, parallel slits in each tongue ½ inch from the outside tip. After lacing, pull through the new slots and tie as usual.

A way to save disposable diapers
- If you ruin the adhesive tab on a diaper, simply tape the diaper with masking tape.

Dull diaper pins
- Simply stick the pins into a bar of soap.

Graduating from crib to bed
- Eliminate fears of injury when your child graduates from crib to full size bed by putting the crib mattress on the floor next to the bed. If the child falls out, he'll be startled but not hurt.

Making a door for baby
- Attach an extra handle near the bottom of the screen door. Your child will then be able to pull the door open himself without calling for help.

Bathing
- Use baby's infant seat for bathing in the bathtub. Remove the pad and buckle strap and place a large folded bath towel on the seat and on the bathtub floor (to prevent slipping). Place baby in seat, and run water into tub. Now you can use both hands.
- When a child is past the baby stage, but is too small for the tub, a plastic clothes basket with holes in it is ideal. Run several inches of water into the tub, place the basket in it and set your child in the basket.
- Put small pieces of soap into a white sock and tie up the open end. Children prefer it to a bar of soap and it will not slip from their hands.

When you are out of baby shampoo
- Shampoo will not run into eyes if you put petroleum jelly on baby's eyebrows and eyelids. The soap will run sideways instead of downward.

- Or, put a diving mask on your child. It's fun and he can watch the bubbles run down the mask without getting soap in his eyes. Peek-a-boo, I see you.

Calming the angry child
- Whispering works wonders when a child is angry. Simply whisper gentle words into his ear. He will stop crying so he can hear what you're saying. And, 100% effective on husbands.

Saving your child's artwork and the appearance of your walls
- Give each drawing a good coating of hairspray and it will prevent the colors from fading or wearing off.

- To display his works of art, hang fishnet over one wall. Instead of ruining the wall by taping or tacking, simply pin his artwork to the fishnet with clothespins or pins.

Cleaning stuffed toys
- Clean with dry cornstarch. Rub in, let stand briefly and brush off.

Soak up spills before they happen
- To eliminate messy spills when children are using paint or glue, cut an opening in the center of a sponge and insert the container. The sponge keeps the container from tipping over, and absorbs any overflow.

Eliminating milk spills
- Your child will be able to hold onto a glass of milk better if you place two tight rubber bands around the glass an inch or so apart. This makes it easier for little hands to hold.

Lost and found
- Before leaving for a day at the zoo, fair or circus, tag each child with a stick-on label that gives his name, address and telephone number.

Keeping art supplies fresh
- Wrap new crayons with masking tape and there will be less chance of breaking.
- For fresh, smooth paste, moisten the lid with water before screwing the lid back on.

Ideas "to boot"
- To avoid lost boots, cut two matching shapes of colored tape and stick on the backs of each boot heel. Your child can easily spot them, even in a jumble of 30 pairs at school.
- Putting snow boots on over tennis shoes can be a real struggle. It's simple if you slip plastic bags over the tennis shoes before sliding the boots on.

The growing jacket
- The life of a winter jacket can be lengthened by sewing knitted cuffs (available in notion departments) to the sleeves. Hopefully, your child might make it through another winter in last year's jacket.

Removing gum from hair
- Rub ordinary cold cream into the hair. Pull down on the strands of hair several times with a dry towel.
- Or, rub in a dab of peanut butter. Massage the gum and peanut butter between your fingers until the gum is loosened. Remove with facial tissue.
- Freeze the hair with ice cubes and peel gum off hair.

Mirror, mirror on the wall
- To make your child's grooming chores less complicated, and out of respect for the little one, hang a second mirror at his eye level in the bathroom.

All dressed up and staying that way
- When you want to keep your children looking fresh for those special occasions, spray knees, cuffs and collars with fabric protector. The spills will bead up and wipe off easily to keep mom happy.

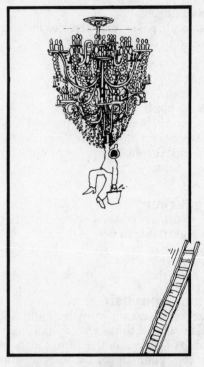

The Best of Hints for Cleaning the Miscellaneous

Artificial flowers
- Pour some salt into a large paper bag with the flowers. Shake vigorously. The salt won't look soiled at first, but wait until you see its color when you run water on it.

Ball point pens
- If your ball point becomes clogged with excessive ink and fuzz, insert it in the filter portion of a cigarette. Just a few quick turns ànd it's ready for use.

Candles
- Sponge with a piece of cotton dampened with rubbing alcohol.
- Did you know? Candles burn more slowly and evenly with minimum wax drippings if you place them in the freezer for an hour before using.

Candle holders
- If your candle holders are coated with wax, place in the freezer for an hour or so. The wax will peel off in a jiffy with absolutely no injury to the silver.
- Or, run under very hot water and dry with a paper towel.

Canvas awnings
- Make old canvas look like new by painting with canvas paint (available at paint stores).
- Eliminate bird droppings with a stiff brush that has been run over a bar of naphtha soap and sprinkled with dry washing soda. Hose well to rinse.

Cigarette smoke
- Soak a towel in water, wring it out thoroughly, and swish it around the room. Smoke will disappear quickly.
- Put small bowls of vinegar in 4 corners of the room where smokers are congregating.
- Or, place activated charcoal in small dishes to remove post-party odors.
- Also, burn candles to eliminate the smoke.

Chandeliers

- Here is a method of cleaning crystal chandeliers which does not require disassembling the fixture. The area underneath the chandelier should be protected by a drop cloth. Fill a water tumbler with 1 part alcohol to 3 parts water. Raise the tumbler to each pendant until it is immersed. The crystal will drip-dry without leaving water spots, lint or finger marks. The crystal parts not accessible to the tumbler can be wiped with the solution.
- Or, wear cotton work gloves and dip your fingers in ammonia water and clean away.

Combs, brushes and curlers

- Add 3 tablespoons baking soda and 3 tablespoons household bleach to a basin of warm water. Swish around, rinse and drip-dry.

Diamonds

- Add some mild white soap flakes and a few drops of ammonia to a pot of boiling water. Place your diamond in a wire strainer and dip it into the boiling water for a few seconds. Let it cool, then rinse. Finally, soak it in a small bowl of alcohol for 10 minutes before drying on a piece of tissue paper.

Draperies

- Before sending the drapes to the cleaners: As you remove the hooks, mark the places where the hooks were inserted with pink nail polish. These dots wil remain through the cleaning process.
- For draperies that hang on particular windows, number the panels, starting from left to right. Use colored thread and mark on the wrong side of the bottom hem. No. 1 panel, 1 long stitch; No. 2 panel, 2 long stitches, etc. Be sure to knot the stitches well so that they will remain throughout the cleaning.

Eyeglasses

- To clean eyeglasses without streaks, use a drop of vinegar or vodka on each lens.

Fireplaces
- There is less need to scrub the fireplace if you throw salt on the logs occasionally. This will reduce the soot by two-thirds.
- Vinegar will clean brick tiling around the fireplace. Dip a vegetable brush in white vinegar and scrub quickly. Immediately sponge to absorb the moisture.
- Rub smoked areas with an artgum eraser. This works especially well on porous, rock front fireplaces.
- For smooth stone or brick fireplaces, wash with a strong solution of trisodium phosphate (½ cup to 1 gallon water). Apply with sponge. Use this solution only after all smoke possible has been erased by an artgum eraser.
- For big jobs: Add 4 ounces of naptha soap to 1 quart of hot water. Heat until soap dissolves. Cool, then stir in ½ pound of powdered pumice and ½ cup of household ammonia. Mix thoroughly. Remove as much of the smoky deposit as you can before applying a coat of the soap mixture with a paint brush. Allow it to remain on for 30 minutes. Scrub with a scrub brush and warm water. Sponge with plenty of water to rinse.

Frames
- Wipe with a soft sponge moistened with turpentine. If the gilt seems a bit sticky after you finish, let dry for a day of two without touching.

Garage floors
- To remove oil dripping from concrete: Soak with mineral spirits for 30 minutes and then scrub with a stiff brush as you add more mineral spirits. Immediately after the scrubbing, absorb the grease with oil towels or newspaper. Allow concrete to dry. Then, wash with a solution of laundry detergent, 1 cup bleach and 1 gallon of cold water. Repeat until stains are removed.
- Spread several thicknesses of newspaper over the area where quite a bit of oil has spilled. Saturate the newspaper with water and press firmly against the floor. Allow to dry thoroughly, remove, and the oil spots will be gone.
- To eliminate oil spots, sprinkle the area with sand or kitty litter. They both will absorb the oil, and you can sweep it up.

Garden tools
- Quickly and easily remove rust by rubbing tools with a soap-filled steel wool pad dipped in kerosene or turpentine. Rub briskly with a piece of wadded aluminum foil.

Grills
- Barbecue grill: Tear off a sheet of heavy-duty aluminum foil large enough to completely cover your grill. Press foil shiny side down on grill and fold sides under, covering as tightly as possible. When coals have nearly reached their hottest point, place grill over coals for ten minutes. Remove foil and any charred grease or food on your grill should drop off leaving your grill clean and shiny.
- Before ever using your barbecue grill, spray it heavily with vegetable oil.
- Restaurant grills: A fast and effective way to clean a grill is to use left-over brewed coffee. Pour it on a hot or cold grill. Wipe off and you will be amazed at the results.

Guitar
- Rub toothpaste on your guitar, let it dry, then buff for a super shine.

Household odors
- Here's a way to kill household odors and always have a fresh smelling house for just pennies. Put a few drops of winter-green oil (available at drug stores) on a cotton ball and place it in a glass container. It will last for months and is as effective as room sprays.
- Toss dried orange and lemon rinds into your fireplace for a spicy aroma.

Iron
- To remove mineral deposits from the inside of a steam iron, fill it with equal part of water and white vinegar. Let it steam for several minutes, then disconnect and let set for 1 hour. Empty and rinse out with clear water.
- Remove brown or burned-on spots by rubbing with a heated solution of vinegar and salt.
- Remove wax build-up by rubbing with very fine sandpaper. Next, polish with a piece of fine soapless steel wool, then wipe off with a damp cloth.
- Or, clean the outside of your iron with toothpaste or silver polish.

Jewelry
- Clean with a soft cloth dabbed in toothpaste.

Pewter
- One of the best ways to clean pewter is to rub with cabbage leaves.
- Or, try a homemade mixture of wood ashes moistened with water.

Piano keys
- Apply toothpaste to a well dampened cloth. Rub the keys well, wipe dry and buff with a dry soft cloth.

Radiator
- Hang a damp cloth behind the radiator, then blow with the blower end of your vacuum cleaner. The dust and dirt will be blown into the damp cloth.

Telephone
- Clean your telephone with rubbing alcohol to keep it new looking.

Vases with small openings
- Dampen the inside of vase and add any toilet bowl cleaner. Let stand for 10 minutes and stains will disappear.

The Best
of Hints for
Clothing/Jewelry/
Shoes

Longer lasting panty hose
- Before you ever wear a new pair of hose they should be frozen first. No kidding, they will last longer if you wet them thoroughly, ring out gently, place in a plastic bag and toss in the freezer. Once frozen, thaw in bathtub and then hang to dry. It's a wild and crazy hint, but it's true!
- Or, starch them very, very lightly. This helps resist runs and they will also go on easily.

Stopping a run
- Apply hair spray or rub with a wet bar of soap. Of course, the old standby, clear nail polish, is still a good run stopper.

Before ever wearing a new garment
- Touch the center of each button (front and back) with clear nail polish. This will seal the threads and buttons will stay on much longer.

Clinging dresses
- Starch your slips to prevent dresses from clinging.

- Run a wire coat hanger between your dress and nylon slip. This will draw out the electricity and eliminate some of the clinging.

A wrinkle-free idea
- Hang your wrinkled garment on the curtain rod in your bathroom and run the hottest water possible from your shower. Close the bathroom door and let the water run for a while. This allows the steam to penetrate the material, thus eliminating the wrinkles. When traveling this hint should be remembered.

A great cover-up
- If you are in a hurry and notice a stain on your white suit, cover it up by rubbing baby powder into the stain.

Shave away fuzz balls
- Remove those little balls of fuzz from an old shirt collar by going over the surface with a clean shaver. It will not harm the fabric.

The above trick works on sweaters too!
- Remove knots and balls from sweater by shaving with a regular razor (very gently) or an electric shaver.
- Or, remove by rubbing with a very fine piece of sandpaper.

Sticky zippers
- They will slide easily if rubbed with a lead pencil.

Removing hem creases
- White vingar will help remove a permanent crease. Sponge the material liberally with the vinegar and press with a warm iron.
- Try this trick when lengthening old jeans: The white hem lines will disappear if you mix permanent blue ink with a little water (keep adding water until you get the perfect shade). Then, apply with a small brush. Let dry and no more telltale hemline.

A quick pair of ski jeans
- Convert regular jeans into ski pants by spraying with a waterproof fabric protector.

In case you need it... here's another jean trick

- Many times the cuffs on jeans will turn up after they have been washed. To correct this, affix a wide strip of iron-on mending material (the kind used for patching) to the inside of the cuffs. You will have no more problems with cuffs turning up.

Simple jewelry re-stringing

- Use the finest fishing line to re-string a broken necklace. The line is firm enough so that you do not need a needle, but soft enough to hand string beautifully.
- When re-stringing beads of graduated sizes, tape down a strip of cellophane tape (sticky side up) on a smooth surface. Arrange beads in order before re-stringing.

Eliminating a knot

- If a necklace chain is knotted, put a drop or two of salad oil on a piece of waxed paper, lay the knot in the oil and undo it by using 2 straight pins. It should unknot easily.

These "Shoe" Be Great Hints . . . and more to "boot"

Polishing and cleaning

- Nail polish remover is excellent for removing tar and grease from white shoes. Do not use on plastic.
- Use a solution of equal amounts of vinegar and water to remove salt from shoes and boots.
- Give your patent leather shoes a bright shine by rubbing with a dab of petroleum jelly.
- Use household window spray or furniture polish as a speedy shoe shine for all types of leather.
- Your white shoe polish will go on evenly if you rub the shoes with rubbing alcohol or a raw potato before applying the polish.
- White shoe polish will not smear if you spray the shoe with hair spray after it has dried thoroughly.

Drying tips

- A sure way to dry children's boots fast: Drop the hose of a portable hair dryer into the boot. Let it run until the boot is completely dry.
- To dry a pair of shoes quickly, hang them under a chair by hooking the heels on the chair rungs. They will be out of the way and still receive circulation of air on both sides.
- Keep rain-soaked shoes from becoming stiff by rubbing well with saddle soap before they have dried. Dry away from direct heat. When thoroughly dry give them a good polishing.

Some hints you should know about canvas shoes

- Spray new canvas or rope trimmed shoes with a fabric protector to keep them looking new.
- To clean rope trimmed canvas shoes, rub with a toothbrush that has been dipped in rug shampoo.
- Keep new white tennis shoes looking new by spraying heavily with starch.

The Best of Hints for the Floor

Hints That Will "Floor" You

A good cleaning agent
- For varnished floors or woodwork of any kind, rub with cold tea.

Eliminating marred floors
- When moving furniture slip old heavy socks over their legs.

A fast cover-up
- Renovate floors which have become faded in spots by mixing brown shoe polish with floor wax and applying to spots. It will give the floor an antique look.

Silence squeaks forever
- Silence floor squeaks by dusting talcum powder or dripping glue into the cracks.

Rub those scratches away
- With a piece of very fine steel wool dipped in floor wax.

Rocking without worries
- Your rocker will not scratch waxed floors if you line the rocker arcs with adhesive tape.
- Or, wax the arcs of your rocker at the same time you do the floors.

Removing heel marks
- Wipe the spots with kerosene or turpentine.
- Or, try an ordinary pencil eraser.

Removing tar spots
- Use paste wax. This also works on shoes.

Nail polish spills
- To remove nail polish from waxed floors or tile, let it solidify before attempting removal. When the polish is barely solid and pliable it can be peeled off. Smears are removed by wiping up the polish before it has dried, or by using a solvent on completely hardened polish.

Removing crayon marks
- Remove from vinyl tile or linoleum with silver polish.

A quick shine between waxings
- Mop with a piece of waxed paper under your mop. The dirt will also stick to the waxed paper.

Nylon stockings for dusting
- Place a nylon stocking over your dust mop. Discard the stocking and you will have a clean mop.

Loose linoleum edges are easy to fix
- Work linoleum cement (available at hardware stores) under the loosened edge of the corner, using a dull knife. Put a few heavy books over the area and let dry for 24 hours.

To seal linoleum seams
- Run a strip of cellophane tape down the full length of the crack. Shellac over the tape and the surface will hold up indefinitely.

A faster working carpet sweeper
- Dampen the brushes of your carpet sweeper before using and it will do a much better job of picking up lint and string.

Cleaning your floor polisher
- If wax has built up on the felt pads of your floor polisher, place the pads between several thicknesses of paper toweling and press with a warm iron. The towels will quickly absorb the old wax.

The Best
of Hints for
Furniture

Fantastic furniture polish

- Use ⅓ cup each boiled linseed oil, turpentine and vinegar. Mix together and shake well. Apply with a soft cloth and wipe completely dry. Wipe again with another soft cloth. Do not try to boil your own linseed oil—it is not the same. Buy it at a hardware or paint store.
- Or, add a teaspoon of apple cider vinegar to your favorite liquid furniture polish.

To remove polish build-up

- Mix ½ cup vinegar and ½ cup water. Rub with a soft cloth that has been moistened with solution, but wrung out. Dry immediately with another soft cloth.

Polishing carved furniture

- Dip an old soft toothbrush into furniture polish and brush lightly.

Is your seat sagging?

- Tighten a drooping cane chair seat by giving it a hot water bath and placing it outside in the sunlight to dry and shrink. After it has dried thoroughly, apply either lemon or cedar oil to prevent cracking and splitting.
- Sagging springs in chair: Turn the chair upside down. Make a pattern of the upper-structure frame. Transfer the pattern either to a piece of scrap masonite or plywood (⅛ inch). Nail to the upper structure. By doing this, the springs are pushed back into the chair, eliminating the sag.

Cigarette burns

- Burns can be repaired with a wax stick (available in all colors at paint and hardware stores). Gently scrape away the charred finish. Heat a knife blade and melt the shellac stick against the heated blade. Smooth over damaged area with your finger. But always consider the value of the furniture. It might be better to have a professional make the repair.
- Or, make a paste of rottenstone (available at hardware stores) and salad oil. Rub into the burned spot only, following the grain of the wood. Wipe clean with a cloth that has been dampened in oil. Wipe dry and apply your favorite furniture polish.

Removing paper that is stuck to a wood surface
- Do not scrape with a knife. Pour any salad oil, a few drops at a time, on the paper. Let set for a while and rub with a soft cloth. Repeat the procedure until the paper is completely gone.
- Old decals can be removed easily by painting them with several coats of white vinegar. Give the vinegar time to soak in, then gently scrape off.

Scratches
- *Make sure you always rub with the grain of the wood when repairing a scratch.*
- *Walnut:* Remove the meat from a fresh, unsalted walnut or pecan nut. Break it in half and rub the scratch with the broken side of the nut.
- *Mahogany:* You can either rub the scratch with a dark brown crayon or buff with brown paste wax.
- *Red Mahogany:* Apply ordinary iodine with a number 0 artist's brush.
- *Maple:* Combine equal amounts of iodine and denatured alcohol. Apply with a Q-tip, then dry, wax and buff.
- *Ebony:* Use black shoe polish, black eyebrown pencil or black crayon.
- *Teakwood:* Rub very gently with 0000 steel wool. Rub in equal amounts of linseed oil and turpentine.
- *Light finished furniture:* Scratches can be hidden by using tan shoe polish. However, use only on shiny finishes.
- *For all minor scratches:* Cover each scratch with a generous amount of white petroleum jelly. Allow it to remain on for 24 hours. Rub into wood. Remove excess and polish as usual. Or, apply a product called Liquid Gold (available at grocery stores).
- *For larger scratches:* Fill by rubbing with a wax stick (available in all colors at your hardware or paint store) or a crayon that matches the finish of the wood.

Two solutions to remove white water rings and spots
- Dampen a soft cloth with water and put a dab of toothpaste on it. For stubborn stains, add baking soda to the toothpaste.
- Make a paste of butter or mayonnaise and cigarette ashes. Apply to spot and buff away with a slightly damp cloth. Polish as usual.

Marble table-top stains
- Sprinkle salt on a fresh cut lemon. Rub very lightly over stain. Do not rub hard or you will ruin the polished surface. Wash off with soap and water.
- Scour with a water and baking soda paste. Let stand for a few minutes before rinsing with warm water.
- For horrible marble stains, try this: Place the marble table in hot sunlight. If this is not possible, heat the marble for 1 hour or more under a hot spotlight (never a sun-lamp). Then, swab on white household bleach. Continue this every hour or so until discoloration is gone. (Sometimes this may take a couple of days). Rinse with water and dry. Move to shade and polish with paste carnauba wax. Never use oil polish or soft waxes on marble; they can cause discoloration.

Removing candle wax from wooden finishes
- Soften the wax with a hair dryer. Remove wax with paper toweling and wash down with a solution of vinegar and water.

Proper cleaning and care for leather table tops
- Remove all wax build-up with a vinegar and water solution (¼ cup vinegar and ½ cup water). To raise any indentations such as pressure points from lamps or ash trays, apply lemon oil to the leather twice a day for a week. To maintain results, use lemon oil monthly.

Plastic table tops
- You will find that a coat of Turtle Wax is a quick pick-up for dulled plastic table tops and counters.
- Or, rub in toothpaste and buff.

Glass table tops
- Rub in a little lemon juice. Dry with paper towels and shine with newspaper for a sparkling table.
- Toothpaste will remove small scratches from glass.

Chrome cleaning
- For sparkling clean chrome without streaks, use a cloth dampened in ammonia.

Removing glue from furniture
- Airplane or cement glue can be removed by rubbing with cold cream, peanut butter or salad oil.

Tips for wicker
- To keep wicker furniture from turning yellow, wash with a solution of warm salt water.
- To prevent drying out, apply lemon oil once in a while.
- Never let wicker freeze. This will cause cracking and splitting.
- Wicker needs moisture, so use a humidifier in the winter.

Removing rust on metal furniture
- A good scrubbing with turpentine should accomplish the job.

Proper cleaning and care of vinyl upholstery
- Never oil vinyls because oil will make the vinyl hard. If this happens it is almost impossible to soften it again. For proper cleaning, sprinkle baking soda or vinegar on a rough damp cloth. Then, wasn with a very mild dishwashing soap. Body oil will cause vinyl to become hard so it should be cleaned once in a while.

Leather upholstery
- Clean with a damp cloth and saddle soap.
- Prevent leather from cracking by polishing regularly with a cream made of 1 part vinegar and 2 parts linseed oil.

Removing blood stains from upholstery
- Cover the spot immediately with a paste of cornstarch and cold water. Rub lightly and place object in the sun to dry. The sun will draw the blood out into the cornstarch. Brush off. If the stain is not completely gone, try, try again.

Grease and oil stains
- Sprinkle talcum, cornstarch, or fuller's earth on a fresh stain. Rub in well and let stand until the stain is absorbed. Brush off and wipe with a damp cloth.

Soiled cotton upholstery
- Try rubbing the soiled areas with artgum squares. Purchase at any stationery store.

Ready-to-use upholstery cleaner
- Shaving cream is one of the most useful upholstery cleaners for new stains and ordinary dirt.
- Make your own by mixing ½ cup mild detergent with 2 cups boiling water. Cool until it forms into jelly, then whip with a hand beater for good stiff foam.

The Best
of Hints for
the Handyperson

Wobbly chair legs
- Secure a loose chair leg by wrapping the loose end with a small strip of nylon hose or thread before applying the glue, then re-insert.
- A few drops of wood expander will achieve the same results.

Wobbly table
- If your table wobbles because of a short leg, put a small amount of Plastic Wood on waxed paper. Set the short leg on it and allow to dry. Trim down with a sharp knife and smooth with sandpaper.

Sticky dresser drawers
- They will slide easily again if you rub candle wax or soap on the runner of the side that seems to be sticking.

Is your screw loose?
- Stick a wooden kitchen match in the screw hole and break it off. Then, put the screw back in.
- Wind a few strands of steel wool around the threads of the screw before screwing it in.
- Paint the screw of a wobbly drawer knob with fingernail polish before inserting it. When the polish dries, it will hold the screw tightly.
- Or, dip in glue or putty and it will hold tight.

Difficulty loosening a tight screw
- Heat the edge of a screwdriver to its hottest point before loosening a screw.
- Or, put a few drops of peroxide on the tight screw and soak for a few minutes.

Remember this
- Left is loose and right is tight.

Loosening a rusted bolt
- You can often loosen a rusted bolt by applying a cloth soaked in any carbonated beverage.
- A drop or two of ammonia will loosen it right up.
- Before screwing it back in, wrap thread around it and coat with vaseline to avoid future rusting.

Not just another screwy idea

- Should metal screws on your home appliances keep coming loose, a dab of shellac placed under the heads before tightening them, holds them securely in place.

To loosen joints

- Put vinegar in a small oil can and apply liberally to joints to loosen old glue.

Longer lasting sandpaper and easier sanding

- Sandpaper will last longer, work better and resist cracking if the paper backing is dampened slightly, then wrapped around a block of wood.

Mending a leaking vase

- Coat the inside with a thick layer of paraffin and allow it to harden. The paraffin will last indefinitely and the vase will not leak.

Cutting plywood

- Prevent plywood from splitting by putting a strip of masking tape at the point where you plan to start sawing.

How to find a wall stud

- Hold a pocket compass level with the floor and at a right angle to the wall. Slowly move it along the surface of the wall. Movement of the compass needle will indicate the presence of nails and reveal the stud location. Wall studs are usually 16 inches apart, center to center.

Preventing nylon cord and rope from fraying

- Shellac the ends of the rope and it will not unravel.
- To prevent nylon cord or twine from fraying at a cut end, heat the end over a small flame. The strands will bond into a solid unit. Knots can be prevented from working loose by this same method.

Preventing rust on tools

- Place a piece of charcoal, chalk or several mothballs in your toolbox to attract any moisture.

- Wax tools with an automobile paste wax. A light coat will ward off corrosion for quite some time.
- Or, store small tools in a bucket of sand.

Preventing a screwdriver from slipping
- Rub chalk on the blade.

Stop squeaks
- Use nonstick vegetable spray to lubricate squeaky hinges, sticky locks, bicycle chains, roller skate wheels and so on.

After sanding a surface
- Pull an old nylon stocking over your hand and rub lightly over the wood. You will be able to locate the slightest rough spot.

Finding a gas leak
- Lather the pipes with soapy water. The escaping gas will cause the soapy water to bubble, revealing the damaged areas. You can make a temporary plug by moistening a cake of soap and pressing it over the spot. When the soap hardens it will effectively close the leak until the gasman comes.

More hints for the handy person
- For accuracy in drilling metal, use a small drill first.
- When drilling hard metal, add a drop or two of turpentine to the drill point instead of oil for lubrication.
- A small quantity of kerosene will help ease a hand saw through a tight cut.
- Thaw a frozen water pipe with a hair dryer.
- To prevent snow from sticking to a shovel, cover shovel with spray wax.

Picture Perfect

For cockyed pictures try these:
- Wind some adhesive tape around the center of the picture wire. The wire will be less likely to slip on the hanger.
- Place masking tape on the back four corners of your picture and press against the wall.
- Or, wrap masking tape (sticky side out) around the middle of a rounded toothpick and place a few near the bottom, back side of the frame.

Preventing experimental holes when hanging pictures
- Cut a paper pattern of each picture or mirror that you plan to hang and pin to the wall. After you've found the correct positions for the hangers, perforate the paper with a sharp pencil to mark the wall.
- Before you drive nails into the wall, mark the spot with an X of cellophane tape. This trick will keep the plaster from cracking when you start hammering.
- A wet fingerprint shows the exact spot for the hanger. The print dries without a mark.

Finishing unfinished picture frames
- Stain them beautifully with ordinary liquid shoe polish. Apply one coat and let dry. Follow with another coating. Then, wax with a good paste wax. Brown polish gives the wood a walnut glow and oxblood polish emulates a rich mahogany. Tan polish will appear as a light maple color.

The Best
of Hints for
the Laundry

Did you know?
- The basic ingredient of many commercial spot removers is 2 parts water to 1 part rubbing alcohol.

Cleaning your machine
- Fill the washer with warm water and pour a gallon of distilled vinegar into it. Run the machine through an entire cycle. The vinegar wlll cleanse the hoses and unclog soap scum from them.

Ring around the collar
- Use a small paint brush and brush hair shampoo into soiled shirt collars before laundering. Shampoo is made to dissolve body oils.
- Mark heavily with chalk. The chalk will absorb the oils and once the oil is removed, the dirt will come off easily. This method may require a few applications if the yellow line has been there for some time. If the shirt is new, one application should do it.
- Or, apply a paste of vinegar and baking soda. Rub in and wash as usual. This method also removes dirt and mildew.

No more lint
- To remove lint from corduroy, wash and allow to dry very slowly. While clothing is still damp, brush with a clothes brush. All the lint will come off, but remember, the clothing must be damp.
- You will eliminate the lint problem by adding 1 cup white vinegar to the final rinse cycle.
- Or, put a yard of nylon netting into the dryer with wet clothes to act as a lint catcher.
- If the lint, under and around the filter of dryer seems damp, it means the outside vent is clogged. You better clean it out before the machine breaks down.

The final rinse cycle

- To make sure clothes receive a thorough rinsing, add 1 cup white vinegar to the rinse cycle. This will help dissolve the alkalines in soaps and detergents. Plus, it will give you soft and sweet smelling clothing for just pennies.
- The vinegar is a must for hand washing. It cuts down soap so fast you will only have to rinse 2 times.
- A teaspoon of Epsom salts to a gallon of rinse water will help keep most materials from fading or running.

Creme rinse your sweaters

- For the best results when hand washing sweaters, put a capful of creme hair rinse in the final rinse water.
- Or, rinse wool garments in lukewarm water and a few tablespoons of glycerine. This will keep them soft and will also help prevent itching when they are worn.

Accidentally washed woolen item

- Soak in tepid water to which you have added a good hair shampoo. Sometimes this will soften the wool fibers enough to allow for a reshaping. It's worth a try.

Washing feather pillows
- First check for any open or weak seams. Place the pillow in a pillowcase. Wash 2 pillows at a time for a balanced load or add towels for balance. Fill your washer with warm water and push pillows down to saturate them completely before turning on the gentle cycle. Stop the washer halfway through the washing and turn pillows over. To dry, put feather pillows (not foam rubber) into dryer along with a clean tennis shoe. Drying will take up to 2 hours.

Renovating feather pillows
- Set dryer on air setting and let pillows tumble for 15 minutes. However, make sure there are no holes in the pillows or the feathers will work through.

Make your own fabric softener sheets
- Pour a few capfuls of any fabric softener into a small bowl of water. Swish a washcloth in the solution. Ring it out and toss into the dryer along with the wet clothes. It's that simple. But best of all, it is a lot less expensive than using the tear-off sheet brands.

Machine washing dainty garments
- Drop your dainty garments into a pillowcase and fasten the loose end with a plastic bag tie. Place in washer and wash on a gentle cycle.

Too many suds
- Any time your washing machine overflows from too many suds, pour in a little fabric softener. Suds will disappear.

Procedure for cleaning velvet
- To clean, raise nap and remove wrinkles. Hold garment (pile side up) over steaming water to which a little ammonia has been added. Finish by brushing well and ironing lightly on the wrong side.

Renovating stiffened chamois
- Soak in warm water to which a spoonful or so of olive oil has been added.

When the red wine spills
- Sprinkle the spill immediately with lots of salt. Dunk into cold water and rub the stain out before washing.

Cleanest work clothes ever
- Add ½ cup of household ammonia to the wash water.

Removing grease from suede
- Sponge with a cloth dipped in vinegar or club soda. Restore nap of suede by brushing with a suede brush.

Getting white cotton socks white again
- Boil in water to which a slice of lemon has been added.

A fast way to dampen clothes
- Place clothes in dryer and add 2 thoroughly wet bath towels. Set dryer on a no heat setting and let clothing tumble until desired dampness.
- If you have dampened ironing that you can't finish, stick it in the freezer until you are ready to catch up.

Faster ironing
- Place a strip of heavy duty aluminum foil over the entire length of the ironing board and cover with pad. As you iron, heat will reflect through to the underside of the garment.
- Starch your ironing board cover. This also helps the cover stay clean longer.

Ironing embroidery
- Lay the embroidery piece upside down on a turkish towel before ironing. All the little spaces between the embroidery will be smooth when you are finished.

Removing alcoholic beverages
- Soak fresh stains in cold water and a few tablespoons of glycerine (available at drug stores). Rinse with white vinegar and water. These stains turn brown with age so treat immediately.

Blood
- Cover area with meat tenderizer. Apply cool water to make a paste. Wait 15–30 minutes, sponge with cool water.

Chewing gum
- Place garment in plastic bag and put in freezer. Scrape off frozen gum.
- Or, loosen gum by soaking in white vinegar or rubbing with egg white before laundering.

Candle wax or crayon
- Place the stained area between clean paper towels or pieces of a brown paper bag and press with a warm iron.

Grease on double knit
- Club soda works wonders for removing grease from double-knit fabrics.

Ballpoint ink
- Apply hairspray liberally to stain. Rub with a clean dry cloth and the ink usually disappears. This works exceptionally well on polyester fabrics.
- Or, try rubbing alcohol on the spot before laundering.

Rust
- Apply lemon juice and salt, then place in the sun.
- Rust can also be removed from white washables by covering the stains with cream of tartar, then gathering up the ends of the article so that the powder stays on the spot. Dip the entire spot into hot water for about 5 minutes. Ordinary laundering will complete the job.
- A commercial rust remover by the name of Barkeeper's Friend may be used.

Mildew
- Dry in the sun after moistening with lemon juice and salt.
- Treat by adding ½ cup of liquid Lysol to the wash water.
- On leather, sponge with equal amounts of water and rubbing alcohol.

Perspiration
- Soak the garment in warm vinegar water.

Scorch
- On whites, sponge with a piece of cotton which has been soaked in peroxide. Use the 3-percent solution sold as a mild antiseptic.
- For linen and cotton, dampen a cloth with peroxide, lay it on the scorched area and iron with a warm iron.

Shoe polish
- Remove with rubbing alcohol. Use 1 part alcohol and 2 parts water on colored fabric. Use it straight on whites.

Tar
- Rub the tar spot with kerosene until removed, then wash with detergent and water. The kerosene will not take the color out of most fabrics, but you better test it first.

The Best
of Hints for
the Painter

Painting windows

- To eliminate window scraping try these tips: Dampen strips of newspaper or any other straight-edged paper with warm water. Spread strips around each window pane, making sure that the paper fits tightly into corners and edges. The paper will cling until you have finished with the paint job.
- Rub a bar of softened soap around the window panes.
- Or, swab on liquid detergent with a paint brush (a few inches from the frame). When the windows dry, paint away.
- Before painting windows, remove the hard-to-get dirt out of nooks and crannies with an old paint brush.

Spattered paint on windows and woodwork

- If the paint spatters on windows use nail polish remover. Allow to soak for a few minutes then rub off with a cloth and wash with warm suds. The paint will usually disappear, no matter how long it has been there.
- Soften old stains with turpentine and scrape off with a razor blade. This method also works on putty stains.
- Wash freshly dried paint off glass with a hot vinegar solution.
- Apply a coat of lemon oil on woodwork before painting. If paint speckles appear they will rub off easily.
- Coat door hinges, doorknobs, lock latches and other hardware with a coating of petroleum jelly. This will eliminate a lot of scraping after.

Drip catchers

- When painting the ceiling, you can prevent drops from landing on your head by simply sticking the paint brush through the middle of a paper plate and securing with Scotch tape.
- Before painting a chair or table, place jar lids under each leg to catch paint drips.
- To prevent drips of paint from falling on your light fixtures, tie plastic bags around them.

Storing leftover paint

- To prevent scum forming on leftover paint, place a disc of aluminum foil directly on the paint surface. To make the disc the correct size, set the can on the foil and cut around it.
- Keep oil base paint fresh by adding 4 tablespoons of mineral spirits only to the top layer of the paint. Do not mix until the next paint job.

- Tightly fit the lids of paint containers and store upside down. Scum will not form on paint.
- Always mark the paint level and color on each can before storing.
- Use nail polish or shoe polish bottles for leftover paint and label. They are excellent for small touch-ups.
- When tiny touch-ups are necessary, use throw away Q-tips instead of soiling a dry paint brush.

Cleaning paint brushes

- A new paint brush will last longer and be much easier to clean if it soaks in a can of linseed oil for 12 hours before it is ever used.
- To soften hard paint on brushes, soak in hot vinegar. Follow with a wash in warm, sudsy water.
- After washing brushes and rollers, use a fabric softener in the final rinse water. It helps them stay soft and pliable.
- Use a coffee can when cleaning paint brushes with paint thinner. After the brushes have been cleaned, cover the can and let stand for a few days. The paint will settle to the bottom and you can pour the clean thinner into a can and re-use.

Fast clean-ups

- When working on a paint job which takes a couple of days, save time by thoroughly wrapping brushes in several layers of foil and freezing (stick them right into the freezer compartment of your refrigerator). Let brushes defrost an hour or more before returning to the job.
- Put a large plastic bag over your roller pan before putting the paint in. When you are through, throw the bag away.

Banishing paint odor

- Add 2 teaspoons of vanilla extract per quart of paint.
- Place a large pan of water which contains a tablespoon of ammonia in the freshly painted room. Leave overnight.
- Or, place a large cut onion into a big pan of cold water. Paint odors will sponge into the onion within a very short time.

Lumpy paint

- The best strainer of all is an old nylon stocking.
- An old egg beater is excellent for stirring paint.
- Cut a circle from an old screen slightly smaller than the can lid. As the screen settles, it will carry all lumps to the bottom.

Stick it!
- After painting, apply some of the paint to a popsicle stick. It is a handy color guide to matching colors when shopping.

Preventing white paint from yellowing
- Stir a drop of black paint into any good white paint.

Paint removers for face and hands
- Cooking oil or baby oil is a better way to remove paint because it will not burn the skin.
- For easy removal, rub Vaseline on exposed skin.
- Before painting, give fingernails a good coating of bar soap for the fastest wash-up ever.

Before puttying windows
- Mix putty with the paint that matches the woodwork.

Antiquing furniture
- Try using a small piece of carpet to work in the glaze. It gives a beautifully grained effect.

The Best
of Hints for
Pets/Pests

What to do about those doggy spots

- Blot up as much moisture as possible. Rub with a solution of vinegar or lemon juice and warm sudsy water. Blot and blot some more. Then pour straight club soda over the spot. Blot again. Place a dry towel over the stain and put a heavy book on top of it. If the towel becomes soggy, immediately replace with a clean, dry one.

What if the cat makes a mistake

- Follow the above procedure, but once the spot has dried, rub with a cloth dampened in ammonia. This will not only take the offensive odor away, but it will prevent the cat from ever doing it again in the same spot.

Dry cleaning your dog

- Instead of always giving your dog a regular bath, rub baking soda into his coat thoroughly and then brush off. It deodorizes as well as it cleans.

More rub-a-dub-dub hints

- A creme rinse is helpful for dogs whose fur tangles when wet.
- To cut soap film and wash away strong soap odors, add vinegar or lemon juice to the rinse water.
- For whiter and brighter fur, put a little bluing in the shampoo or rinse water.
- If your pet is shedding, place a tea strainer in the tub drain to keep pipes from clogging up.

Removing burrs

- Remove burrs by working oil into the tangle or by crushing the burrs with pliers. Crushed burrs lose their holding power and can be combed out.

Giving your dog a pill

- Most dogs love chocolate candy, so if yours refuses to swallow a pill, push the tablet into a piece of candy. You could also hide the pill in a chunk of dog food.

Chewing puppy

- If your new pup is chewing on your table and chair legs, solve the problem by putting a little oil of cloves (available at drug departments) on the wood with a piece of cotton. If the odor does not keep him away, the bitter taste will.
- Help prevent damage to rugs and shoes by giving him a thoroughly washed out plastic bleach bottle to chew on.

Whining puppy

- Your puppy probably misses his mother. So make him feel at home by putting a warm hot water bottle, wrapped in a towel, and a ticking clock in his bed. Sometimes a radio playing soft music will help also.

If the skunk got "Fido"

- In a well ventilated area, wash the pet down with tomato juice before washing thoroughly with shampoo and water. Rinse with a gallon of water to which a few tablespoons of ammonia have been added. Rinse the pet thoroughly with clear water.
- Another good solution is equal amounts of vinegar and water. Wash thoroughly and rinse with clear water, followed by another good dousing of the vinegar and water solution. However, for this rinse, make it weaker.

Keeping the cat off your favorite chair
- Cats hate plastic coverings! Cover your chair until your cat realizes the chair is a no-no.

Fleas will "flee"
- If you place some fresh pine needles in his doghouse or underneath his bed pad.
- Or, salt the crevices of his dog house and wash him periodically with salt water.

A safety tip for "Rover"
- Tape reflector tape on your dog's or cat's collar to help cut down the danger of its being struck by a car at night.

When the ants come marching in
- Place small sponges soaked in sugar sweetened water wherever ants have been seen. Collect the sponges periodically and plunge into hot water.
- Rid red ants from your pantry by putting a small quantity of green sage on the cupboard shelves.
- Ant hills outside the home can be destroyed by pouring a kettle of boiling water down each opening.

The best cure for the No. 1 household pest
- A 1 pound can of boric acid compound can effectively keep a house cockroach-free for a year. It will not kill roaches as rapidly as some pesticides, but it has by far the longest lasting effect. (If they do not pick up a toxic dose of other pesticides in their first contact, they learn to stay clear. Boric acid will not repel roaches, so they keep going back into it over and over until they die). Simply sprinkle it in cracks, crevices, under sinks and in other dark places. To rid them immediately, spray with a pesticide and after a few days start using the boric acid method.

Keeping the flies and stray dogs away from the garbage
- To prevent flies from swarming around garbage pails, hose them down and allow to dry in the sun. Then, sprinkle a little dry soap into them.

- If you are hounded by stray dogs attacking the garbage, sprinkle full strength ammonia over the garbage bags before placing them in the pail.

Silverfish
- Sprinkle a mixture of boric acid and sugar on affected areas.

There's a bee in the house
- If a wasp or bee gets into the house, reach for the hairspray. Most insect sprays only infuriate them, but the hairspray stiffens their wings, immobilizing them immediately. This works on all winged insects.

How to treat bug bites
- Treat insect bites with a poultice of either cornstarch or baking soda, mixed with vinegar, fresh lemon juice or witch hazel.
- Apply a paste made of meat tenderizer and water.
- Or, rub bites with wet bar soap to help relieve itching.

Bee stings
- Apply a poultice of baking soda and water.
- Or, try applying a fresh cut slice of raw onion to the sting to help draw out the poison. Hold the onion in place with tape.

The Best
of Hints for
Plants/Flowers/
Gardens

Watering houseplants
- Use water at room temperature. A plant can be injured by cold water.
- Let tap water stand for 1 day to rid water of chlorine. This will help avoid brown tips.
- Stick your finger 1 inch into top soil, if it feels moist, delay watering.
- The water you boil eggs in is filled with minerals and is a good "drink" for your plants.
- Or, drop egg shells into a jar of water and cover. Let set a day before watering. Do not store egg shells for any length of time, because they will spoil and cause the worst odor.
- Top choice fertilizers are old aquarium water and water in which fish has been frozen.
- Don't throw away your fizzless club soda. It has just the right chemicals to add vigor and color to your plants.
- Once in a while, if you wish to water plants in hanging baskets without making a mess, try using ice cubes. They will not drip through before being absorbed. But only once in a while.
- Bulb plants should always be watered from the bottom. Fill a saucer or kitchen sink with water and let the plant sit in it.
- If you have a room full of plants, a small portable vaporizer is a must for addition of moisture in the wintertime.

Snow your plants with kindness
- Scoop up some clean snow and let it melt. Use it for watering because there are wonderful minerals in snow.

"Love 'em and leave 'em"
- To water houseplants while on vacation, stand plants on bricks submerged in water in the tub. The bricks absorb water, keeping the plants happy.
- Or, place all houseplants in the bathtub on old thickly folded bath towels, in a few inches of water. They will absorb moisture as needed.
- You might want to try this hint: Place one end of a clothesline into a pail of water and bury the other end in the plant soil. Make sure the water pail is higher than the plant.

To keep indoor plants growing straight
- Frequently rotate the pots about a quarter of a turn so they absorb the sunlight evenly. Plants lean toward the strongest light.

Ailing houseplants—"They'll reflect all the love you give them"

- Your houseplant will come out of its slump if you cover it with a plastic bag, along with a pest strip. Make sure the entire plant is under the bag. Remove the bag in a few days and you will find it in good health. This is excellent to do when transferring plants from outside into the house.
- Give your plant a shot of Geritol on a regular basis for 3 months. Within a month you will notice new leaves have begun to appear.
- Or, feed your plant a tablespoon of castor oil, followed by a good drink of water.

Bug beaters

- *Aphids & Spiders:* Wash total plant off with mild detergent and water.
- *Black flies:* Combine ½ tablespoon of plain ammonia and 1 quart of water. Water soil.
- *White flies:* Mix 2 tablespoons of dishwashing liquid in 1 gallon of water and spray on leaves.
- *Scales:* For instant removal of slugs, place plant in pot of water.
- *Pests of all kinds:* Plant a garlic clove along with your plant. As it grows, simply keep cutting it down so it will not disturb the appearance of the plant. Garlic will not harm the plant, but the bugs hate it.

House plant on the mend
- A tiny splint made of toothpicks and tape will often save the broken stem of a plant.

Cleaning plant leaves
- Dust with a feather duster.
- Glycerine is one of the best substances to use if you wish to put a gloss on the leaves of your plants. Put a few drops of glycerine on a cloth and swab the leaves with it. It is much better than olive oil or mayonnaise, since it is not a dust collector.
- A half and half mixture of milk and water also makes a fine solution for glossing leaves.

Homemade trellises
- Snip off the hook of a wire coat hanger, bend remaining wire into a fun, creative shape, such as a heart or a star. Then, push ends into the pot to make a miniature trellis for your ivy to grow on.
- Support tall plants with old adjustable brass-like curtain rods.

Eliminating the scratches
- Corn pads are terrific coasters for plant pots. Simply stick them on and you will be able to use that pot that has been scratching your table for years.

Another planting hint
- For good drainage use: broken clay pot, cracked walnut shells, fruit pits, marbles, charcoal or stones on the bottom of the pots.

Ferns love tea parties too!
- A good tonic for ferns is to water them with weak tea. In addition to their tea break, plant a wet soggy teabag along with your fern.
- Let worm infested ferns meet their "match". Stick matches into the soil with the sulphur end down. For an ordinary size plant, use 4 matches and for a large one use 6.
- Ferns enjoy the nitrogen content in a very weak solution of ammonia and water.

Ways to help your cut flowers last longer

- Always cut stems at an angle with a very sharp scissors or knife.
- Split the ends of thick stems before putting them in a vase. Split ends give stems a better chance to absorb moisture.
- Always cut stems under water. That way, no air bubbles can form to stop the free flow of water into the stem.
- Remove leaves below the waterline, as decaying vegetable matter poisons the water.
- Aspirin tablets, pennies and ice cubes are all said to lengthen the lives of fresh cut flowers. However, the best preservation is 2 tablespoons of white vinegar and 2 tablespoons of cane sugar in a quart of water. The vinegar inhibits the growth of organisms and the sugar serves as food.
- Refrigerate each night. This alone can double their lives.
- Flowers will last longer if not crowded in the vase.

Reviving wilted flowers

- Cut stems and place in hot water. Let them rest in a dark place until water cools. Then, transfer into cold water.

More tips on flowers

- If you have ever smelled a marigold which has been in a vase of water for a few days, you will appreciate this tid bit. Add a teaspoon of sugar to the water to eliminate the odor.
- Carnations will last longer if placed in water containing a little boric acid.
- Feed geraniums rinsed coffee grounds.
- Place a crushed paper napkin or towel in the bottom of your flower vase if it's too deep for displaying flowers.
- If you have any birth control pills left, dissolve them in water and water violets.
- To add length to short stemmed flowers, slip stems into drinking straws before placing in vase.
- Put a layer of gravel on the top of window boxes to prevent rain from spattering dirt on windows.
- Drop a penny into the vase, so tulips will stand erect and not open too wide.
- To keep water from clouding in a clear vase, add 1 tablespoon of liquid bleach to 1 quart of water.
- Hold long-stemmed flowers erect in a tall wide mouthed vase by crisscrossing transparent tape across the top.
- Hair rollers tied together and placed at the bottom of a vase make an ideal holder for your arrangement.

Preserving flowers and leaves
- Spray any cut flower with hair spray to make it last longer without shedding. Hold the spray can about a foot away from the bouquet and spray in an upward direction, so as not to cause the flowers to droop.

How to dry flowers
- Mix 10 parts white cornmeal to 3 parts of borax. Bury flowers into the mixture. Let set for 2 weeks and your dried flowers will last for years.
- Another fine preservation method for dried arrangements: First hammer the ends of the branches or the stems of their leaves. Then stand the branches or stem ends in a jar containing a solution of ⅔ water and ⅓ glycerin, enough to reach 3 or 4 inches up branches or stems. (You can also lay leaves in the solution.) Allow a week or so for the solution to be absorbed. Some foliage may change color, but the leaves will last for years.

Food coloring tints flowers
- You can change the color of cut flowers by mixing food coloring in warm water and placing stems in the solution. The stems absorb the colors and by morning you will see pretty designs and different colors on flowers.

Spring is busting out all over
- In winter when flowers are scarce, go out and prune some twigs or branches of forsythia, crab apple, hawthorn, lilac and other flowering trees and shrubs. Put the stems in a bucket of warm water, then drop in a cotton ball saturated with ammonia. Put the pail and branches in a plastic bag and tie securely. Soon the ammonia fumes will force blooms on the branches.

Goodbye to unwanted grass and weeds
- Salted boiling water will immediately kill grass or weeds growing between sections of cement walk.
- To keep grass from growing between bricks in a walk, sprinkle the spaces with salt.

Clearing away poison ivy
- Spray the area with a solution of 2 gallons soapy water and 3 pounds of salt. A few dousings will kill it.

A good deed for your feathered friends...
They'll love you for it!
- Help make their nesting easier and provide building materials. Collect lint from your dryer, bits of string, yarn from your sewing basket and hair from your brush. Fasten together very lightly and attach to a tree branch.

A "pine" treat for the birds in the winter
- Cover pine cones with hardened bacon grease or other type of fat. Roll in bird seed or bread crumbs. Hang from a tree branch or tuck into bushes.

More ideas for the birds
- To attract birds to an outdoor birdbath, drop in a few colored marbles.
- When you cannot find a funnel to put bird seed in the feeder, use the cut-off top of a bleach jug or an old milk carton.

A perfect seed row marker
- Mark the planting date on each seed packet. Then, slip small plastic bags over each seed packet and secure with a twist-tie. You will never have doubts about which plants are which if you follow this procedure.

Aid tomato plants with pantyhose
- To avoid cutting into your prize winning tomato plants, tie the stalks with pantyhose that have been cut lengthwise.

Assuring baby tomatoes a good start
- Mix fireplace ashes into the surrounding soil. Remove the top and bottom lids from coffee cans and set a can over each plant. (Step firmly on the can to set it into the ground.) Remove cans when plants are a few weeks old.

The know-hows of organic gardening
- Herbs are nature's insecticides. Include a variety of them in your garden.
- Basil near tomatoes repels worms and flies.
- Mint, sage, dill and thyme protect cabbage, cauliflower, broccoli and Brussels sprouts from the cabbage moth.

- Onions and garlic protect your plants from Japanese beetles, carrot flies and aphids on lettuce and beans. Onions should be planted near carrots and beets.
- Plant horseradish near potatoes. The potato beetle hates horseradish.
- Anise and coriander discourage aphids.
- Radishes planted near cabbage repels maggots.
- Do not plant garlic near peas, nor cabbage near strawberries. They do not like each other.
- Rabbits hate talcum powder. Just dust a little on or around the plants, and it works like a charm in repelling flea beetles. When the rain washes it away, apply more.
- Dried coffee grounds add acid to the soil.
- Soapsuds are a fantastic insecticide. Spray them on liberally.
- Compost piles are important. They are a must for the organic gardener.
- Make an additional fence around your garden with a row of vegetables. The roots secrete oil which many pests refuse to cross.
- Toss crushed up egg shells on your garden for plant growth.
- For a quick end to ants, pour boiling water on each ant hill.
- Scatter mothballs around your garden to discourage rabbits and other pests from feasting.

That's all "fern" now!

The Best
of Hints for
Sewing

An easy way to hem a dress

- A sink plunger is a handy gadget to use when marking a skirt for hemming. Mark the handle at the desired length, then move the plunger around the hem. It stands by itself, leaving your hands free to mark or pin.

Threading a needle

- Spray a bit of hair spray or spray starch on your finger when threading a needle and apply it to the end of the thread. The thread stiffens just enough to ease the job of finding the eye.

Sharpening a machine needle

- Stitch through a piece of sandpaper.

Make heavy seams "seam" easy

- Rub seams with a piece of hard bar soap. The machine needle will go through the material with ease.

Storage for sewing tools

- Use an empty thermometer case as a holder for extra long and fine needles that are hard to store in a sewing box.
- Use plastic pill bottles with snap-on tops to hold the extra small buttons.

Pins and needles all over the place

- Safety pins can be gathered and threaded onto a pipe cleaner. Then, bend the pipe cleaner into a circle and twist the ends together.
- Keep a small magnet in your sewing basket and use it to pick up pins and needles that drop to the floor while you are sewing.

Reusing a zipper

- Spray it heavily with spray starch and it will sew like new. Zippo! It works.

Buttons and buttonholes

- Here's a tip for keeping those four-hole buttons on longer. Sew through only two holes at a time, breaking the thread and knotting it for each pair of holes. This way, should one set break loose, the other side will still hold the button.

- Use dental floss or elastic thread to sew buttons on children's clothing. The buttons will take a lot of wear before falling off.
- If you have trouble removing a button from a garment, slide a comb under the button and cut with a razor blade.
- To make a straight cut for a buttonhole on heavy fabric, lay buttonhole section over a bar of soap and cut with a razor blade.

A red hot idea for belt holes
- Poke with a red hot steel knitting needle.

"Snappy" ideas
- Sew the snap point on first. Then take a piece of chalk and touch this little point. Turn the material over, rub it with your finger, and you will find that you have marked the exact place where the snap should be sewed on.

A quick trick for sewing on emblems
- Use a few dabs of any good white glue on the back of the emblem and press it in position on the clothing, then let it set for a few minutes. The emblem can then be stitched by hand or machine without any worry that it will turn out lopsided. The glue subsequently washes out.

Creeping machine foot pedal
- Glue a piece of foam rubber to the bottom of a portable sewing machine foot control and it will not creep on the floor.

Worn elastic

- Whenever elastic that is sewed on a garment becomes worn or stretched, just baste cord elastic through the worn elastic. Pull it up and knot.

Eliminating the knot

- When sewing with a single thread, does it constantly knot? If so, try this: After you thread the needle, be sure to knot the end that was cut off closest to the spool.

After oiling the sewing machine

- Stitch through a blotter several times to avoid surplus oil from damaging your fabrics.

"Darn it"—Two different ways

- Use a glass marble as a darning egg when mending fingers of a glove.
- One of the easiest ways to mend a hole in a garment is to place a thin sheet of paper under the hole and darn back and forth with the sewing machine. When the garment is washed the paper will dissolve. This is ideal for bedsheets with big tears or rips.

A handy pin cushion

- A bar of soap makes an ideal place to stick needles and pins. It lubricates them so that they will go through stiff fabrics with ease.

Great balls of yarn

- When you are working with more than one ball of yarn, put the balls in a plastic bag with small holes, like the bag potatoes come in. Thread the different yarns through various holes in the bag. The yarn will stay clean and untangled throughout the project.

Sewing on plastic

- Put wax paper over the seam and the sewing machine will not stick to the plastic nor pucker. The wax paper will tear off easily after the job is done.

Avoiding the slips and slides when sewing on nylon

- When repairing seams on nylon jackets or lingerie, make the job a lot simpler by placing a piece of paper underneath the section you are going to sew. Stich through the fabric and paper. When finished, tear the paper off.

How to make your patterns last longer

- Spray a new pattern with fabric protector. The pattern will last longer, rip less easily and resist wrinkles.

The Best of Hints for Storing/Saving/ Spending

Damp closets
- To help prevent dampness in a closet, fill a coffee can with charcoal briquets. Punch holes in the cover and place the container on the floor. For larger closets use 2 or 3 one-pound coffee cans.
- You can also cut down on dampness by wrapping and tying together 12 pieces of chalk and hanging them in your closet.

Musty smells
- For sweet smelling closets, hang an old nylon stocking filled with cedar chips in the closet. This also serves as an excellent moth repellant.
- To remove musty odors from a trunk, place a coffee can filled with kitty litter deodorizer inside the trunk overnight.

Helping prevent moth damage
- In addition to mothballs, put whole cloves in pockets of woolen coats or in bags with sweaters when storing for the off season. They help prevent moth damage and have a nice spicy odor.
- Before storing blankets for the summer, wash them and add 2 cups of mothballs to the rinse water.

This hint "can" solve your problem
- Store out of season clothes in large plastic lidded trash cans. Not only will your clothes be moth-proof, they will stay dry in damp basements.

Storing fine china plates
- Insert paper plates or paper napkins between fine china plates as you stack to prevent scratching.

Before applying contact paper
- Make patterns of the shelves and drawers with newspaper. Transfer the patterns to the contact paper before cutting and you will have an excellent fit.

Tips for storing jewelry, belts and handbags
- Egg cartons serve as excellent storage containers for jewelry.
- Place a piece of chalk in your jewelry box to prevent costume jewelry from tarnishing.

- To avoid tangled chains and necklaces, screw cup hooks to the inside of your closet door for tangle-free hanging.
- Hook large shower curtain hooks over the clothes rod for hanging handbags and belts.

No spills
- Tack a piece of sewing elastic across the inside of a drawer to keep small bottles (nail polish, ink...) upright in your desk or dresser drawers.

How to preserve a favorite news clipping
- Dissolve a milk of magnesia tablet in a quart of club soda overnight. Pour into a pan large enough to accommodate the flattened newspaper. Soak clipping for one hour, remove and pat dry. Do not move until completely dry. Estimated life: 200 years.

Wrapping packages
- To premeasure the length of gift wrapping paper from a large roll, wrap a string around the package first, then cut off the desired length and use it as a measuring guide.
- Before tying a package for mailing, wet the string or cord with water. This method prevents the string from slipping, and when dry it will hold extra tight.

Here's more
- Keep clear plastic wrap in the refrigerator to prevent it from ever sticking together.
- When mailing cookies, pack in popcorn to help keep them from crumbling.
- Sometimes mildew can be removed from papers and book pages by a good dusting with cornstarch. Allow the powder to remain on for several days before giving it the brush-off.
- Your favorite photo negatives can be stored behind the actual print in your scrapbook for safekeeping.
- Empty soft drink cartons are ideal for storing light bulbs.
- When postage stamps are stuck together, place them in the freezer. They will usually come apart and the glue will still be usable.
- Extension cords can be conveniently stored without tangling, by simply winding the cord loosely and slipping it into a cardboard tube (from paper towels or tissue paper).

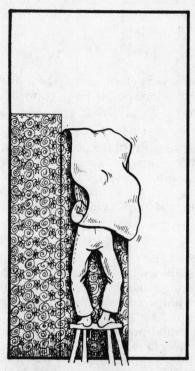

The Best
of Hints for
Wallpaper/
Woodwork

Removing wallpaper
- Use equal parts of vinegar and hot water. Dip roller or sponge into solution and wet paper thoroughly. After two applications the paper should peel off in sheets. Note: Use a paint roller. It is much more effective than using a brush.

Before repapering a wall
- Cover all grease spots with shellac and allow to dry thoroughly. This effectively prevents the grease spots from coming through on the new paper.

How much wallpaper?
- Try this formula to determine how many rolls of wallpaper will be needed to paper a room. Multiply the distance around the room (in feet) by the height of the room, then divide by 30. Deduct 2 rolls for every ordinary-sized opening such as windows and doors. The answer will equal the number of rolls needed. This allows for matching patterns.

Wallpapering the bathroom or kitchen
- After papering steamy rooms, paint all joints with clear varnish to prevent peeling.

A quick way to replace vinyl wallpaper
- When taking down the old paper, number each strip from left to right or vice versa. When cutting the new paper, use the numbered strips as a pattern. However, make sure the old and new papers are of the same width. You will save yourself a lot of measuring time with this method.

Patching wallpaper
- When you are tearing (never cut) wallpaper to make a patch, tear toward the wrong side of the paper. The patch will be almost invisible.

Removing unsightly bulges
- Slit the bulge with a razor blade. Using a knife, insert some paste under the paper. Smooth with a wet sponge.

Grease spots on wallpaper
- Make a paste of cornstarch and water. Let it remain on the spot until dry, then brush off. If the stain persists, try, try again.
- If the above method fails, try a paste of Fuller's Earth and carbon tetrachloride (both available at hardware stores) and use it in the same way.
- Or, apply a piece of clean blotting paper to the grease spot and press with a warm iron. Do more than once, using a fresh blotter each time. Remove any lingering traces by rubbing with a cloth dipped in borax.

Removing crayon marks
- Treat as a greasy spot.
- Rub lightly with a dry soap-filled steel wool pad. Do not wet.
- Or, rub very gently with baking soda sprinkled on a damp cloth.
- Crayon marks on vinyl can be removed with silver polish.

To remove everyday smudges
- Erase away light marks (pencil, fingerprints, dirt) with art-gum squares (available at stationery stores).

Removing cellophane tape
- Put a blotter against the tape and press with a warm iron.

An easy tip to avoid expensive plastering bills
- If the plaster is cracking on the ceiling, try this: Mix some Elmer's glue with baking soda, making a paste. Apply to cracks with fingers. If the ceiling is colored, add food coloring to match. This trick could help postpone replastering for months.

Plaster with no lumps
- If you add plaster to water, instead of water to plaster, the mixture will be lump free.

Another plaster tip
- You can slow the hardening of plaster by adding a little vinegar to the mixture.

How to hide nail holes from the landlady
- Rub toothpaste into the hole and smooth with a damp sponge.

Cleaning rough plastered walls
- Instead of using a cloth or sponge, try using nylon or Banlon socks. No small pieces will be left behind as you work.

A crack filler
- Fill cracks with steel wool or newspaper before finishing off with plaster.

The best wall cleaner
- Combine ½ cup ammonia, ¼ cup white vinegar, ¼ cup washing soda and 1 gallon warm water for the perfect solution for cleaning walls.

Brushing away cobwebs
- Slip a sock or two over the end of a yardstick. Secure with a rubber band. Also good for cleaning under the refrigerator and radiators.

The Best
of Hints for
Windows

Take the "pane" out of washing your windows
- Never wash windows on sunny days. They will dry too fast and show streaks.
- Never use soap.
- Add ½ cup ammonia, ½ cup white vinegar and 2 tablespoons of cornstarch to a bucket of warm water for a perfect window washing solution.
- For fast clean-ups, wash with a cloth soaked in white vinegar. This method is great when washing only a few indoor windows.
- Shine with newspaper instead of paper towels. It is cheaper and some feel easier. Be sure you have read the papers or the project could take all day.
- No more guess work when drying the inside panes with vertical strokes and the outside panes with horizontal strokes, or vice versa—you will notice quickly which side has the smudges.
- After windows have dried, rub a clean blackboard eraser over them for a really fine shine.

Before washing the inside windows
- To avoid taking down drapes, drape them through a clothes hanger and hang from the curtain rod. Drapes will be safely out of the way.

Keeping Jack Frost off windows
- The problem of ice covered windows can be solved by adding ½ cup rubbing alcohol or anti-freeze to each quart of water used.
- Rub the inside of windows with a sponge that has been dipped in rubbing alcohol or anti-freeze. Polish with paper towels or newspaper.
- Try a cloth moistened with glycerine, rub on, leaving a little of the glycerine on the inside of the glass.
- Or, head south.

Window and mirror cleaner
- Duplicate the "blue kind" by filling a spray bottle with 3 tablespoons of ammonia, 1 tablespoon vinegar and cool water. Add a drop or two of food coloring.

Spotted window sills
- Pour a little diluted rubbing alcohol on a soft cloth and rub the entire surface. The spots will not only disappear, but the sills will look freshly painted.

Some rather "shady" ideas
- Rub unwashable window shades with a rough flannel cloth which has been dipped in flour or corn meal.
- A soft eraser may remove spots and stains.
- Keep parchment shades clean by waxing them.

Are your tiebacks straight?
- A foolproof way to get tiebacks straight across from each other when hanging curtains is to use your window shade as a measuring guide.

Window shade tears
- Repair with colorless nail polish. This works wonders on small tears.

Cleaning screens
- For a thorough job, brush on both sides with kerosene. Wipe with a clean cloth. This method will also prevent rust from forming. Be sure to dust the screens with a small paint brush before you begin.
- For small jobs, rub a brush-type hair roller lightly over the screen and see how easily it picks up all the lint and dust.

Cleaning sliding door tracks
- Generally, the tracks of sliding glass doors are very hard to clean. Try wrapping a small cloth around an eraser and rub dirt away.

Cleaning aluminum window frames
- Try a cream silver polish.

Venetian blinds
- To repair a venetian blind tape that has broken, simply tape the side that faces the wall with heavy duty packing tape. Apply white canvas shoe polish.

- To brighten up the tapes on your blinds, simply rub in white shoe polish with a damp sponge.
- You can quickly clean venetian blinds by saturating a cloth with rubbing alcohol and wrapping around a rubber spatula. It will easily reach into the tiny slats.

Eliminating sticky windows

- Once a year, dip a small brush in petroleum jelly and paint it on the inside molding.
- If it is stuck, the divider is probably bent. To fix easily rap the divider to one side.
- Sometimes a vigorous snap to the window rope or chain will do the trick.

Replacing a pane of glass

- To loosen the old pane of glass, pass a red-hot poker slowly over the old putty.

Cheap drapery hem weights

- Use old door keys.

Easy moving curtain rods

- After washing traverse or curtain rods, wax them. They will move much better. This applies to new rods as well.

Inserting drapery hooks

- A soap coating will make drapery hooks much easier to push into the fabric.

Mary Ellen's
Best of
Helpful
Hints
Book II

by
Mary Ellen Pinkham

Dedication

This book is dedicated to my hinterrific staff:

Stan Ginsburg, editor-in-chief
Ruta Bruvelis
Steve Chain
George Cleveland
John Jacobson
Dick Madden
June Mattson
Sandy Mattson
Tom Morgan
Cindy Owen
Dana Pinkham
Sherman Pinkham, Sr.
Kathy Rice
Linda Riedl
David Smith, associate editor

and Lynn Johnston,
the creator of the syndicated cartoon
"For Better or for Worse"

Contents

Introduction

We've been at it again to bring you the "best" all-around hints to help you manage that busy life and household of yours. We've had a busy time of it ourselves, testing and reading more than 100,000 hints that came our way last year from all over the world.

We've selected the "best" 1,000 to bring you what we feel is our most "helpful" collection ever—*Mary Ellen's Best of Helpful Hints Book II.*

Happy Hinting!

Part 1
Home Stuff

Cleaning the
Miscellaneous

A Potpourri of Cleaning Hints

Ashtrays
- Ashtrays (not glass) will be easier to clean if polished with furniture polish.

Ballpoint-pen marks
- Clean ballpoint-pen marks off woodwork and painted walls with distilled white vinegar. First dab it on with a clean rag, then blot. Repeat as many times as necessary.
- For wallpaper, dampen the spot with water, then apply a very light coat of hair spray. Let it set a minute, then blot with a dry rag.

Barbecue grills
- When the grill is cool, place it inside a plastic garbage bag and add enough powdered dishwasher detergent and hot water to cover the grill. Tie the bag shut and let it sit outside for a few hours. Rinse it completely before using it again.

Bathroom bonuses
- Eliminate overcrowded drawers and messy medicine chests by hanging a large shoe bag on a wall or behind the bathroom door to hold toiletries and cosmetics. Childproof it if necessary.
- Or use a spice rack placed at adult eye level.
- Hang a roll of paper towels in the bathroom. You'll quickly find many uses for it.

Ceiling
- Wrap a cloth around your broom head and secure it with a rubber band. Just sweep away dust and cobwebs.

Cutting board
- Scrub it with a solution of two tablespoons of bleach per quart of warm water. Rinse under hot running water. Wipe immediately with paper towels.

Dacron curtains
- You can eliminate most of the ironing after washing Dacron curtains. Add one packet of unsugared gelatin dissolved in plain hot water to the final rinse water.

Doors
- To get at dust on louvered doors, wrap a cloth around a ruler, spray with your favorite dusting spray, and run the flat end across each louver.

Draperies
- Remove wrinkles from draperies: Spray them with a fine-mist plant sprayer as they hang.

Fiberglass tubs and shower walls
- Use the cleaner especially made for cleaning fiberglass boats.

Fireplace
- Clean the smoke film from glass fireplace doors by rubbing on fireplace ashes with a damp cloth. Buff with another damp cloth and the glass will come clean.
- To prevent soot from settling all over the house, dampen fireplace ashes with a plant mister before cleaning them out. Then shovel ashes into a box and cover it with wet newspapers.
- Rub a candle stub along the track of your fireplace screen to keep it sliding easily.

Golf balls
- Soak them in one cup of water and one-quarter cup of ammonia.

Golf clubs
- Rub the shaft and club heads lightly with a dry steel wool sponge.

Humidifiers
- A copper scouring pad in your humidifier will prevent lime buildup.

Kitchen exhaust-fan grill
- Wash it in the dishwasher.

Knickknacks
- Don't dust each knickknack individually. Collect them in a dishpan and bathe them in a little detergent and water. Rinse and dry them with a hair dryer.
- For delicate figurines that can't be washed, use artist's red-sable paintbrush #2 or #4. The long handle lets you get to hard-to-reach places and the little brush allows you to dust without breaking the object.

Light bulbs
- Get more light from light bulbs by keeping them dust-free.

Linens: a new wrinkle
- Store seldom-used linens by folding them wrong side out. Dust won't show on the crease lines.

Marble
- Try covering the stained area with 3 percent hydrogen peroxide. Let it set for several hours and wipe up with a dampened cloth. Marble stains are difficult to remove but this hint is worth a try.

Mattresses
- Use an upholstery shampoo to remove mattress stains. Spray the area with disinfectant air freshener to prevent mustiness.

Microwave oven
- To clean spills in a microwave oven, cover the spill with a damp paper towel and turn the oven on high for ten seconds. The mess will wipe up easily when the oven cools.

Odors: nothing to sniff about
- Make the whole house fresher: Put a solid room deodorizer next to the return vent of your forced-air heating system.
- To eliminate odors in home humidifiers, pour three or four capfuls of bottled lemon juice in the water.
- Get rid of sink odors by pouring a strong saltwater solution or a cup of bleach down the drain. Then let the water run to be sure no bleach remains to erode the pipes.

Pictures
- By using eyeglass-cleaning tissues (instead of a wet cloth) to clean the glass on a small picture, no water can seep under the glass or damage the frame.
- Dust oil paintings every few months with a soft brush. Never rub the painting with a cloth.

Plastic
- When cleaning plastic, try using a rag dampened with lemon oil to prevent smears.

Plastic hanging beads
- Put them in a pillowcase and run them through the washing machine along with a batch of cold-water wash.
- Or rinse them in a solution of warm water and vinegar.

Pleated lampshades
- Blow dust away with a hand-held hair dryer.
- Or use an old shaving brush.
- Or try a paintbrush.

Radiators
- Place a wet towel under the radiator and vacuum excess dust from fins. Blowing down through the fins with the blower end of the vacuum gets rid of even more dust. The wet towel beneath the register collects the excess.

Roller skates

- A good soaking in kerosene will remove dirt and grease from the bearings. Be sure to apply new grease before using them again.

Screens

- Clean screens with the dusting attachment of a vacuum cleaner.
- Or brush with carpet scraps that have been nailed to a wooden block.
- For a thorough job, dust the screens and brush with kerosene on both sides. Remove excess with soap and water.
- Take hopelessly dirty window screens to a do-it-yourself car wash. The high-pressure hoses shoot streams of hot, soapy water to clean off all dirt and grime.

Stainless-steel ware

- You can get rid of brownish stains on stainless steel by rubbing it with a dishcloth dipped in household ammonia.
- Or try oven cleaner. Be sure to rinse well.

Silver
- Use a pipe cleaner dipped in silver polish to remove tarnish from between the tines of silver forks.

Sinks
- Use an old toothbrush for cleaning off mold and dirt around the base of faucets and for cleaning the groove around your vanity basin.

Soap holder
- Use a sponge to hold soap. When you wash, wet and squeeze the sponge for suds—and there's no soap dish to clean.

Teflon
- Remove stains from a nonstick-finish utensil by boiling in it two tablespoons of baking soda and one cup of water for fifteen minutes. After the pan has been rinsed and dried, coat it with vegetable oil.

Venetian blinds
- Use an art-gum eraser (available at stationery stores) to remove smudges from venetian blinds.
- An old sock makes a great dusting glove.
- When blinds are really dirty, hang them on a clothesline and hose them down.
- Or hang them under the shower.

Walls behind stoves
- After you clean the painted wall behind your stove, apply a generous coating of furniture polish. Buff well. The next time you clean, grease spatters can be wiped away with a dry paper towel.

Clothing Care, Accessories, and Laundry

Feet First

The best shoeshine
- Use both liquid and cake-wax polishes. The liquid polish covers up scuff marks; the wax polish adds the shine. Apply the liquid first, let it dry, then apply the cake-wax polish and buff. It really does make a big difference.

More shine hints
- Soften hardened shoe polish by heating the metal container in a pan of hot water.
- A clean powder puff is a terrific shoe-polish applicator.
- And when your shoe brush becomes caked with polish, soak it for one-half hour in a solution of warm, sudsy water and a few teaspoons of turpentine. Rinse and let dry.

Shine in the boss's eyes
- For that quick polish at the office, rub a little dab of hand cream on each shoe and buff thoroughly.

Scuff marks
- Cover scuffs on white shoes with white typewriter correction fluid (available at stationery stores) before polishing.
- Acrylic paint or paint used to touch up car nicks is helpful in restoring badly scuffed shoes.
- Light scuff marks can be removed from most light-colored leather shoes with an art-gum eraser (available at stationery stores).
- Scrub scuff marks on silver and gold shoes with a toothbrush and white toothpaste; the marks will vanish.

Boots

- Make your own boot tree: Tie together two or three empty paper-towel tubes; stand them in the legs of your boots to hold them upright.
- Or use large soda bottles or rolled-up newspapers or magazines.
- Or hang them up with a clamp-type pants hanger.
- Rubber boots will slip on and off easily if you spray the inside with furniture polish and wipe them clean.

Cowboy boots

- Spray the inside of cowboy boots with silicone spray (available at hardware stores) and you'll slip in and out of them without a struggle. (It also holds down foot odor.)
- To prevent cowboy boots from turning up at the toes, clip the sole at the tip of the toe to a clipboard, then weigh the heels down with a few heavy cans inside the boot.

Suede shoes

- Remove scuff marks or rain spots from suede by rubbing with very fine sandpaper.
- Keep those suede shoes looking like new; rub thoroughly with a dry sponge after they've been worn.
- Steam-clean suede the easy way. First remove all dirt with a suede brush or dry sponge, then hold shoes over a pan of boiling water. Once the steam raises the nap, stroke the suede with a soft brush in one direction only. Allow the shoes to dry completely before wearing them.

Tennis shoes

- Clean grimy tennis shoes by rubbing them with a wet, soap-filled scouring pad.
- After they've been washed and dried, stuff the toes with paper toweling. Then dab undiluted liquid starch on the toes and let dry. They'll keep their shape and wear longer.
- When the crepe sole of a washable canvas shoe becomes loose, spread clear silicone glue (available at paint and hardware stores) between the sole and the shoe. Hold them together with rubber bands or tape for twelve to twenty-four hours.

Shoelaces
- Don't come unglued if the plastic tip comes off the end of a shoelace. Dip the frayed end in glue and shape to a point. Let dry before using.
- Leather shoelaces stay tied longer when a few drops of water are sprinkled on the knot.

New shoes
- Sandpaper the soles of new shoes to make them less slippery.
- Or rub the soles across the sidewalk before wearing them.

Wet shoes
- Coat rain-soaked shoes with saddle soap while they are still wet. Stuff the inside with black-and-white newspaper and leave the soap on for at least twenty-four hours. Dry shoes away from direct heat to prevent stiffness.

Tight shoes
- Saturate a cotton ball with rubbing alcohol and rub the tight spot on the inside of the shoe. Put both shoes on immediately and walk around. Repeat until the tight shoe feels comfortable.
- Or purchase a shoe-stretching product from your shoe-repair shop.

Underneath It All

Panty hose
- Have a soft touch: Liquid fabric softener, because it lubricates the fibers, adds life to hosiery. Keep some handy in a leftover dishwashing-detergent squirt bottle and add a dash to the final rinse.
- Panty hose bounce back into shape if you rinse them in a basin of warm water and three tablespoons of vinegar.
- To quick-dry panty hose, hang them on a towel rod and blow-dry them with a hair dryer.

- Instead of storing hose or nylon knee-highs in a dresser drawer, put each pair in a small plastic sandwich bag. It's easy to pick out the right color and the bags are snag-proof.

Got a run?
- Cut the other leg off the panty hose and pair it with another one-legged pair.

Slips and bras
- To rejuvenate dingy white slips and panties, dye them in hot, strong tea until the fabric is a shade darker than desired. Rinse until water runs clear. The color will not wash out.
- How to wash those delicate lace items? Shake them up in a jar filled with warm, mild, soapy water.
- To get the wrinkles out of lace, iron on waxed paper.
- Keep bra straps from falling off your shoulders by sewing lightweight thin elastic from one strap to the other.
- Rub a fresh fabric-softener sheet over slips and hose to prevent dresses from clinging.

Hints for Those Who Wear the Pants

Slacks
- To remove those little fuzzy balls between pant legs, try this: Stretch the area as taut as possible over your knee, then rub fabric with a clean plastic-mesh pot scrubber. Don't be afraid to rub hard.

Jeans
- If you don't want the color to fade from new designer jeans, soak them for an hour in a solution of cold salt water (two tablespoons per gallon of water) before washing them. Use the cold-water setting for both the wash and rinse cycles.
- And before laundering, turn the pant legs inside out to reduce wear from friction.
- Rejuvenate a pair of faded jeans by washing them with a pair of new jeans that have never been laundered. You'll be amazed how the dye and sizing that wash out of the new jeans add color to the old ones.
- To prevent the cuffs from rolling up on blue jeans, fold and crease the bottom of the pant legs and secure each with two paper clips before putting the pants in the dryer. Dry the pants separately to prevent snagging other clothes.
- Or if a denim hem keeps folding up no matter how much you press it, iron on some mending tape just inside the hem edge.
- Rescue jeans with muddy knees and bottoms by rinsing them under the faucet and letting them soak overnight in a plastic tub of water with one-quarter cup of ammonia and one-quarter cup of your favorite detergent. Wash them as usual and ground-in mud should be gone.

Hints to Pull the Wool over Your Eyes

Sweaters
- If shedding angora sweaters are getting your goat, put them in a plastic bag in the freezer for a while before they're worn.
- When the cuffs and waistline of your woolen sweaters are stretched out, dip them in hot water and dry with a hot blow dryer. They should shrink back to normal.
- Hand-wash sweaters in your favorite cold-water wash product. Then fill the washing machine with cool water and add a little fabric softener. Swish the sweaters around by hand until they are thoroughly rinsed. Drain the tub and set it on the final spin cycle. The sweaters can now be spread on towels without leaving puddles.

- After hand-washing woolen sweaters, rinse with one-quarter cup of white vinegar in cool water to remove detergent residue.
- To dry and block sweaters, take a framed window screen and outline the unwashed sweater in chalk on the screen. After washing the sweater, block it to the outline and set the screen on bricks or across the backs of two chairs. Air freely circulates underneath for quick drying.
- Fix a snag by taking a wire needle threader and pushing it through the sweater from the wrong side. Catch the loose thread in the tip of the threader and pull it back through the fabric. If the thread is long enough, knot it to keep it from working loose again.

"Skin" Care Hints

Leather
- Remove ink from leather by rubbing out the stain with baking soda. As the powder absorbs the stain it becomes discolored. Reapply the baking soda until the stain disappears.
- To remove grease stains rub with a thick mixture of Fuller's paste and water. When dry, brush paste off.
- Using cold cream is an inexpensive way to clean and soften leather items. Just rub the cream into the leather with fingertips, then wipe clean with a dry cloth.
- Never put a sticky name tag on suede or leather garments.

Suede
- Clean suede by gently rubbing, in a circular motion, ground oatmeal into the stain with a clean cloth. Brush out all the powder with a wire brush. Repeat if necessary.

Hints to Top It Off

Fur real
- Use a wire brush to fluff up dry, matted trim on fur coats.

- Caught in the rain? Shake your fur coat and hang it in a well-ventilated area away from direct heat.
- Allow furs to breathe. Don't cover them with plastic or smother them between other coats in the closet.
- Put a pest strip in the closet instead of mothballs. Mothball odor clings to fur and is very difficult to eliminate.

Hats
- To reshape an old straw hat, soak it in salt water until it's soft. Then shape it and let dry.
- The limp veil on your hat will perk up after being sprayed lightly with hair spray.
- Or iron it under a sheet of waxed paper.

Gems for Jewels

No more tangles
- Hang long necklaces and chains on a small bulletin board and secure each piece with a push pin.
- Or hang chains on men's tie holders. Fasten the tie holder to the inside of a closet door.
- Or hang them on small cup hooks that can be easily screwed to the inside of your closet door or to a free wall in the closet.
- Or put them in drinking straws, then fold each end.
- Or wrap chains around a hair roller and secure them with bobby pins.

Untangling
- To untangle a thin chain, try rubbing it between your hands for a minute or two.
- Or dust the knot with talcum powder and untangling will be easier.
- Or put a drop or two of salad oil or baby oil on a piece of waxed paper, lay the knot in the oil, and undo it with two straight pins.

Storing

- Egg cartons, plastic silverware trays, and plastic ice-cube trays make excellent storage containers for jewelry.
- Fasten pierced earrings through the holes of a small button so they won't get separated or lost.
- Or line your jewelry box with foam rubber and stick the posts into the foam.

Diamonds

- Here's a formula gemologists use to clean diamonds, rubies, and sapphires: Mix in a bowl one cup of water, one-quarter cup of ammonia, and a tablespoon of dishwashing detergent. Scrub the jewelry lightly with an old toothbrush. Ammonia won't hurt gold or silver settings. *Do not* use this formula for cleaning soft, porous stones, such as opals, pearls, turquoise and coral.
- Or clean gems with a soft toothbrush and Prell shampoo.
- Or soak them in club soda for a while.
- To remove remaining soap film after cleaning a ring, dip it in a small bowl of rubbing alcohol, then let it dry without rinsing.

Gold

- In a bowl combine one-half cup of clear household ammonia and one cup of warm water; let chains or rings sit in the solution for ten to fifteen minutes. Scrub jewelry with a soft brush and rinse under warm water with the sink drain closed.

Pearls

- Soak pearl rings and pins in a bowl of mild soap and water. *Never* use ammonia. Rinse in clear water, with the drain closed, before drying them with a soft flannel cloth.
- *Don't soak* a *string* of pearls in water. Dampen a soft cloth with soapy water and rub pearls gently until clean.
- And to help keep pearls lustrous, gently rub them with a little olive oil and wipe dry with a piece of clean chamois cloth.

Silver
- Soak it in a mild solution of Dip-It coffeepot cleaner and water.
- Or rub silver with dry baking soda and a soft cloth. Rinse it in water and towel-dry.
- Or try rubbing silver with a soft cloth that has been dipped in fireplace or cigarette ashes.

Super-clean jewelry
- After the jewelry has been soaked in the appropriate solution, squirt it with the water jet of your jet oral-hygiene appliance, using clear water. It drives dirt out of the crevices and leaves the jewels sparkling clean. (Make sure the sink drain is closed just in case any gem settings are loose.)

Ring around the finger
- Clear nail polish applied to the inside of an inexpensive ring prevents a green ring from forming around your finger.
- If you have an allergic reaction to a favorite ring or pair of earrings, apply one or two coats of clear nail polish around the inside of the band or to the part of the earring that touches the ear. Before applying nail polish to earrings, clean them with rubbing alcohol.

Ring removal
- Help loosen a ring when your finger is swollen by placing your hand in a bowl of ice-cold soapy water.
- Or rub hand cream around the band of the ring.
- Or rub soap on the ring and finger.
- Or try holding your hand above your head for a few minutes, allowing the blood to drain.

An ounce of prevention
- Don't lose that pin. Cut a wide rubber band to a length of one-half inch. Push the pin through clothing, but before locking it, put the pin through the rubber. If the lock opens, the rubber band will help prevent the pin from falling off.
- Be extra cautious when attaching charms to a charm bracelet. Place a drop of clear glue on the small ring opening to prevent loss.

Washday Wisdom

Lint regulations
- To keep lint from clogging your drain, secure an old nylon stocking over your washing-machine hose with a heavy-duty rubber band.
- Or cut a piece of window screening big enough to cover the bottom of the sink. To remove lint from the screen, simply scrub with a damp brush.

A time-saver
- If your laundry room is in the basement, set your kitchen timer to the length of time it takes each cycle to be completed. Now you can avoid those unnecessary trips up and down the steps to check your wash. This goes especially for apartment dwellers.

Sorting
- Set a small wastebasket in each child's room to use as a minihamper for soiled socks.
- Save yourself the trouble of sorting dark socks. Make a small laundry bag for each family member, using dish towels or mesh fabric with a drawstring top. Personalize the bags by making each a different color. Toss the bags into the washer and when they come out of the dryer, the socks are already sorted.
- For faster sorting, mark underwear and T-shirts with a different color indelible ink for each family member.

Prewash treatments
- A bar of Fels naphtha soap wrapped in a nylon onion bag provides the cleaning power as well as the abrasion for pretreating most stubborn laundry spots.
- Remove spots cheaply by applying automatic-dishwasher detergent to wet fabric. Scrub gently with an old toothbrush. Rinse.
- To prevent nylon from turning yellow, presoak it in a tubful of warm water to which you've added one-half cup of baking soda.

- Before washing a garment with a drawstring, safety-pin the string to the clothing. Now you can toss it safely into the washer.

The best way to clean whites
- Pour one gallon of hot water into a plastic container and add one-half cup of automatic-dishwashing soap and one-half cup of bleach. Mix well. Soak clothing overnight, then, in the morning, dump solution and clothes into the washing machine and wash as usual. Add one-half cup of white vinegar to the rinse water. (If you use this formula on nylon or synthetics, allow water to cool a bit, as hot water sets wrinkles.)
- To whiten old or dull white polyester, soak it overnight in a bucket filled with one gallon of water and one cup of automatic-dishwasher detergent. In the morning toss the polyester into the machine and wash as usual. It's a great way to get uniforms sparkling white.

Colorfasting
- When setting the dye in clothing, always do each article separately. Add one-half cup of vinegar and one tablespoon of salt to one-half gallon of water. Soak fabric for one hour. If rinse water still shows some color, repeat.

The best washing compound
- Dissolve one pound of washing soda and one-half pound of borax in two gallons of water. Store mixture in a large plastic jug. Add a cupful for a tub of soiled clothes.

Rinse cycle
- Add a sprinkling of your favorite bath salts to the last rinse water when washing blankets, robes, and spreads. Let fabric soak about ten minutes and it comes out sweet-smelling.
- Keep plastic items such as shower curtains or baby pants soft and pliable. Add a few ounces of glycerin when rinsing them.

Solar power
- An ideal place to dry your laundry in the winter is a screened porch with a southern exposure. Completely cover all screened windows and doors with plastic. When the sun shines through the plastic, the temperature on the porch can reach 75 degrees.

Old softies
- After fabric-softener sheets have been used twice, store them in a jar with some liquid fabric softener. When drying a load of clothes, just squeeze out the excess liquid from one of the sheets and toss it in the dryer.

Drying
- A plastic hanging plant pot makes a great weatherproof clothespin holder for the clothesline. When it rains, the water will drain out of the holes in the planter's bottom.
- Does your clothesline sag? Put a link chain at one end, and instead of having to bother with retying, just move the chain up one or two links.

For Pressing Engagements

Wrinkles
- If permanent-press clothes are wrinkled, set the dryer for ten minutes and toss in a wet towel.

Starching
- If you like collars, cuffs, and button bands extra stiff, fill an empty, clean roll-on deodorant bottle with liquid starch and apply the desired amount. (To remove the roll-on ball from the bottle, gently pry the top off with a nail file.)

Dampening clothing
- Don't use cold water to dampen your clothes for ironing. Clothes dampen more evenly and quickly with warm water.

Faster ironing
- For smoother ironing, frequently run your warm iron over waxed paper. Be sure to run the iron over a clean cloth or a paper towel before ironing again.

Lint removers
- Use a pompom made of nylon net to remove lint quickly from clothes while ironing. Brush the net ball over the clothes and the lint will disappear. For handy usage, attach the net to the ironing board with string.
- Or use a large synthetic sponge to take lint off synthetic clothing. This works especially well on polyester double-knits, which seem to attract lint in the wash.

Sweet smells
- Add a little witch hazel to the water in your steam iron. Your clothes will smell fresh and sweet.
- Or add a few drops of your favorite cologne.

Creaseless sleeves
- To press a jacket or dress sleeve without making a crease, roll up a thick magazine, cover it with a cloth, and insert it in the sleeve. The magazine immediately unrolls enough to make a firm pressing pad.

Pressing pleats
- Hold pleats in place with paper clips while ironing.
- When pleats are pressed, the folds sometimes leave marks on the pleats above. Avoid this by placing long strips of brown paper under each pleat.

Sharp pant creases
- Use a dampened brown grocery bag (with no lettering) for pressing sharp creases. It's especially good for pressing seams on tailored garments.
- For a sharp, permanent crease in slacks, steam-iron them as usual, then turn slacks inside out and run a candle along the crease. Turn pants right side out and steam-iron them again. This method is great for wash-and-wear fabric.

Press on
- When ironing large flat clothing, use the wide end of the board and rest the iron at the tapered end. You'll have more room to iron each section.
- Revive velvet or corduroy by pressing it facedown on a piece of the same fabric.

Stop the presses
- Remove blouses from the dryer while still wet. Hang them on hangers, smooth out at the buttons, and spray with starch. Let dry and pressing is eliminated.

Putting clothes away
- If you could use more help sorting and returning clean clothes to their owners, put up a shelf in the laundry room. Set plastic dishpans on it and label each pan with a family member's name. On washday each person can collect his own clothing.
- Put up a floor-to-ceiling plant pole in your laundry room to hang freshly dried clothes. Let everyone retrieve his own clothing.

Dear dry cleaner
- Before sending a freshly stained garment to the cleaner, attach a note saying what caused the stain.

Storage ideas
- Line dresser drawers with colorful quilted fabric instead of shelving paper. Measure the drawers and hem the fabric to fit the drawer. Apply with double-faced carpet tape.
- Dresses with spaghetti straps will not slip off hangers if you wrap both ends of the hanger with thick rubber bands.

- Used fabric-softener sheets can be reused as sachets in dresser drawers.
- Or put empty perfume bottles in lingerie drawers.
- Did you know that bar soap lasts longer when unwrapped and left to dry before it is used? While drying it out put it in a linen drawer to add a fragrance that will linger.

Going into storage

- Preserve treasured clothing that you plan to hand down by storing in plastic bags that seal. After washing and drying an item, fold it and place in one of the large-size bags, squeezing as much air out as possible. This will keep the bag airtight and bug-proof.
- Worn sheets make excellent garment covers, especially for fur, suede, and leather clothing, which must breathe.
- And don't store leather or suede purses in plastic. Wrap them in old pillowcases.
- Fill those empty clip-on baskets (used in the dishwasher to prevent water spots) with mothballs. Replace the cap and hang the baskets in your garment bags to prevent moth damage.

Coming out of the closet

- To remove mothball odor from clothing, tumble each item separately in the dryer for about ten minutes with air only and no heat.

- Or air clothing outdoors on windy days. To ensure that the clothing stays on the hangers, hang each item on two hangers with the hooks turned in opposite directions. The hangers won't fall off the line. To make clothing doubly secure, clip the garment to the hangers with clothespins.
- After removing your winter or summer clothes from storage, hang the garments on the curtain rod in your bathroom and cover with clear plastic dry-cleaner bags. Run the hottest tap water possible from the shower for a few minutes. The steam will penetrate the clothing and remove most of the wrinkles.

Furniture
and Floors

Good–Wood Care

Polishing tools
- A shoe buffer polishes tabletops to a high luster.
- A terry-cloth oven mitt does double duty. One side waxes; the other polishes.
- Chair rungs are easier to clean if you use a discarded cotton sock with spray wax on it.

The best dustcloths
- Add two teaspoons of turpentine to a quart jar of hot, sudsy water. Put clean, lint-free cloths in the jar and let them soak overnight, then wring them out and hang to dry. Your cloths will attract dust as well as if they'd been sprayed with any commercial product.
- Or put a cloth in a solution of one-quarter cup of lemon oil and two cups of hot water. Let the cloth dry, and go to work.
- Capture dust balls from under and behind furniture with a damp mop.

Removing wax buildup on wood
- Wax can be softened by using a few drops of turpentine on a soft cloth. Rub hard, allow turpentine to dry, and buff wood with another cloth.

High-gloss shine
- After polishing, sprinkle on a little cornstarch and rub wood with a soft cloth. The cornstarch absorbs excess polish, eliminates fingerprints, and leaves a glossy surface. Your finger should leave no trace when you run it over the surface.

Out of circulation
- Cut down on the dust circulating through your home by spraying the furnace filter with Endust.
- Or cut used fabric-softener sheets or pieces of nylon to fit your floor registers. Slip them under the vent as air filters.

Turning the tables
- Because exposure to sunlight affects color, the dining-room table should be turned a few times a year to help maintain even color.
- Leaves should be put in the table occasionally. This exposure to light will help them maintain the same color as the table.

Home Furnishings

Wicker furniture
- Wicker will not turn yellow if washed in a solution of mild salt water.
- Tighten a sagging seat by washing it outdoors with hot, sudsy water. Rinse with a hose and let it dry in the sun.
- A paintbrush sprayed with furniture polish is ideal for dusting wicker. The brush reaches into crevices while the polish removes the dust.
- Mildew on wicker? Rub the spots with a cloth dipped in diluted ammonia. The wicker won't become discolored as long as you do not saturate the wood.

Lawn furniture
- Tubular aluminum outdoor furniture won't pit if you apply paste wax. Repeat every year.
- And keep old metal furniture from rusting by drilling a few small holes in the seats. Rainwater will drain out.
- To help prevent moisture damage to cushions, first cover them with plastic, then put the covers on.

Wrought iron
- If rust appears, remove all traces with steel wool or a wire brush.
- Coat with aluminum paint before covering with two coats of outdoor paint.
- A coat of paste wax will give extra protection.

Chrome furniture
- Spiff up chrome table legs by rubbing them with a piece of smooth, damp aluminum foil, shiny side out. The foil will turn black, but the chrome will sparkle.
- Leftover club soda is great for cleaning chrome. Ask your friendly bartender.

Glass-top tables
- A capful of liquid fabric softener in a quart of water makes a great lint-free cleaner for glass and Plexiglass tabletops.

Double-duty sofa
- When it's time to have the sofa upholstered, have one side of each cushion covered with plastic. When company comes, just flip the cushions over.
- Because the seat wears faster than other parts, cover each seat cushion with two sets of covers.

Nonslip arm covers
- Keep all arm covers in place by laying a sheet of art foam (available at art-supplies stores) between the arm covers and the arm rest.

Pianos
- If you are going away for a length of time, crumple some newspaper and place inside the piano to absorb moisture, then cover the top with a blanket.

Sectional furniture: keeping it all together
- To keep sectional furniture pieces from drifting apart, fasten a screen-door hook and eye to the back legs.

Loose caster
- Wrap a rubber band or some string around the caster stem before pushing it back into the leg.

Having a fit?
- Use a rubber spatula to push the material into the corners and sides when fitting slipcovers.

Worn piping
- When the fabric wears off the piping on your sofa or chair, color it with matching indelible ink.

Upholstery tricks
- Space tacks evenly on upholstered furniture by fastening a tape measure along the tack line.
- When hammering a decorative furniture tack, place a wooden thread spool against it to avoid damaging the head.
- Stick a few extra tacks to a hidden spot on the frame so they are available when needed.
- After recovering a piece of furniture, put some of the upholstery scraps in an envelope and staple it to the bottom of the piece. The material is there when a patch-up is needed.

Linoleum

Mop to glow
- Floors will shine between waxings if mopped with a mixture of one-half cup of fabric softener and one-half pail of cold water.
- Or quick-shine floors, after they have been swept clean, with a mop and a piece of waxed paper underneath. The remaining dust will also stick to the waxed paper.

Quick-drying waxed floors
- Dry floors quickly with a portable fan set at one end of the room.

Repairing floor tiles
- A linoleum floor tile may come loose or develop a bulge. Put a piece of aluminum foil over the tile and run a hot iron across the top a few times to soften the glue. Then put a couple of heavy books on the tile to flatten it.
- The same method can be used to remove floor tile.

- To patch a hole or gouge in linoleum, grate a scrap of matching tile in a food grater, then mix the dust with white glue. Fill the hole with the mixture. Let it dry and sandpaper it smooth.
- Or make a paste of finely chopped cork and shellac. Fill the hole, sandpaper it, and touch it up with paint to match the color of the linoleum.

Cleaner mops
- Rinse soiled string or yarn mops in a bucket of sudsy water and a little chlorine bleach as long as the strings aren't coated with cellulose.
- Don't be fazed if you can't shake a dust mop outside. Shake off dirt and dust after placing the mop head inside a large grocery bag.

Clean sweeps
- Dust and dirt collect easier after spraying the bristles of the broom with some furniture polish or water.

Dustpans
- Put a coat of wax on your dustpan; dust and dirt will slide off easily.

Broom care
- Stiffen the bristles of a new broom by soaking them in hot salt water.
- To renew the shape of an old broom, put a large rubber band around the bottom.
- Put a hook in the end of your broomstick and hang it in your cleaning closet. If you stand a broom on end, it might ruin the bristles.
- Cut the finger off an old rubber glove and slide it over the handle. The broom won't fall down if you have to lean it against the wall for a moment.

Carpet

Vacuuming
- A straightened wire coat hanger will unclog your unattached vacuum hose.
- Some vacuum bags can be used many times. When full, just cut off the bottom and empty it.•Then fold and staple.
- Save steps when vacuuming. Carry all your attachments in a carpenter's apron.

Vacuuming under dressers
- Take out the bottom drawers from a dresser that is too heavy to move. If the dresser does not have a wooden bottom, the vacuum hose will fit through the opening.

Longer carpet life
- Don't use leftover carpeting as an area rug on your new carpet unless it's backed with rubber. Because the bottom is rough, it acts like sandpaper, wearing down the pile whenever someone walks on it.

Throw-rug care
- Shampoo large area rugs outdoors on the picnic table, then just rinse with a hose. Rugs will dry flat with no clothesline creases.

No slipups
- Throw rugs won't slip out from under you if a few strips of double-faced carpet tape are placed under the corners.

Rugs on the mend
- To repair a rug with frayed edges, snip off the loose threads and dab some transparent glue along the entire edge. When the glue dries, it won't be noticeable.
- Has your braided rug split apart? Sew it back together again with clear plastic fishing line.

The
Handyperson

Handy Dandies

Taming of the screw
- If you've already tried loosening a stubborn nut or screw by soaking it in ammonia, penetrating oil, or hydrogen peroxide, try this: Heat the nut or screw with an iron and rap it with a hammer. Use goggles for eye protection.
- Keep a bolt tight simply by putting another nut on the bolt and tightening it against the first one.
- Or put a few drops of clear nail polish on the bolt just before giving it the final turn with a screwdriver.
- A screw will be easier to insert if you push it into a bar of soap first.

No magnetic screwdriver?
- Start a screw in a hard-to-get-at place by pushing the screw through a narrow piece of masking tape, sticky side up. Fold each end of the tape so that it sticks to the side of the screwdriver blade.
- Or glue the screw to the screwdriver with a drop of rubber cement. When the glue has dried enough to hold the screw, put it in place and tighten it. Then just pull on the screwdriver and the blade will easily break loose from the rubber cement.

Avoid smashed fingers
- Use a bobby pin to hold a nail or tack in place as you hammer.

Eliminating hammer and plier marks
- When pulling a nail out of wood with a claw hammer, slip a small piece of wood or a magazine under the hammerhead. This protects the wood surface and gets better leverage.

- Or use a spatula or a bowl scraper.
- To prevent vise jaws from leaving clamp marks, pad them with plastic coffee-can lids.
- Or use a kitchen sponge or carpet scraps.
- For pliers, cut two fingers off an old pair of rubber gloves and slip them over the jaws.

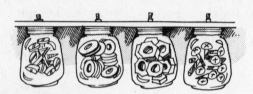

Storing small parts
- Separate nails, screws, bolts, and other small items and put them into baby-food jars with screw-on tops. Then punch a hole in the center of each lid, screw it in place under a work shelf, and screw the jar to the lid.
- Keep nuts and washers together by slipping them over the open end of an extra-large safety pin. Close the pin and hang it on a nail.

Storing larger tools
- Hang a shoe bag with pockets above your workbench.
- Store your circular saw blades in record-album covers and line them up in a record rack. Label the covers clearly and keep rack where children can't get at it.

Storing tools often used
- The tools used most frequently should be stored in an old lunch box. The box is ready at hand in case of an emergency.

Storing tools seldom used
- Before storing seldom-used tools, spray them with silicone lubricant, then wrap each tool tightly in aluminum foil.

A "hefty" apron
- Make a quick apron for those messy jobs by cutting holes for your arms and head in a large garbage bag.

Gluing clamps
- Use a spring-type clothespin to hold a glued object in place as it dries.
- Or use a clamp-type pants hanger.
- And for a very small item, try an old screw-type earring.

Gluing joints
- When gluing a joint, put a strip of tape along the edge. If any of the glue is forced out of the joint, it will stick to the tape. When the job is done, just peel the tape off and any excess glue will come off with it.
- For a stronger bond mix a few steel-wool shavings in the glue before applying.

No tape measure?
- Use string to take measurements in awkward places or around corners. Fasten one end with tape.
- Spread your fingers wide apart and measure the distance between your little finger and your thumb. When you don't have a ruler, this "quick reference" can serve to approximate a measurement.
- If you're alone and have to measure something long with a tape measure, tape one end down with masking tape.

Keep this hint on file
- Clean a file by putting a piece of masking tape over the length of the blade and press down firmly. Pull the tape off and the shavings will come off with it.

Substitute whetstone
- Dampen the bottom of a clay flower pot.

Keeping track of small parts
- Before taking apart an item that has a lot of small pieces, stick a strip of double-edged tape on your worktable. Place the parts on the tape in the order of removal so that everything will be in line for reassembly.

Slick oil tricks
- Put a drinking straw over your oil-can spout when oiling hard-to-get-at places.
- Or after soaking the tip of a pipe cleaner, bend it to fit into any hard-to-reach spot.

Uses for petroleum jelly
- It's a great rust preventive for tools. Spread it heavily on tools that aren't used much.
- Use as a lubricant whenever oil or grease is not handy.
- And apply a glob to the end of a long stick to retrieve a small item from an unreachable place.

Razor blades
- Don't cut yourself when working with a double-edged razor blade. Make a holder by sliding a piece of cork over one edge.
- Or cover one edge with the bottom fold of an empty matchbook. When you're done, close the cover, mark it "razor blade," and store it in a safe place.
- To sharpen blades, use the matchbook striker.

Ladder matters
- Drive spikes through the bottom of tuna-fish cans into the ground and put the feet of the ladder inside the cans.
- And for extra safety, wrap a piece of burlap around the bottom rung. Wipe your shoes on it to remove moisture

and mud that might cause you to slip as you climb.
- Tools won't fall off a stepladder platform if molding is attached to the edges of the platform.
- Make a tool holder for use on a straight ladder by wrapping and nailing an old belt to the top ends of the ladder. Then slip your tools beneath the belt before you put the ladder up.
- Or use thick rubber strips from an old inner tube.

Lumber hints
- To prevent moisture damage, stack your shop lumber on top of a couple of old tires.
- Your shop floor becomes a giant ruler for measuring lumber by painting inch and feet intervals on it. Start at a wall so that wall and boards can abut.

Light bulbs
- To remove a broken light bulb, turn off the lamp, then press a thick, dry sponge onto the jagged bulb base and twist gently.

Finding the right switch in a fuse box
- You want to turn off the power to a certain room but you don't know which switch to flip. Try this: Plug in a portable radio in that room, turning it up loud enough to hear at the fuse box. When you flip the right switch, the radio will shut off.

A new way to find a wall stud
- Gently run an electric razor along the wall. When the razor runs across the stud, the tone of the buzzing will change.

Door hinges
- Hanging a door will be a lot easier if you rest it on a small stack of newspapers or magazines while you put the hinges on the frame.
- Remove a door by taking off the bottom hinge first, then wedge a book under the door and remove the top hinge.

Windows
- Stop window rattles! Glue corn pads to the window frames.

- To safely remove a broken windowpane, glue newspaper to both sides of the glass, let it dry, then gently chip away the putty. The pane will come out without scattering glass splinters.
- Repair a small hole in a windowpane by filling it with clear shellac or nail polish. Put a few drops in the hole, let it dry, then put in a few more drops until the hole is filled.

Floorboard squeaks
- Squeeze liquid soap into the cracks.

Squeaky bed springs
- A shot of spray wax will often silence the squeak.
- If springs rubbing against the frame cause the squeak, pad the frame with small pieces of sponge.

Screen test
- How do you fix holes in a screen? For small holes dab them with clear nail polish. Use thin coats to prevent drips.
- Or use a few drops of airplane glue.
- For larger holes cut a patch from a piece of old screen and glue the edges in place with airplane glue.

Frozen padlocks
- Keep an outside padlock from freezing by covering it with a plastic sandwich bag and sealing the top with a rubber band.
- Or cover the keyhole with a piece of masking tape.
- To thaw a frozen lock, cup your hands around it and blow on the keyhole.

Plumbing
- Checking for a silent leak in the toilet-tank valve? Pour some bluing into the tank. Don't flush for an hour or more. Then if blue water appears in the bowl, seepage has occurred and either you or your plumber should replace the valve.
- Put some petroleum jelly around the rim of your plunger to provide a seal for better suction.
- If your toilet is clogged and you don't have a plunger, try pouring six to eight buckets of very hot water into the bowl as fast as they will go down without overflowing. Do not flush between buckets.

Clogged sinks
- Clogged kitchen sinks are usually caused by grease caught in the sink trap. This problem is easily solved if you put a heat lamp or a hair blow dryer (turned to HOT) directly under the sink trap until the grease has melted. Flush the drain by running hot water for a few minutes.
- To unclog a stopped-up sink or drain, run your garden hose into the house and push the nozzle as far into the drain as possible. After wrapping a towel around the hose to fully close the drain opening, hold on tightly while someone else turns on the outdoor faucet. Whatever is clogged should be forced out by the water pressure.

Repairing stereo-speaker rattles
- Take the speaker apart and you'll probably find a crack in the paper cone. A dab of clear nail polish will mend it well.

Repeat performances
- Your appliance or car refuses to make its peculiar noise for the serviceman! Then tape-record one of its better performances and let him listen.

Restoring a picnic table
- Glue leftover pieces of floor tiling to the top. Choose a matching color paint for the legs, and you will have an almost-new table at very little cost.

Get a handle on it
- Make a new pot-lid handle. Paint an old thread spool and secure it on top of the lid with a bolt and nut.

Warped records
- Place the record between two sheets of picture-frame glass and leave it in the sun for a day on a flat surface. When the sun goes down, remove the record. If it wasn't too badly warped, it should be as good as new.

Letter perfect
- Renew the worn dial on a washer or other appliance by rubbing the knob with red or black crayon until indentations (letters and numbers) are level. Wipe off excess crayon and the print will be readable again.

Painting

Hinterrific Paint Jobs

Cover ups
- An old pair of socks slipped over shoes protects them from paint spatters.
- Keep a couple of plastic sandwich bags handy to slip over hands if the doorbell or telephone rings.
- Or wrap a rag around the telephone receiver and fasten it with rubber bands.

A better paint bucket
- A portable lightweight paint bucket can be fashioned from an empty, clean plastic milk or bleach bottle. Opposite the handle cut a hole for the paintbrush to fit through easily.

Eliminating paint-can messes
- Don't use the side of the can to remove excess paint from your brush. Use a straight piece of wire coat hanger fastened across the opening of the can. To hold it in place, bend the wire at right angles, inserting the ends in two nail holes punched at opposite sides of the rim.
- Before pouring paint from a can, cover the rim with masking tape. After pouring, remove the tape: The rim will be clean and the cover will fit tightly.
- Or poke holes around the inside of the rim with a hammer and nail so paint will drip back into the can.

Paint "stores"
- Store leftover latex paint in an empty, clean plastic milk or bleach jug; put the cap on tightly. Shake the jug the next time you use it and the paint will be ready.
- You've got just a little paint left in a large can. Pour it into a small glass jar and seal it tightly. Use for touch-ups and nicks.

Good to the last drop
- A worn-out plastic bowl scraper gets the last bit of paint out of the can.

A stirring idea
- Several holes drilled in the end of your paint paddle makes stirring easier.

Comb and brush
- Run a comb through the brush before painting and those loose bristles won't come off in the paint.

Hands off
- Protect hands from paint solvent by putting the brush and the solvent into a strong plastic bag. Work the solvent into the brush through the plastic.

Right ways to clean brushes
- Never let paintbrushes rest on their bristles in a can of solvent because they will bend and lose their shape. Put solvent in an empty coffee can, cut an X in the plastic lid, and push the brush handle up through the slit. That way you can let the brush hang in the can.
- There's a way to clean several brushes at one time. Suspend them in the solvent from a piece of wire coat hanger slipped through the holes in the brush handles.
- And to clean small brushes, poke the handles through a piece of cardboard, then lay the cardboard over the top of a small can of solvent.
- Give clean brushes a pointed edge by hanging the bristles between clamp-type hangers.

Cleaning paint thinner
- After you have cleaned the brushes, cover the coffee can full of paint thinner and let it stand for a couple of days. The paint will settle to the bottom of the can and the clean thinner can be poured into its original can to be reused.

Shake it off
- The neatest way to shake solvent out of your brush is to squeeze the top of a bag around the handle and shake the solvent into the bag.

Stop-and-start situation
- If you can't finish a latex-paint job, store the paintbrush or roller for several days by slipping it inside a plastic bag, pushing the air out, and tying the end shut. The paint won't dry out.

Ways to clean rollers
- Fill an empty quart milk carton with solvent, put the roller inside, crimp the ends shut. Give the carton a few shakes, then let it sit for a couple of hours.
- Or use a tennis-ball can.

Bugging off
- Have you ever been "bugged" by flies and other insects landing on a freshly painted outdoor surface? Try squirting some bug repellent into the paint before applying.

Painting wrought iron
- Use a smooth piece of sponge. When the piece starts to get tacky, toss it and use a fresh one.

Screens
- Tack a small piece of carpeting to a wood block and dip it in the paint. You'll use less paint, and it will spread quickly and evenly.
- And always dry screens horizontally so the paint won't drip into the mesh.

Stairways
- You can use your stairway while painting it. Paint every other step on one day, and the rest on the next.
- Or paint just half of each step at a time.

Painting the small stuff
- An old lazy Susan makes an ideal rotating work area for repairing or painting small appliances and other items.

Baseboards
- Press down carpeting with a dustpan as you paint along.

Preventing paint peels
- To keep paint from peeling off concrete floors and sheet metal, put a coat of vinegar on it before you paint.

Removing paint spatters
- Very fine dry steel wool will remove spatters from woodwork.
- For spatters on tile and porcelain, use a pumice stick (available at hardware stores).
- To get paint and varnish off chrome hinges and door pulls, simmer them for a few minutes in baking soda and water, then wipe off the solution with a rag.

Keep a color-code record
- On the back of the light-switch plate, write down the color and amount of paint used in each room.

Faster plaster
- Plaster hardens faster if mixed in warm water. Cold water slows down the hardening process.

Homemade patching compounds
- Fill nail holes before painting or wallpapering by mixing equal parts of cornstarch and salt. Add water until it's the consistency of putty.
- An easy way to repair a hole in plaster is to mix paint or food coloring in the plaster to match the color of the walls.

Removing the last bits of wallpaper
- With a piece of sandpaper wrapped around the pad of a wax mop you can scrape off the last bits of wallpaper.

More on wallpaper
- Always apply an oil-based primer before putting up wallpaper. If you don't, the paper will be nearly impossible to remove when it's time to replace it.
- Wallpaper paste will spread quickly and easily if applied with a short-napped paint roller.
- Use the back of a spoon to smooth down a loose seam.
- A squeegee is a handy tool for smoothing the lumps out of vinyl wall coverings.

Marking nail holes
- Put a finishing nail (the kind without a head) into the holes where pictures hang. As you come to these areas push the nail through the paper.

A foolproof idea
- If, like most walls, yours are slightly uneven, dab the corners with a quick coat of paint of the same color as the wallpaper. This will hide any spots where the paper edges don't quite meet.
- Use a plumb line to make sure you're hanging the paper straight.

How to store leftover wallpaper
- Store some leftover scraps of wallpaper by stapling them to an attic wall. When you need to repair a worn spot, your patches will be just as faded as the paper on the wall.

As great as it "seams"
- Before you install paneling, approximate where the seams will join and paint a matching stripe two inches wide. Later, if the seams separate, the old color won't show through.

Lawns, Gardens, Plants, and Flowers

It Pays to "Mother" Nature

The right way to water
- A little water is worse than no water at all when it comes to watering your lawn. Don't even start the job unless the ground is going to be drenched, and the soil wet at least an inch below the surface. Light watering causes the roots of grass to turn up and become shallow. A thorough watering once a week does a lot of good, whereas light watering every day or every few days does a lot of harm.

Soaking wet
- If soaker hoses will not lie flat on the lawn, tape pieces of a yardstick to the bottom side.
- If the soaker hose is longer than the stretch of lawn that needs watering, shut off the extra portion of hose with a clamp-type pants hanger.
- A coat hanger can be fashioned into a good support for a hand-held hose.

Tricks for old hoses
- Punch a few more holes in it and turn it into a lawn soaker.
- Slit sections and, with super-hold glue, attach them to the edges of your youngsters' swing seats. The hose acts as a bumper if the swing accidentally hits one of the kids.
- Cover swing chains with garden hose for a steadier grip.
- Insulate a lug wrench and a jack handle and your hands won't freeze when using these tools during the winter.

Fertile ideas

- Be smart: Buy fertilizer on the basis of nitrogen content rather than price per bag. Inexpensive fertilizer may have a low nitrogen content.
- It's a matter of leverage! Use a broom or snow shovel to move a heavy sack of fertilizer.
- Spread additional fertilizer under trees so the grass can compete with the trees for nutrients.
- Make your own fertilizer spreader from a large coffee can by punching lots of holes in the bottom. Cover with the plastic lid and shake the can.

Hints for mowing with knowing

- A squirt of an octane booster (available in auto-parts stores) will quickly start a stubborn lawn-mower motor.
- To keep screws from vibrating loose on power motors, apply some weather-stripping sealer to the ends of screws. Screws will hold tight but are easily removed when necessary.
- Be sure the blades are sharp. Dull blades will rip rather than clip the grass and cause leaf tips to turn brown.
- Spray mower blades with vegetable oil to keep grass from sticking.
- Unplug the spark-plug wire on the mower so youngsters can't start it when you're away.
- Hang a trash bag from the handle of the mower to fill with debris as you go.
- Wear golf shoes when mowing on a wet or steep hill and aerate the lawn at the same time.

No need to weed

- Why clip the grass that grows along walls by hand? Make a mowing strip around fences and walls to eliminate hand-trimming chores. Strips can be made from stones or bricks placed even with the soil.
- Or dig a shallow trench and fill it with a mixture of sand and used motor oil or strips of plastic covered with dirt.
- If you find that weeds are still growing between your mulch or gravel, try this: Lay plastic over the area and place the mulch on top.

Dandelion exterminator
- Don't let dandelion seeds blow all over your yard: Hook a vacuum cleaner up to a grounded long extension cord and vacuum the seed heads.

Garden tools
- Here's a handy tool carrier! Cut off the top of an old bleach bottle above the handle.
- Or cut if off below the handle—use it as a scoop for pesticides and fertilizer.
- Inches marked off on your garden trowel with red nail polish conveniently show proper depth for planting seeds and bulbs.
- Make a waterproof kneepad for gardening from an old pillow wrapped in plastic.
- Paint the handle of all your garden tools in the same bright color so you can easily see them. If anyone borrows a tool, the color will be a reminder to return it to you.
- Tools won't rust if you store them in a box of sand mixed with old motor oil.
- Use a toy rake to reach those difficult spots underneath bushes and shrubbery.

Tree don'ts
- Don't plant trees too close to the house; they may cause damage to the foundation.
- Don't plant them near a garden where they will block out sunlight and soak up nutrients.
- Don't dig the planting hole without laying a sheet of plastic next to it. When you're ready to fill the hole, just lift the edge of the sheet and the dirt will slide right back in.
- Don't plant a tree in soil that has poor drainage. Check by filling the hole with water. If it hasn't drained in twelve hours, think twice.

Patching bare spots
- Use moss to cover bare spots under trees (such as evergreens). Lay it on bare patches and water it well, and it should take hold.
- If you seed a bare spot on your lawn and don't have a roller, cover the patch with a wide board and walk on it.

Sure shrubbery
- To make sure your hedges are trimmed in a straight line, tie a string to a branch at one end and run it across to the other end. Stand back to make sure the string is straight before you start cutting.
- Keep your pruning shears sharp, as dull blades leave ragged cuts that may not heal.
- Protect your hands while pruning. Use barbecue tongs or pliers to hold thorny branches.
- Put a sheet of plastic beneath the shrubs when clipping. Pick up the plastic for easy disposal of the trimmings.

On the vine
- When putting up a trellis, attach a hinge to the bottom so it can be pulled away from the house when it has to be painted.

An old-seed test
- How do you tell whether old seeds are still good? Count out about fifty seeds, placing them between two layers of wet newspaper covered with a plate. After five days, count the number of seeds that have germinated to determine how thick they will have to be spread. If half are no longer good, use twice as many as you normally would.

Feeding time
- There is nothing better than compost to feed a garden. It can't be bought; it can only be made. Grind leftover vegetables, onion skins, and eggshells in a blender, then sprinkle compost around the garden. Use coffee grounds, too.
- Large plastic ice-cream containers make fine storage bins for collecting compost in the kitchen.
- Pile leaves and grass clippings in a corner and cover them to prevent scattering. As the leaves decompose they create a rich mulch for your garden.

Reflect on this
- If you live in a colder climate give Mother Nature a hand. Walls and fences lined with a reflective surface, such as aluminum foil, will reflect heat and light on the garden plants.

Fast cleanups
- For fast cleanups from your outside faucet, hang a bar of soap in an onion net bag on it. Wash your hands without even taking the soap out of the bag.
- Fasten a broom clip or pound a nail above the outside faucet. Whenever you take the nozzle off the hose, just hang it and it won't get lost.

Chives alive
- The next time you cook with green onions, use only the green tops. Save the bottom three inches (the white bulbs), plant several of the bulbs in a pot and place on the kitchen windowsill. Water daily. As the onions grow, snip off the fresh green tops when needed. They'll always grow back.
- Or use a fresh onion that has begun to sprout and plant it in a small pot to use as you do chives.

Happier ferns
- They don't like to be moved from place to place, so keep them happy and in one spot.

This hint gels
- Dissolve one envelope of unflavored gelatin in hot water and stir. Then slowly add three cups of cold water. Use this mixture instead of water once a month, and you'll see healthier plants. Prepare only as much of the mixture as you plan to use at one time.

Tips for watering
- A newspaper or umbrella held behind the plant protects walls and furniture when spraying it.
- Never put clay pots directly on wooden furniture because water will seep through the porous clay.

Plant sitter

- If you're going away for about a week keep your plants healthy in a homemade miniature "greenhouse." First thoroughly water the plant, then loosely wrap part of a plastic dry-cleaning bag over the plant and around the bottom of the pot.
- If you have many plants, fill the bathtub with about one-quarter inch of water. Set each plant on a saucer so that the pot doesn't touch the water and cover the whole tub with a dry-cleaning bag.

Plants like showers, too

- Plants thrive in the humid atmosphere of a bathroom. The next time you take a hot shower, invite them into the room with you to soak up the steam.

Flower power

- Cut flowers will last longer if you keep them in equal parts of water and 7-Up with one-half teaspoon of chlorine bleach added to each quart of this solution.
- Put a piece of charcoal in the water and cut flowers won't develop a bad odor when the stems begin to rot.
- The plastic baskets that strawberries come in, turned upside down, make great holders for cut flowers in low, round bowls. (Such holders are called frogs.)

To the rescue

- If your local university has an agriculture department, the staff will often provide information and even do tests free of charge. For example, they'll test soil samples or try to solve an insect-control problem.

Part II
You
and
Yours

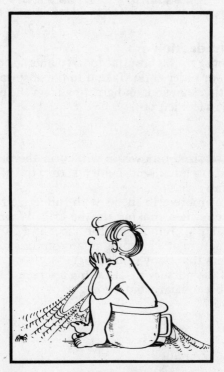

The Children

Baby Talk

Special introduction
- Before going to the hospital to have another baby, wrap a gift for your older child. Take it to the hospital and send it home with a snapshot and greeting from the new baby. No one likes to feel left out.

Bedtime
- A standard-sized pillowcase will cover the pad in a bassinet. In case of late-night accidents, turn the pad over to the fresh, clean side.
- Use two or more crib sheets with rubberized flannel pads in between when making up the crib. When baby's bed needs changing, remove the top sheet and pad.
- Hang a picture of a sleeping infant on the nursery door to alert others that baby is napping.
- Pet-proof the nursery by installing a screen door and you'll still be able to hear what's going on.

Temperature control
- To cool a hot baby bottle, store extra formula in a sterilized jar in the refrigerator. Add a small amount to the too-hot bottle.
- Speed up heating water for baby's late-night bottle by filling an airpot or Thermos with boiling water before going to bed.
- Place an uncapped cold baby bottle in the microwave for thirty to sixty seconds for a fast warm-up.
- Add a teaspoon of vinegar to a glass jar filled with water to sterilize nipples in a microwave oven.

Bottle odors
- Rid sour milk smells from plastic bottles by filling the bottle with warm water and adding one teaspoon of baking soda. Shake well and let set overnight.

Bottoms up
- Cornstarch is a good, inexpensive substitute for baby powder.
- Or if you like the smell of baby powder, mix it with an equal amount of cornstarch.
- Use a flour shaker for convenient application but don't shake the powder on lavishly. It can be harmful to the lungs if baby inhales it.
- Or put powder in a clean dusting-powder box and apply with a clean puff.
- Crisco vegetable shortening is as effective as petroleum jelly and does the same job.
- An old card table becomes a changing table if you cover the top with a plastic foam pad. Attach a patterned skirt around it so that the area under the table can be used for storage.

Cleaner and softer diapers
- Soak rinsed diapers overnight in the washing machine in warm water, with one cup of Ivory Snow or Dreft and a commercial soaking preparation (such as Diaperene). In the morning run the diapers through the entire cycle, then once more without soap for a final rinse.
- Fabric softener can irritate baby's bottom, but adding one-half cup of baking soda to the second washing cycle keeps diapers soft and smelling fresh.

Rash moves
- To treat diaper rash remove wet diapers as soon as possible.
- The best place to change the diaper is on the bathroom vanity. Lay baby on a towel with his bottom near the edge of the sink. Hold his legs up and splash with warm water from the basin.
- Because drying with a cloth can cause further irritation, blow warm (not hot) air on baby's bottom with a non-asbestos hair dryer after each change. Be careful to hold it at least six inches from the skin.

- Exposure to air is the best possible treatment. Try to keep diapers off as much as possible.
- Zinc oxide and cornstarch should not be applied while the skin is inflamed. Use petroleum jelly or a prescribed ointment.
- It's a good idea to acidify washed and rinsed diapers with one cup of vinegar and a washtub of water. Soak for thirty minutes, then spin dry without rinsing the vinegar out.

The baby and the bath water
- With a bath towel wrapped around your neck and pinned on like a bib, you'll keep dry during the bath. It also makes an instant wrap-up for baby.
- Don't startle an infant with cold baby lotion. Warm it first by setting the lotion bottle in a pan of hot water.

Helping the medicine go down
- Even the worst-tasting medicines go down without fuss when you put the prescribed amount in a nipple, then give it to baby just before feeding time. He'll be so hungry he'll hardly realize he has swallowed it.
- Give liquid vitamins at bath time. No more stained clothing to launder.

Read all about it
- Haven't had the time to read the newspaper because baby is fussy? Read it aloud while rocking her. She will think you are talking to her and enjoy it as much as a lullaby.

Toddling Along

Fun foods
- Fill a flat-bottomed ice-cream cone with egg or tuna salad for fun eating.
- If your child doesn't like chunks of fruit in his gelatin dessert, add pureed fruit. It's also a good way to sneak in some pureed raw vegetables for extra nutrition.

Fast foods
- Use a pizza cutter to cut up food.
- An egg poacher is ideal for warming several foods at once.

High-chair cleanup
- The best place to clean a high chair is outdoors with a garden hose.
- In the winter place it under the shower and let hot water spray over it for several minutes.

Breaking the habit
- Every week snip off a piece of the pacifier until it's all gone. The shrinking pacifier may make the end easier.
- Or tell your toddler that when his last pacifier is lost or worn out, that's it.

Be a good example
- A simple rule that will save a lot of disciplining in the future is: Never do anything with a child that must be corrected later. For example, don't stand a child on a chair or bed while dressing her. Later she must learn not to stand on the furniture.

Charmin' squeeze
- Little children love to watch a new roll of toilet tissue spin off the roll. To prevent roll-offs, before inserting it on the holder, squeeze the roll together so it's no longer round.

Safety measures
- Perhaps your child, when riding his tricycle on your driveway, rides too close to the street for safety. A white line painted across the driveway at a safe distance from the street might help. Tell him it's the finish line and he's not to go any farther.

- Tie two pieces of yarn to each side of your child's car safety seat and to each attach a favorite toy. While you concentrate on driving, your securely strapped-in toddler can retrieve his own toys.
- Hang a towel over the top of the bathroom door to prevent lock-ins.

Comforting suggestions

- Keep a tray of juice-flavored ice cubes on hand when baby is learning to walk. If she falls and bumps her lip, let her suck on the flavored cube to reduce the swelling. It tastes so good she might forget about the fall.
- Clean a cut or scrape with a red washcloth. The blood won't show and the child won't be frightened.
- Don't apply salve or liquid antiseptic directly to a cut. It's less traumatic if it's put on the bandage before applying it to the skin.
- If you can't see the splinter in a finger, touch the spot with iodine. The splinter will darken and be easier to locate.
- Make a table for a child's sickbed with an adjustable ironing board.
- To help eliminate spills, place a damp washcloth under the plate on a tray for serving children in bed.
- When using a cool-mist vaporizer, the stream of cool mist will be directed where you want it if you tape a three-foot (or more) piece of vent pipe to the vaporizer opening.
- When bathing a child, keep a plaster cast dry by covering it with a plastic bag secured with waterproof electrical tape.

Easy eyedrop application

- Have the child lie down and close his eyes, then place the eyedrops in the corner of each eye. As he opens them the drops spread gently throughout.

Growing Up

Show and tell

- For days when you don't have time to read a story, record several on a blank tape. Don't forget to ring a bell so the child will know when to turn the pages of his book. Label each tape with the book title.

Quick learners
- Here's a great way to teach a child the concept of time. If you plan a trip to the zoo in five days, for example, make a chain of five paper links and have him take one off every day.
- Teach a child the difference between right and left by playing this game. Say "right" or "left" whenever possible in a sentence and cheer if he turns the correct way or shows the correct hand.

Instant clubhouses
- Draw doors and windows on an old sheet and lay it over a card table.
- Or cover the top of an old wooden playpen with a well-secured sheet of plywood. Remove four slats from the side to make a door.
- Or hang an old bedspread over the clothesline, securing it with clothespins on top and small stakes on the bottom. another instant hideout.

Watercoloring
- Put a teaspoon of food coloring in a bottle of water and let your kids spray designs on snow and snow-covered shrubbery.
- Add a few drops of food coloring to your child's bubble bath for a nice surprise.

Finger-paint protection
- Always add about one-quarter teaspoon of liquid dishwashing detergent to finger paints. It won't stop spills, but they'll be easier to clean.
- The key to cleaning these paints off washable fabric is to let them dry. Once dry, most of the paint can be brushed off and the material washed as usual. But remember not to machine-dry because this will set any remaining stain.
- For paint on walls and woodwork, blot up as much as possible with a damp rag. Then gently rub the area with baking soda on a damp cloth.

Fun in the sun
- If your child's slide has lost its "slide," rub a sheet of waxed paper on it and watch him scoot.
- On hot days let the kids cool off in a plastic swimming pool placed at the bottom of the slide.

- Fill an empty, well-rinsed plastic detergent bottle with water for a great squirt gun.
- Carry beach toys in a plastic laundry basket so you can easily rinse off all the sand from them when it's time to leave the beach. Just dunk the filled basket in the water.

Red alert
- For a day at the fair or zoo, dress each child in brightly colored clothing (red is great) to help keep track of them.

Clock watchers
- Kids won't keep popping in and out of the house to find out the time if you put a clock in the window.

Look what's under the bed
- An old twin-bed mattress makes an extra bed for sleepover friends. Slide it under a bed for easy storage.

Picture this
- Be sure to wash the bottoms of small children's shoes before professional photos are taken. Kids are almost always posed sitting with their legs folded, and the bottoms of the shoes show.
- As the children bring their school pictures home each year, put each one in a frame right in front of last year's picture. It's a safe place to store them and it's fun to look at the whole series every year.

The guest of honor
- The reward for a good report card doesn't always have to be money. Bring out the good china and silverware, set his place at the head of the table, make a cake decorated with a candle for each A or B. He'll feel like a king.

Grow-along clothes
- To get more use from outgrown sleepers with feet, cut off the feet.
- Cut off worn or too-short sleeves from padded jackets to make a fast vest.
- Buttoning clothes will be easier if all the buttons are sewn on with elastic thread.

Winterwear
- To store mittens and stocking hats in one place, hang a shoe bag on the inside of the closet door nearest the entrance.
- Sew a loop of elastic into the cuffs of sweaters to keep the sleeves from pushing up when kids put on their coats. Be sure it isn't too tight.
- Attach some sort of trinket to a snowsuit zipper. It will be easier to identify and the snowsuit will zip up without a struggle.
- Recycle an old heavy sweater by turning it into mittens. Place your child's wrist on the waist ribbing and trace his hand. Cut around the thumb and hand outline, using double thickness. Stitch together, press, and you've got new mittens for nothing.

Happy Birthday

A golden rule
- To limit party invitations let the child invite six friends if he is going to be six years old, seven guests if he is going to be seven, and so on.

Place cards
- Make your own. Write each guest's name in chocolate on a cookie iced in white.
- Or print the name of each child on a paper cup to eliminate mix-ups.
- Or stick a balloon with a child's name on it to the back of each chair.

Free flicks
- Give your child a special birthday treat. Your local library has a fine selection of free children's films. Sound projectors can also be rented for a small fee. Make lots of popcorn and invite the kids in for an afternoon.

Remember this
- Save the front page of the newspaper on your child's birthday and glue it in a scrapbook. It's fascinating to look back at yesterday's headlines.

Family
Business

It's Your Move

A picture is worth a thousand words
- Planning to sell your home in the winter? Make sure you have pictures of its special summer features to show buyers. Take a picture of the apple tree and roses in full bloom or of a family picnic under the shade tree.
- Before moving to a new house, take photos of your old house, your children's friends, the old school, and of anything else the family will have fun looking at later.

Read all about it
- Supply friends with self-addressed, stamped postcards. It's a nice way to hint that you'd love to hear from them.
- While you're still in your present home take a one-month subscription to the newspaper of the community where your new home is located. You'll get a feel for your new community before you move in.

First things first

- Set off a bug bomb in the new house a day or two before moving in. Even the cleanest house sometimes has unseen bugs and this will be your last chance before moving in the food, dishes, kids, and pets.
- Have area rugs and slipcovers cleaned before you move. They'll come back neatly rolled in paper, ready for moving. If you're moving locally, the cleaner will deliver them to your new address.

Start packing

- Label all boxes so they can be taken directly into the proper room.
- Make sure the items you'll want first, such as beds, get packed in the moving van last.
- Cover each mattress with a fitted sheet to prevent damage if it's dragged or dropped.
- Stuff plastic bags with crumpled newspaper and use them as buffers in packing cartons.
- Sectioned cardboard boxes from liquor stores are great for packing glasses and other fragile items.

All the essentials

- Mark one packing box SPECIAL. Fill with things you'll need immediately, such as bedding, light bulbs, a change of clothing, and other indispensables. Move it yourself so it doesn't get misplaced.

Bits and pieces

- Collect all casters, screws, and brackets in a plastic bag and tape them to the piece of furniture they came from.
- When removing pictures, attach the hooks to the back of the frame with masking tape.

Moving the heavyweights

- Put four carpet tiles under the legs of heavy appliances when moving them. Turning the carpeting foam side up keeps the appliance from slipping off, and the carpet side slides easily over vinyl floors.
- When there just doesn't seem to be any place to grip a heavy piece of furniture, buckle several heavy leather belts together and slip them over an end or corner.

Tax deduction for moving

- Remember that moving expenses may be tax-deductible. Keep a file of bills of lading, packing certificates, travel expenses, and so forth.

Maximum Security

Open and shut cases

- For extra window security, drill holes through the frames where the upper and lower halves of windows come together. Put nails in the holes so they slip in and out easily. Insert them when you don't want windows to open, and remove them when you do.
- To prevent a burglar from lifting a sliding door out of its track, put a two-inch corner brace on the inside top of the door.
- Or put a length of wooden dowel or a broom handle on the track and the door can't slide open.
- If you have an attached garage, install a peephole viewer in the door connecting the house to the garage. That way you can investigate a noise without opening the door.
- Another way to keep a prowler out of your garage is to put a C-clamp (ask for it at a hardware store) on the track in front of the roller. The garage door won't budge with the clamp in place.

Cover your tracks

- Make your home a little safer after a light snowfall by taking the time to walk back to your doorstep before leaving. One set of footprints leaving your home could be an invitation for an unwanted guest.

House keys
- The best place to keep a spare set of house keys is with a trusted neighbor.
- Or bury a set of keys nearby in a film canister.
- To avoid fumbling around for your house key, drill a second hole near the edge of the key so it will hang slightly off center on your ring.

Smoke detectors
- When installing smoke detectors, be sure to put one in the basement, too. A fire that starts here may not trigger the other alarms in your home until it's too late.

Under lock and key
- Take photographs of household valuables, furniture, and other items and keep them in your safe-deposit box. In case of fire or theft, you'll have evidence for your insurance claims.
- And make photocopies of your credit cards in case they are misplaced or stolen.

The Family Secretary

Pens and pencils
- When ink erasers become smudged, use fine sandpaper or an emery board to clean them.
- Your ballpoint pen won't write and it's not out of ink? Lightly rub a pencil eraser across the paper and the pen will write more easily.
- When a marking pen seems to be dried out, remove the cap from the bottom and add a few drops of water, then shake it as you would a thermometer.
- And always store felt-tipped pens with the point down to keep them from drying out.

Typewriters
- To cut down on typewriter noise, put a rubber mat under the machine.
- Clean typewriter keys with cotton dipped in rubbing alcohol.
- Vinegar will remove typewriter correction fluid from most surfaces.

At the touch of a finger
- You don't need rubber fingers to thumb through stacks of paperwork. Rub a little toothpaste into your fingertips and let dry.

Drying wet books
- Dry the pages and keep them from wrinkling by placing paper towels on both .sides of every wet page. Close the book and let it sit overnight with a heavy book on top.

Underline this hint
- When writing on unlined stationery, put your unlined paper over a piece of lined paper and use it as a guide. If the lines don't show through, darken them with a pen.

Stormy weather
- In rainy weather you can leave mail sticking out from a mail chute for the postman if you put the letters in a plastic bag.

Phone numbers

- Write emergency phone numbers on a small card and tape it to the telephone. Cover the card with clear plastic tape. This can be a lifesaver.
- Make your address book easy to update. Write all addresses and phone numbers in pencil.
- And to change addresses written in ink, use mailing-list labels (available in stationery stores).

Stamp Acts

Getting in your licks

- When a postage stamp won't stick, just rub it across the gummed part of an envelope that's been slightly moistened.
- Fill a used, clean shoe-polish container with water and use the brush applicator to moisten stamp backing.
- Or dampen a kitchen sponge with water.

Ungluing stuck stamps

- Run a warm iron over them, but separate the stamps quickly before the glue sets again.
- Or place in a shallow dish filled with water. Let soak, then pull apart gently under slow running water. Dry them facedown on paper toweling.

Signed, sealed, and delivered
- Cover the address on a parcel with cellophane tape. This prevents the address from smudging.
- To prevent damage to photos, place the pictures between two pieces of corrugated cardboard and slip a hairpin diagonally through the corrugations at each corner. This will add rigidity.
- When sending get-well greetings to a hospitalized friend, write his home address where your return address would normally go. That way, if your card arrives after he's.been discharged, it will automatically be sent to his home.

Past History

Kids' stuff
- Store your youngsters' artwork, school papers, and other memorabilia in large boxes in their closets. Once a year, go through the boxes, discard unwanted items, and keep the precious ones. Cover the boxes, label them, and store your memories in a safe place.

Picture perfects
- Store family photos in a file box and use tab dividers to label them by year, event, or subject.
- And put the negatives in envelopes and keep them in the box right behind the prints.
- Make slide shows go smoothly as follows: First ensure that all the slides in the holder are right side up, then run a marking pen across the tops of the slides. Next time you need only look for the mark when putting slides in the holder.

Family lost and found
- A small box in a convenient place may serve as a catch-all for the little things found in odd places around the house.

Lookin' Good

Hand Aids

A treatment for rough, red hands
- Place one-half teaspoon of sugar in the palm of your hand and cover sugar with mineral or baby oil. Massage hands briskly for a few minutes. Wash hands with soapy water and they'll feel like silk.

Overnight sensations
- No hand lotion will ever take the place of pure glycerin (available at drugstores). Apply it every night before retiring and almost overnight your hands will turn beautiful. And to get the most benefit from glycerin or lotion, first soak your hands in warm water before applying it. (Warm water opens the pores and the lotion is absorbed better.)

How to remove super-hold glue from your hands
- Don't try to peel it off. Soak the glue-covered area in nail-polish remover until the glue disappears.

Nail Savers

Repairing a broken nail
- Out of nail-mending paper? Cut a piece of paper from a tea bag to fit the nail. Apply a generous coat of clear polish to the tea-bag paper and press it gently against the break, making sure you also work it under the crack. Then cover with colored nail polish.

For stronger and longer nails
- Apply white iodine (available at drugstores) over the entire nail surface three times a week. If yellowing occurs, don't worry. It isn't harmful and will disappear when the iodine treatment is cut down to only one application a week.

Weak and brittle nails
- Gelatin *does* help strengthen nails! Research has proven that drinking three or four tablespoons of unflavored powdered gelatin mixed into a glass of water each day results in stronger nails within a couple months.

An emergency emery board
- When a nail file isn't available, smooth nail edges with the striking part of a matchbook.
- When the edges of an emery board become worn, trim off about one-eighth inch on both sides and use the inner portion.

Hair "Ways"

Waterless hair wash
- Sprinkle cornstarch or baby powder lightly on oily hair and brush out. To restore the sheen and remove more dirt, put a nylon stocking over the bristles and continue brushing. This hint is very helpful for anyone bed-bound or who doesn't have time for a shampoo.

Formula to control oily hair
- Boil one quart of water with four teaspoons of spearmint leaves. Cool and use as an after-shampoo rinse.

Removing sticky hair-spray buildup
- Wash hair as usual, but work a tablespoon of baking soda into the lathered hair. Hair spray will dissolve.

Out of cream rinse?
- Try a little dab of fabric softener in a glass of warm water. It leaves hair soft and snarl-free.

Final rinse cycle
- Leftover tea makes a great final rinse for brunettes. It will help remove soapy film and leave hair shining.

Dandruff exterminator
- Try shaking table salt into dry hair. Massage salt into the scalp before shampooing. Dandruff should disappear.

Some blues you can use
- Add a bit of bluing (the kind used in the laundry) to the final rinse water to prevent gray hair from yellowing.

Down with frizzies
- When fly-away hair is a problem, rub a fabric-softener sheet over your hair and it will stay in place.

A microwave hot-oil treatment
- For a professional hot-oil treatment, saturate hair with olive oil. Place in a microwave oven, for two minutes, two wet towels that have been thoroughly wrung out. Wrap hair in plastic or aluminum foil and apply hot towels. Let sit for twenty minutes and then remove oil with two good washings.

Believe it or not
- If you lighten your hair, it could turn green when you swim in a chlorinated pool. Prevent this by dissolving six aspirin tablets in a large glass of warm water and rubbing the solution into wet hair. The green will disappear.
- Or rub in tomato juice.

Let's Make Up

Get the most out of your makeup
- Revive dried-up mascara by holding the closed tube under hot, running water for a few minutes. The mascara inside will soften and you'll have more to use.
- Your foundation will last longer if you mix it with moisturizer in the palm of your hand before applying.
- For a sharp point on lipstick and eyeliner pencils, without as much waste, put them in the freezer for a few minutes before sharpening.
- To thin nail polish that has become thick and gooey, add a few drops of polish remover.
- If your blushing powder has broken, crumble and smash it thoroughly. Then keep it in a small, wide-mouthed jar for future use.
- Stretch your dusting or face powder by mixing it with an equal amount of cornstarch.
- Instead of costly makeup brushes use high-quality artist's brushes.

The best makeup remover
- Vegetable shortening (such as Crisco) is an economical and very effective makeup remover. Massage it into skin and wipe off with tissue.

Makeup organizers
- Unclutter your dressing table by putting the cosmetics on a lazy Susan or purchase a two-tiered turntable (available at hardware stores). The turntable will double your space.

Skin Do's

Getting rid of a blemish
- Rub a styptic pencil (used for razor cuts) on a pimple three times a day and it will dry up quickly.

Vinegar astringent

- All you need is one-quarter cup of apple-cider vinegar, one-half cup of water, and one teaspoon of cream of tartar. Mix cream of tartar with water. Add vinegar. Shake thoroughly. Apply with cotton pads. You must shake this formula before each use.

Deep pore mask

- Grind about two ounces of blanched almonds in the blender, then add just enough witch hazel to the powdered almond meal to form a thick paste. Before applying, open pores by steaming your face with a washcloth wrung out with hot water. Leave mask on for fifteen minutes. Rinse with cool water.

Moisturizing mask

- Beat one teaspoon of mayonnaise with one egg yolk. Spread mixture evenly on face. Remove with warm water after twenty minutes. Close pores with a cold-water splash. If you are allergic to the ingredients of the mask, it's not for you.

Make your own bubble bath

- Combine two cups of vegetable oil, three tablespoons of liquid shampoo, and a thimbleful of your favorite perfume. Beat solution in a blender at high speed for several seconds.

Soften hard bath water

- Just add one-half cup of baking soda.

For men only
- Give yourself a facial massage each morning by using an electric razor instead of a blade. It's great for keeping firm, healthy skin and avoiding the jowls that appear as we grow older. Also, rather than shaving lotion, apply a good moisturizing cream so as to lubricate your skin instead of drying it.

Fresh Ideas

Problem perspiration
- If underarm deodorants irritate your skin, no matter how gentle the product, try applying hand cream before the antiperspirant. The lotion won't interfere with the effectiveness of the deodorant.
- Make your own inexpensive and convenient roll-on deodorant by adding two tablespoons of alum (available at drugstores) to one pint of water. Shake mixture well and pour it into a clean, empty roll-on deodorant bottle. (To remove the ball from the bottle, run it under cold water and pry off gently with a nail file.)

Tweezing hints
- Take the pain out of tweezing your eyebrows. Hold the eyebrow between the thumb and index finger and roll firmly for fifteen seconds. This will numb the area and allow you to tweeze in comfort.
- When tweezers won't close firmly, wrap both tips of the tweezers with small rubber bands. The rubber grips better and makes the tweezer more efficient.
- Or apply a commercial product used to numb the gums when a baby is teething.

Pets

K–9 Ideas

Puppy love
- When caring for a litter of puppies or kittens, place them in an old mesh playpen. For pens with wooden slats, tape fine screen around the pen so they don't fall out.
- Put some of your old clothes in puppy's box so he'll pick up your scent and be comforted by it.

Housebreaking
- Hang a bell on the doorknob and jingle it when you want to take puppy outside. He'll soon be jingling it himself when he needs to go out.

Portable dog anchor
- Make a portable dog anchor by tying his leash around an old tire and putting a few bricks inside.

In the doghouse
- Make an entrance flap for a doghouse out of a piece of indoor/outdoor carpeting. Cut it to size, slit it up the middle, and nail it in place.
- Or use a rubber floor mat. Guide your dog through the flap a few times until he learns how to do it himself.

Bathtime
- Fill a tub with warm water and put a rubber mat on the bottom for secure footing.
- Put cotton in your dog's ears to keep out water and a little petroleum jelly around his eyes to protect them from soap.
- Add a little baking soda to the rinse water to make your pet's coat softer, shinier, and odor-free.
- Baking soda or dry cornmeal is a good dry shampoo for any furry pet. Rub it in well, then brush it out. Baking soda is a deodorizer, too.

Quick drying after bathtime
- Use a blow dryer with the temperature set at warm, not hot.

Fleas will flee
- Brewer's yeast rubbed on your dog's coat prevents fleas.

Snow problem
- Snow-melting chemicals may not only be irritating to a dog's paws, but licking at the substance may make him ill. Therefore, wash your dog's feet in a solution of baking soda and water to remove the chemicals.

Chowtime
- Your pet's dish won't slide across the floor while he eats if it's set on a rubber mat.
- Or glue a rubber jar ring to the bottom of his bowl.
- Your dog has a habit of knocking over his water dish? Set an angel-food cake pan over a wooden stake driven into the ground.

"Canned" dog food
- Store big bags of dry dog food in a clean garbage can with a lid.

Let sleeping dogs lie
- If your dog sleeps under your bed, save the time and trouble of removing hair from the box spring by fitting an old contour sheet to the underside. Just wash it when it gets dirty. This is a good idea even if you don't have a pet.

Cat Tales

Finicky felines
- Your cat won't be so choosy if some oil from a can of tuna is sprinkled over his food.
- Or add a teaspoonful of brewer's yeast occasionally. It's healthful because of the B vitamins.

No trespassing
- Keep the cat out of the fishbowl by cutting a square piece of netting (from an orange bag) and securing it over the top of the bowl with a rubber band.
- This also prevents fish from jumping out of the bowl.

Cat Rx
- When your cat refuses liquid medicine, spill some on his fur. He will instinctively lick it off.

A good way to train your cat
- Keep handy a squirt gun filled with water. A few good shots and he'll get the message.

Toys
- Cats love scratching sounds. Crumple a piece of aluminum foil into a ball and let your kitten bat it around on a hard floor.
- Or suspend a Ping-Pong ball on a piece of string from an empty shelf. Cats love to jump up and hit things, and the ball can't roll under the furniture.

Cheaper cat-litter liners
- A box of ten plastic lawn bags makes forty litter-pan liners. Cut each bag into four large rectangular pieces.

Did you know?
- That many cats and dogs go berserk when they hear a violin solo?

Feathers and a Fin

Birdbaths
- Here's how you coax birds into the birdbath: Put some sand on the bottom and a few seeds on the surface of the water.
- And if it's in the sun, move it to the shade. The water may be too warm.
- Get rid of birdbath fungus. Soak some towels in bleach and place them on the sides of the empty bath for half an hour. Remove the towels and rinse both thoroughly.

Keeping squirrels out of a bird feeder
- Cut a hole in the bottom of a plastic wastebasket and slide it upside down on the pole that holds the feeder.

"Cheep" birdseed
- Dried seeds from melons, pumpkins, or squash make great birdseed.
- Transfer birdseed from the original box to an empty salt carton for easy pouring.

When your bird flies the coop
- Turn off the lights and close the drapes. A bird will normally stay motionless in the dark until you can catch him.

Cleaning fish tanks
- Soap should never be used to clean fish tanks. Use nylon netting and noniodized table salt. Rinse tank well to remove all residue.

Sewing

Needles and Thread

Finding the eye of the needle
- Hold an index card behind a machine needle to help you find the eye.
- When threading yarn, put a piece of tape or paper around the end and snip it at a slant. The yarn will fit easily through the needle eye.

Thread lines
- Because thread usually lightens, it's wise to buy thread a little bit darker than the material you're working with.
- To keep a bobbin and matching thread together, run a pipe cleaner through both, then twist.

Buttons and Zippers

Loose buttons
- Touch the center of the button (front and back) with clear nail polish if a button comes loose and you can't repair it right away.
- Or to hold the threads temporarily, put a small strip of transparent tape on them.

Storing buttons
- A handy place to keep extra buttons is with the pattern.
- When removing buttons from a soon-to-be-discarded item, sew them together before storing with your spares. It'll save you the time of having to match buttons later.
- Find buttons easily. Sort them by size or color in the compartments of an egg carton.

Right on the button
- Keep the buttons in place while you stitch: After positioning each button for a shirt, tape them onto the fabric with transparent tape.
- When covering a button with a sheer fabric, the job will be neater if you first cover the button with wool or flannel.

- To avoid cutting into the fabric when snipping off a button, slide a comb between the button and the cloth.

Buttonholes
- Make sample strips of different-sized buttonholes with an automatic buttonholer. Match the button to the sample size when trying to decide which size buttonhole to make.
- When cutting buttonholes by machine, mark the ends of the hole with straight pins to avoid cutting too far.
- To hide interfacing that shows along the edge of a buttonhole, color it with a marking pen to match the fabric.
- Sew the buttonholes horizontally when making children's clothing and they'll be less likely to pop open while they play.

Zippers
- Zippers will be easier to sew if you tape the zipper in place and stitch next to (*not through*) the tape. The tape can be pulled off easily after the zipper is sewn.
- If zipper teeth are broken near the bottom, sew that end closed and make the zipper a little shorter.
- For a zipper that just won't stay closed, sew a small button at the top and make a loop of strong thread through the hole in the zipper pull. When you zip up, just hook the loop over the button.

Patterns and Fabric

Storing patterns
- Your favorite patterns will last longer if you put them in manila envelopes or locking plastic bags.
- The cut-out pieces of a pattern will stay smoother if you hang them on a clamp-type skirt hanger instead of folding them.
- Avoid losing pieces of your pattern as you sew: Clip the pieces together with a spring-action clothespin.

Repairing patterns
- Use a strip of plastic freezer paper to repair a torn pattern. Place a torn section over the freezer paper and press with a warm iron.

Homemade patterns

- Look through a children's coloring book for simple, decorative outlines for quilt patterns.
- Use a coloring book that features your youngster's favorite movie or television character to make a novelty print for a T-shirt or pajama top. Trace the picture onto the garment with tracing carbon, then color it in with ballpoint fabric paint (available at craft stores).
- The peel-away backings from adhesive shelf paper, which are ruled in one-inch squares, make handy guides for enlarging your needlework patterns.

Storing fabric scraps

- Take a plastic garbage can with a lid. Tape a small sample of each piece of fabric to the lid. Now, when you need a certain type of fabric, you can check the lid instead of having to rummage through the whole can.

Sewing Tools
and Tricks

Sewing tools

- A child's game board makes a great sewing board. Put it on your lap when pinning, marking, or cutting.
- For convenience, glue a tape measure to the front edge of your sewing machine.
- A small magnet glued to the end of a yardstick makes it easy to retrieve dropped pins and needles without having to bend.
- Keep a nutpick in your sewing basket. The blunt end is perfect for turning belts, and the sharp end can be used to pull out corners after the belt is turned.

Hemming ways

- To eliminate the white hemline mark after letting down a pair of blue jeans, rub a matching blue crayon on the line and iron the fabric under a pressing cloth, using medium heat.
- Try hair clips instead of basting or pinning a hem in place.
- Before dying a garment, baste a few strands of white thread through it. When finished, remove the threads and wrap them around a spool for future mending or hemming.
- Thread a few needles with basic-colored thread and keep them in a safe, handy place near your washing machine. If you spot a loose hem or a small tear, fix it before you wash the item.

The best way to hem curtains

- Shorten them at the top instead of at the bottom. No one will notice if your job isn't perfect.

"Darn" it all

- Stick a straight wooden clothespin inside the finger of gloves that need mending.
- A ragged hole or tear will be easier to darn if you pull the fabric together as much as possible and iron it between two pieces of waxed paper.
- To repair a hole in a bulky-knit fabric, use the plastic L'Eggs panty-hose egg for a darning surface.

Let's patch things up

- Get the most wear out of your youngster's play pants by turning them inside out and ironing patches on the seat and knees.

Sewing seams

- Always pin across a seam, never parallel with it. That way you can sew over the pins.
- To join straight and bias material smoothly, keep the bias on top.

A pocketful of sense

- A piece of cardboard placed inside the pocket when mending it prevents your needle from catching the other side.
- Use the same color material to make the pockets as that of the slacks. Unsightly white pocket lining won't show every time you sit.
- When sewing the pocket on a new garment, reinforce the top corners with a small piece of the fabric sewn on the inside.

Three cheers for Velcro fasteners

- Velcro fasteners are handy for fastening felt letters and emblems to cheerleaders' outfits. Emblems won't have to be removed and resewn every time you wash the garments, and one set of emblems can be used for several different uniforms.
- Put Velcro fasteners in strategic spots on a wraparound skirt and both waist and hemline will stay even.
- To prevent insulated drapes from gapping between panels, sew strips of Velcro fasteners on adjacent panel hems. Drapes will stay neatly and firmly closed, and keep cold air from entering the room.

Centering pant creases perfectly

- After cutting out slacks pattern, place the front pieces of the material on an ironing board and fold to press a crease. Press with a steam iron on a damp cloth.

This hint is a keeper

- For badly worn collars, take out the stitching at the neck seam and carefully remove the collar, then turn it around and sew it back in. The collar will look like new.

Slide-proof comforter

- Sew a piece of muslin across the bottom of a satin quilt or comforter and tuck that part under the mattress. The comforter won't slide around the bed anymore.

Special Occasions

Wrap-ups

Storing wrapping paper
- Simplify storing and gift wrapping by placing rolled wrapping paper in a tall, narrow wastebasket. Tape a bag to the side to hold tape, scissors, pen, and labels.

How much wrapping paper?
- Wrap a string around the package and measure it, allowing a couple of extra inches for overlap. Use the string to measure the wrapping paper before cutting.

For easy paper cutting
- Pull apart a table with leaves, lay the paper over the slit, and cut with a sharp knife or a single-edged razor.

Making used wrapping paper and ribbon new again
- Wrinkled paper perks back to life! Lightly spritz the wrong side with a little spray starch, then press it with a warm iron.
- Run wrinkled ribbon through a warm curling iron.

Cut to ribbons
- Make your own ribbon by cutting almost any type of fabric into the desired width and length. Striped material is perfect to cut in even widths. Press between sheets of waxed paper with a hot iron. The wax keeps the strips from unraveling and provides enough stiffness for the ribbon to hold its shape when made into a bow.

A handy string dispenser
- Make a hole in the center of a L'Eggs panty-hose container lid and thread the string through the hole.

Original gift wrapping
- Wrap a going-away gift in a large, colorful map.
- A striped kitchen towel makes a great covering for a kitchen shower gift. Instead of decorating the package with a bow, attach a plastic or copper scouring pad or colorful plastic measuring spoons.
- Use a receiving blanket and diaper pins for baby shower gifts.
- Select the newspaper section related to the gift you're giving. Use the real estate section for a housewarming gift.
- The *Wall Street Journal* is ideal for wrapping a book about finances.

- Try sheet music for your musically minded friends.
- The comic strips are perfect for the kids; decorate the package with lollipops or candy canes. How about topping off a Christmas package with a gingerbread man?
- Attach fresh flowers to the bow, but first wrap the stems in damp paper towels and cover them with foil.

Mailing a wrapped present
- Stuff plastic dry-cleaner bags with crumpled newspaper. Use as buffers when packing and newsprint won't rub off on the wrapping paper.
- Protect the bow from being crushed by covering it with a plastic berry basket (like the ones strawberries come in).

Many happy returns
- Always ask the salesperson for two receipts—one for you with the price, the other one with the description of the gift but without the price. Enclose the last one with the gift just in case it has to be returned.

It's the thought that counts
- When your children receive a gift, take a picture of them playing with it or wearing it and send it as a thank-you note.

Inexpensive Gift Ideas

Great expectations

- As soon as you know a friend is expecting a baby, start a scrapbook of current events. Fill it with clippings of new headlines, fashion photos, food and movie ads, pictures of cars and famous people. The final page can be left for the front page of the newspaper on the day the baby is born.
- For the father-to-be, give a waiting-room kit. Fill a box with change for the telephone, telephone numbers of close relatives and friends, cigars, gum, lighter, his favorite magazine, and whatever else you can think of to keep him busy.

The buck pops here

- The kids will love this one. Roll up a dollar bill and insert it into a balloon. Mail it along in a card with instructions to blow up and pop.
- Or insert an invitation to a party with the same instructions to blow up and pop.

Unexpected bonus

- When a friend requests a special recipe, you can turn it into a special occasion by giving one of the expensive ingredients along with a copy of the recipe: a bottle of wine for beef Burgundy, wild rice for a favorite casserole, or shrimp for a dip.

MUSHROOM ELEPHANT CASSEROLE

1 ELEPHANT DICED
17 LBS ONIONS
30 LBS MUSHROOMS
80 GALLONS ELEPHANT STOCK

For the new bride
- Fill an address book with addresses and phone numbers of relatives and friends, and add a special section for birthdays and anniversaries.

The gift of gab
- Telephone companies offer gift certificates they will mail to whomever you wish. This is a perfect way to let friends and relatives know that you'd love to hear from them. The recipient simply mails in the coupon in place of money with the monthly telephone bill. Call your local phone company for more information.

Party Plans

Housewarming party
- If you're expecting guests who have never been to your new home, put a colored light bulb in your yard or porch fixture and tell them to look for it.

Anniversary greeting
- Make your own greeting card in a flash by taking a snapshot of the family holding a sign saying "Happy Anniversary" or any other message.

Bridal shower
- It's fun to have each guest bring her favorite recipe, along with a utensil used for preparing the dish. For example, a Chinese recipe with a wok, an omelet recipe with an omelet pan, a meat-loaf recipe with a loaf pan. The hostess could provide the bride-to-be with a recipe box to store all her new recipes.

Special dinners
- Polish your sterling in advance and wrap it in airtight plastic bags to prevent tarnishing.

- Don't forget to spray your prized linen tablecloth with either spray starch or fabric protector. Spills will be easier to remove.

Celebrating a job promotion
- Bring out the champagne. But if you don't drink it all, here's a way to keep it bubbly for a week longer. Drop a stainless-steel turkey skewer into the bottle and fasten a balloon over the neck with a rubber band. This will trap the carbonation.
- Lost the cork to a wine bottle? Soften a candle stub, wrap it in paper toweling and insert it into the neck of the bottle.

Birthday party
- It's easy to serve punch in a thirty-cup coffee maker. Remove the basket and there's plenty of room for ice.
- Make your ice cubes in advance. After they're frozen, store them in brown paper bags and they won't stick together.

Outdoor fish fry
- You're having a large crowd and want to serve everyone at once? As you fry the fish put them in a Styrofoam cooler lined with paper toweling and put the lid on. Fish will stay hot.

Pool parties
- Make your own coconut cream for piña coladas by pureeing three cups of chopped coconut in a blender with a little boiling water. Squeeze liquid through cheesecloth.

Family picnic
- Bring along a small, lightweight wagon. Load it up with blankets, lawn chairs, and the picnic basket for the trip from the parking spot to the picnic area.
- Fill plastic bags that seal three-quarters full of water and place in the freezer. If your family decides on a picnic at the last minute, just toss a few bags into the cooler to keep food cold. To make small pieces of ice for soft drinks, just hit with a hammer.
- Cut the legs off an old card table to make a perfect picnic table for the beach.

Barbecue
- Use a muffin pan to hold the fixings, such as mustard, catsup, relish, and onions. You won't have to pass around a lot of bottles and jars.
- A sure way to start a charcoal fire: Punch a few holes in the sides of a coffee can, remove both ends, and set it in the grill. Fill with charcoal, add starter fluid and light. When the coals are glowing, remove the can with tongs and set it in a safe place. Spread the coals and replace the grill.
- Keep a few flower pots filled with sand near smokers and stop worrying about their littering the lawn.

Candlelight dinners
- Thin candles won't stand up? Twist a rubber band around the candle base before inserting it into the holder.
- Or keep candles firmly in place with a little florist's clay in the holder.
- Is your candle too large for the holder? Trim the excess with a hot, sharp knife.
- Large, round candles can split and crumble when pressed onto the spike of a holder. Avoid this by making a hole in the bottom of the candle with a hot nail.
- When candles become dull and lose their newness, spray furniture polish on a cloth and wipe them thoroughly. They'll look new again.

Winter get-togethers
- Dazzle your guests—line your driveway with weather-proof lights. Here's how: Save plastic gallon ice-cream containers and coat the inside with vegetable spray. Fill with water and set outside. When partially frozen, insert a thick candle in the center and freeze solid. Remove from container. Light and line your driveway or walk.

Christmas Tree-trimming
- Always buy a fresh tree and check to see if the trunk has been sealed. If it has, you must cut off the bottom before placing it in water to help the tree absorb moisture. The cut should be diagonal, about two inches from the bottom.
- And to help your tree stay fresh longer, drill a hole up through the bottom of the trunk as far as you can, then stuff with strips of sponge. The sponge acts like a wick to soap up water and carry it deeper into the trunk.
- When assembling an artificial tree, dip the ends of the branches in petroleum jelly before inserting into the frame.
- To remove tree pitch from your hands, rub them with salad oil and wipe with a paper towel.

Decorating the tree
- When different strings of tree lights are all tangled together, try this hint: Plug in one set and, by following the lights, untangle one string at a time.
- If you're stringing popcorn on the tree, pop the corn a week ahead of time. The stale kernels will slide onto the needle without breaking.
- Use green pipe cleaners to tie tree lights to the branches.
- Stiffen crocheted Christmas ornaments with a few shots of hair spray.
- A few small bells hung low on the tree will announce that little fingers or paws are busy there.

Taking the tree down
- To prevent tangled tree lights, store them around empty gift-wrap tubes. Push the plug into the tube, then wrap the lights around the outside and secure the end with a rubber band. Several strings of lights can be stored on the same tube.

- Wrap one or two old bed sheets around the tree like a sling and needles won't drop on the carpet. You'll need another person to help you carry it out. Go through the door trunk first.

New Year's Eve
- Here's a nifty way to make your own inexpensive liqueur for the big night. Combine one pound of dried apricots, peaches, or pears, one cup of superfine sugar, and one quart of inexpensive vodka in a large jar. Shake well to dissolve sugar. Cover and let stand for one week, shaking the contents daily. Strain liqueur into a decanter. The fruit can be served over ice cream or cake.
- Make your own superfine sugar from granulated by processing in a blender at high speed.

Part III

Away from Home

The Car

Car Cues

Neater car washes
- All you need are two buckets of water and three Turkish towels. Put soapy water in one bucket, clear water in the other. Start with the roof and work your way down, one section at a time. Use one towel and soapy water to wash, the second towel and clear water to rinse, and the third towel to dry. You'll end up with a clean, dry car instead of a mess.

Three ways for washdays
- On hot, sunny days, wash and wax your car in the shade or at dusk. This will prevent streaking.
- A dust-mop head, worn as a mitten, is great for spreading suds and loosening grime.
- Or use carpet scraps glued to a block of wood.

The shining
- Sprinkle a tablespoon of cornstarch on the wipe rag when buffing your car and excess polish will come off easily.
- Or, for a glittering final finish to a newly waxed car, spray it down with cold water, then towel-dry it.
- Give windows and chrome a super shine by polishing with newspaper.

Interior information
- Wipe vinyl seats and dashboards with a cloth dampened with self-stripping floor-wax cleaner. It removes dirt and also covers scratches and scuffs. Quickly dries to a non-sticky shine.
- Or try a solution of three tablespoons of washing soda and one quart of warm water.
- For those stubborn tar spots on auto carpeting, apply Spray 'n Wash; scrub with an old toothbrush.
- Put floor mats in the washing machine with a few old towels to get them extra clean.

Rust-proofing

- Prevent rust by keeping your car clean—outside, inside, and underneath. Set a lawn sprinkler under the car and turn the water on full blast. This washes off the salt and other chemicals that collect on the car bottom during winter.
- Chipped paint spots? Promptly clean the area thoroughly and apply a coat of clear nail polish to prevent rust.
- Aluminum foil dipped in cola will help remove rust spots from car bumpers.

A new tar remover

- Laundry prewash takes tar off car finishes.

Tires

- Steel-wool soap pads and elbow grease still clean white-wall tires best.
- Test how much tread is left in a tire. Stick a penny in the groove. If you can see all of Lincoln's head, there's too little tread.
- Putting air in your tires should be postponed until absolutely necessary when the temperature is 10 degrees or colder. The valve in the tire may freeze and let all the air out.

Windshield wipers

- When wipers begin to wear down, extend their life by rubbing briskly with sandpaper.
- When dirty wipers streak your windshield, give them a good scrubbing with baking soda and water.

Antenna

- A radio antenna will slide easily if a coat of wax is applied occasionally.
- Or rub it occasionally with waxed paper.

Battery "cents"

- Grease one side of a penny and place that side down on the middle of the battery. Corrosion will collect on the penny instead of on the battery posts.
- Or spray the battery terminals with spray paint.

Repairing seat covers

- Increase the market value of your car. See the Yellow Pages under "vinyl repair" and have those little rips and cigarette burns fixed before selling it.
- For home repair use cement glue and a piece of double-knit material in the same color as the car seat. Work the glued material under the rip until the material surfaces are flat and wrinkle-free. Close the rip and lay a heavy book on top of it until the glue is thoroughly dry.

The silent treatment

- When silicone spray is not available, try silencing a squeaky car door by putting a few drops of transmission fluid on the door hinge with the dipstick.

Trunk take-alongs

- Gloves. Wear them when filling the tank at a self-service station or when changing a tire.
- An old window shade. Unrolled, it serves as a mat to protect clothing if you have to change a tire.
- A bleach bottle. Cut it in half. The top makes a free funnel.
- Reflector tape. Cover a burned-out headlight with it until you can get to a service station.
- A squeeze bottle filled with club soda or cola. Nothing is better for removing grease buildup from the windshield. A must when traveling long distances.
- Baking soda and plastic net bags (the kind onions come in). Sprinkle onion bags with baking soda and rub headlights to remove salt residue in winter. You can also use the onion bags to clear insects from the headlights and windshield.
- A broom with the handle cut down. It's the quickest way to brush snow off a car.
- A piece of plastic rug protector. It's great for lining the trunk to protect against grease smudges and spills.

Glove compartment handies
- Use moistened hand wipes to remove gas odor from your hands after you've filled the tank at a self-service gas station.
- Toss in a few dimes and you'll always have change for a highway telephone booth.

Stash this under the seat
- A large plastic trash bag makes a fine emergency raincoat.

Another tape-reflector hint
- For extra safety put strips of reflector tape on the door sill of the driver's door. When the door is opened, the reflection will alert drivers approaching from the rear.

Wash your hands with these
- Remove auto grease with baking soda and water.
- Or give your hands a good scrubbing with Lux liquid detergent.
- Or, before working on your car, rub dishwashing detergent on hands, elbows, and under fingernails. Let it dry but don't wipe it off. The soap seals pores against dirt and grease. When the job is finished, just wash up with soap and water and your hands will come clean.

Emergency substitutes
- Use a hubcap as a shovel if your car gets stuck in snow, sand, or mud.
- Out of gas? If you have no funnel to pour gasoline from a can, use a map, newspaper, or paper bag to guide the gas into the tank. Don't light a match.
- Your radiator needs water and you're not near a hose? Carry the water in the windshield-washer jug or the radiator-overflow jug.
- Cover a partially used one-quart can of motor oil with the plastic lid from a one-pound coffee can.

Locked out without a coat hanger
- Pull out your oil dipstick, wipe it clean, and push the round end between the rubber door seal and the window. Keep maneuvering until the end catches the lock, then lift.

Better tune-ups
- If you gap your own plugs, use the widest gap that the manufacturer recommends and your car will run better, idle better, and give you better mileage.

Garage floors
- Spread cat litter on garage floors to catch oil drips. Just sweep it up when it becomes saturated.
- Or try to purchase from a friendly service station a sweeping compound that absorbs grease.
- Use a prewash spray to remove grease spots. Spray on prewash and let it stand five minutes. Sprinkle on powdered detergent, scrub with a broom, and hose off.
- Before sweeping out a dirty garage, shred some newspaper and dampen with hot water. To prevent dust from rising and resettling as you sweep, first spread the moist pieces on the floor as you would a sweeping compound.
- Or try fresh grass clippings.

Parking precautions
- Hang a tire at bumper height on the front end of your garage.
- If garage space is tight, put strips of inner tube, foam rubber, or carpeting on the side walls, where your car door hits when opened.

Avoid the hot seat
- When you park in the sun in the summer, cover the car seat and back with a towel.

Frost foilers
- Keep car windows free of ice overnight or for any extended period of time by spreading a sheet of heavy-duty plastic (available at hardware stores) over the windshield. Catch one end inside the door on the driver's side, and secure the other end inside the passenger door.
- Leave one window open a crack to prevent frost from building up on the inside of the windows.

Saving money on auto repairs
- Save up to 50 percent on auto repairs, paint jobs, and engine work by checking with auto-repair schools in your area.
- Most paint shops reduce the cost of painting your car if you remove all trim, door handles, and mirrors yourself.

Before buying a used car
- Call this toll-free government number—800-424-9393—and find out if the car you're interested in has ever been recalled.
- Don't buy a used car on a rainy day. All cars with dull or blemished finishes look better when they are wet.

No butts about it
- To keep passengers from smoking, give them the message by filling your ashtray with change for tolls or wrapped hard candy.

Travel

Pack Facts

Packing an airtight case

- When packing shampoo, mouthwash, and liquid cosmetics in plastic bottles, squeeze the bottle and force out some of the air just before tightening the cap. This creates a partial vacuum and helps prevent leakage.
- Make a handy toothbrush container from a plastic pill bottle. Cut a slit in the top, slip the handle through it, and snap it back on the bottle with the bristles inside.
- Instead of traveling with a bottle of nail-polish remover, which might leak in your suitcase, saturate several cotton balls with the remover and keep them in a small, airtight jar.

Uses for locking plastic bags

- Use them to hold shoes to protect surrounding clothing.
- A large size will hold dirty laundry.
- They'll keep stationery and stamps clean.
- They'll prevent bottles of liquid medication, hair spray, and perfumes from leaking. (Use the kind that seal.)

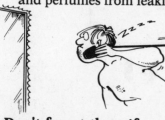

Don't forget these if you're staying in a hotel

- A long extension cord. It won't matter then where the mirror or outlets are in the room.
- High-wattage light bulb. Just in case you need more light when applying makeup or reading.
- Water heater and instant coffee or tea. No more waiting for room service.
- Several clip-type clothespins for clipping slacks and skirts to ordinary hangers.

Do not disturb

- Hang the DO NOT DISTURB sign on your motel or hotel room door when you leave for the evening and chances are you won't have any unwanted guests.

On call
- Two wake-up calls are better than one. The first may be overlooked or you could fall asleep again.

Save on crib rental
- Take along a heavy-duty, flat cardboard box. Set up the box on the floor and line the bottom with a heavy, quilted blanket. The high sides will keep drafts off baby.

Air "Lines"

Nonstop or direct flights
- Be aware of the difference between nonstop and direct flights when booking your reservation. Nonstop flights don't stop. Direct flights, however, may stop many times between your departure and your destination. "Direct" simply means that you don't change planes at a stopover.

For cabin fever
- Airplane-cabin pressurization causes dehydration, so drink a glass of water every hour and you'll feel better when you arrive.
- Wear loose clothing (such as a jogging suit) and shoes because the body tends to swell at an altitude of more than five thousand feet.

Baggage checks
- Put identification tags on both the outside and the inside of suitcases. Bags without outside tags will be opened after three days if they haven't been claimed.
- Never use curbside baggage-checking service. It increases the odds that your luggage will be lost or delayed.
- Most lost luggage is checked in less than a half hour before flight time. So check in early.
- Watch to make sure that each bag is tagged and sent on the conveyor belt or it could be left sitting there.

Quick luggage identification
- Tie brightly colored yarn to the handles of your luggage and you'll be able to identify your bag quickly.

Replacing a broken suitcase handle
- Use a dog collar looped through the metal rings.
- Replace with a dog leash the lost strap used to pull luggage on wheels.

Flying with kids
- Give baby a bottle or pacifier at takeoff and landing to reduce pressure on ears.
- Have hard candy or gum ready for the older kids.
- And remember, a few glasses of cola have as much caffeine as a cup of coffee. Don't give them to the kids if you want them to sleep.

Inspections
- If you are traveling with a gift-wrapped package, wrap the lid and the box separately so the lid can be removed for inspection at the airport. (Use rubber bands to hold the lid on.)

Over there . . .

- When traveling in foreign countries, always carry your hotel matchbook with you. If you get lost, local residents can help you find your way back.
- And carry picture postcards of the places you'd like to visit. Show the cards to cab drivers and there'll be no confusion getting to the right spot.
- Pack a large, collapsible canvas suitcase in the bottom of one of your suitcases in case you go on a shopping spree. When returning from abroad, put all declarable items in one bag and maybe you'll save time going through customs.

Medical standbys

- It's not a bad idea to carry a spare pair of eyeglasses when traveling abroad, and take along a copy of the prescription when traveling in the United States.
- When traveling with prescription drugs, make sure they are in the original containers. Also, carry a copy of the prescription in case you need a refill or have some explaining to do at customs.
- Make note of the generic name of each medicine, since brand names differ in foreign countries.
- Try earplugs and an eyeshade if you can't sleep on planes and trains.

Cameras

- When taking new, expensive, foreign-made cameras, watches, and recorders out of the United States, register them with the U.S. customs before you leave. This way, you can't be asked to pay duty on them when you return.
- Remember that airport security X-ray scanning devices in many foreign countries are more powerful than those in the United States, and may ruin your film. Always unload your camera before passing it through inspection. (Many foreign airports insist on passing the camera through the machine; in the United States you have the right to have it inspected by hand.)

Cruise control
- Remember this general rule for boat cruises: The shorter the cruise, the younger the passengers.

Road "Ways"

Map your route
- After deciding on the route you'll be taking, mark it on the map with a felt-tipped pen.

Saving space and trouble
- Pack bedding in drawstring laundry bags. The bags hold a lot without taking up much space, and they can double as pillows in the backseat for the kids.
- You won't have to empty the whole trunk to get to the jack if you pack it last.

For fast cleanups
- Fill a plastic liquid-detergent bottle (without rinsing it out) with water and keep it in the glove compartment with paper towels.

Keeping the kids busy
- Pack a scrapbook, scissors, and glue. At night the children can paste the day's collection of postcards, menus, and other memorabilia into the scrapbook. The book will not only help with school reports on "What I Did This Summer" but will keep the kids busy collecting souvenirs during the day.
- Bring along a couple of jump ropes so the kids can work off excess energy whenever you stop for food or gas.

Wish you were here
- If you plan to send postcards while on vacation, put all the addresses on sticker labels before you go instead of carrying an address book.

Surefire Camping Hints

Fast food
- Prepare some of the food as far in advance as possible, then seal in locking food storage bags. At the campsite, heat the bags and use the same water to wash dishes.

Fast ways to do laundry
- On camping trips use a clean plunger as an agitator and a plastic bucket as a washtub when doing small laundry jobs.
- Or put dirty clothes, detergent, and water in a large container with a tight-fitting lid. Set it in your car trunk, and while you're driving to the next campsite the dirty clothes will be swishing around and cleaning themselves.

Keeping your trailer hitch rust-free
- Cut a slit in a tennis ball and fit it snugly over the hitch ball. This will keep it dry and rust-free.

Flashlights
- Put a piece of tape over the flashlight switch so it won't get turned on accidentally in the suitcase.
- Protect your flashlight in the rain. Put it in a plastic sandwich bag and close the opening with a rubber band. You can turn it on and off without removing it, and the light shines brightly through the plastic.

Matches
- Wrap kitchen matches in aluminum foil to keep them dry on fishing, camping, and other outdoor trips.

Fishing-trip tips
- Keep your fishing license in an old ballpoint pen. Remove the cartridge, roll up the license, and stuff it inside the pen. Toss it in your tackle box or clip it to your shirt pocket.
- Ever try to pull a worm from the bottom of the can? Take a can with a plastic top and cut out both ends. Put plastic covers on each. When you want a worm, open up the end where it is.

- Wrap a triple thickness of aluminum foil around the hook immediately after taking the rod out of the water. The hook won't stick anybody or get tangled up with other rods in the boat.

This hint gets an A or a B
- Make a note of your blood type on your driver's license in case of an emergency.

Storing suitcases
- To keep suitcases smelling fresh, store them with a fabric-softener sheet or a bar of scented soap inside.
- Or store suitcases with a small packet of activated charcoal (available at your florist) or crumpled-up newspaper inside to avoid musty odors.

Tricks of
the Trade

For those little worries you can laugh about
- When slacks or jeans are too tight to close easily, lie down and zip them up.
- You have trouble getting your children into the tub? Tell them that the last one to take a bath must clean it.
- If you have a garage sale, don't mark prices on the items; let people make you an offer. Often it'll be more than you would have charged.
- When finally you find something after looking all over the house for it, put it back in the first place you looked. That's probably where it belongs.
- To eliminate the mess from cigarettes and cut down on the alcohol bill, invite a clergyman to your party.
- If you need a little help getting that ear-bending friend off the telephone, make a cassette recording of some background noises. Doorbell sounds and children crying are good for starters.
- If you're still in bed when your husband walks through the front door at the end of the day, dab a little liquid cleaner behind each ear. It'll make you smell as if you've been housecleaning all day and deserve dinner out.
- When your house is so messy that you want to throw up your hands in despair, just take off your glasses and things won't look so bad.
- Maybe your kids will brush their teeth without trouble if you tell them the Tooth Fairy pays a lot more for healthy teeth.
- To get children to eat cereal with less sugar, put sugar in a salt shaker.
- If you want to eat less, use chopsticks or eat in front of a mirror.
- When you find yourself in charge of a group of children, have them understand that whoever says, "Me first," is automatically last.

- Your cat will eat only the food from expensive small cans? Try mixing in a little of the less expensive food that comes in the larger cans. Gradually increase the cheaper brand until the cat will eat it without turning up its tail.
- If you want your children to begin helping you with household duties, play the "waiter and waitress" game. Mommy and Daddy are the customers.
- The best way to ensure that your dinner guests will enjoy what you serve is to keep them waiting until they're good and hungry.
- If you can't seem to get your kids to clean up after themselves, hide everything you pick up in a secret place and charge a dime an item as ransom.
- Your hungry mate is due home from work any minute and you haven't started dinner yet! Sauté an onion in a little oil. He'll come home, smell "food" cooking, and won't realize that dinner is going to be late.
- To train children not to complain or tattle, give them a limited supply of complaint tickets. Each time they have a complaint they must give you a ticket before you will listen. The child will have to think twice before using up one of his complaints.
- Chronicle your first year of marriage in a diary because by your tenth anniversary, if you have had children, you will swear that in your entire married life you haven't had ten whole minutes alone.
- Your husband has been complaining about the messy house? Rearrange the furniture and he'll think you've been scrubbing all day.
- If you want to be discreet about the number of birthday candles on a cake, your own for instance, place them in the form of a question mark.
- When a toddler hates to leave the tub, pull the plug.
- Don't make staying in bed too much fun for a child who is ill. You might delay recovery.
- When you're sick, keep a police whistle near your bed to call your husband.

● And remember, one good turn gets the blanket.

Mary Ellen's
Best of
Helpful
Kitchen
Hints

by
Mary Ellen Pinkham

Mary Ellen's Best of Helpful Kitchen Hints

Contents

Introduction

Every day you face problems in the kitchen—and so does everyone else. The meringue on your favorite lemon pie suddenly begins to weep and sink. The cookies stick to the baking pan. You open a carton of eggs, and six of them are cracked. I figured you—and everyone else—needed a book that could help you handle such unpredictable disasters. A book like our first one, *Mary Ellen's Best of Helpful Hints*, but specially designed for kitchen use—a book full of hints that really work, that are easy and fun to look up when you need them most. This is it!

Many of the hints in this book are original, but many also come from you, the people from all over the country who responded to our first book by sharing their own suggestions. I've read and tested them, plus thousands of others, and have organized the very best of them into convenient categories for easy reference when you need a solution to a problem right away.

As you use this book you'll find that what works in the kitchen is often valuable in solving other dilemmas around the home, too. If you're like me, you've discovered that applying to new situations the simple techniques you use in the kitchen can help you in everything from cleaning to child-rearing; and I'm sure that in this collection of over a thousand ideas, you'll find plenty of new ways to save time, money, and trouble—and an expensive trip to the grocery store.

The Best of Helpful Kitchen Hints for Cooking

In the Beginning

Recipes at the ready
- Keep a recipe card upright by placing it in the tines of a fork and putting the fork handle in a glass. Carry the glass with you from counter to range as you cook.
- Or use a small magnet to tack the recipe card to the refrigerator or exhaust-fan hood.
- Or hang a permanent clamp on the inside, or even the outside, of a cupboard door, just for this purpose.
- Or, if you keep your recipe cards in a card-file box, glue a cork to the top of the box. Cut a slot across the top of the cork and simply insert the card you need to use in an upright position.

You'll see right through this
- To keep a recipe book or card clean while you're cooking, place it under an upside-down glass pie plate. The curved bottom also magnifies the print.
- Protect recipe cards from drips by using see-through plastic-covered file cards or by taping plastic wrap over the front.
- Or apply a thin coat of clear nail polish.
- Or spray with hair spray.

Cookbook update
- When you find a better recipe than one in your cookbook, copy it onto a file card and tape it over the recipe in your book. This way, you can use the book's index to find your new, improved recipe.
- Another trick is gluing an envelope to the inside of the front cover to hold new recipe cards and newspaper clippings.

From the Soup

Puree and simple
- Before your extra mushrooms go bad, use your blender to puree them in a little liquid (water, beef, or chicken broth), pour into ice-cube trays, and freeze. Remove when solid and store in freezer in plastic bags. Great for soups, stews, or sauces.
- Keep putting all leftover vegetables in a container in your freezer. When you have a sufficient amount, blend and freeze in ice-cube trays. Just thaw amount needed. Good for adding additional flavor to frozen soups.
- When cooking a beef roast, save pan juice. Pour it into ice-cube trays and freeze. Wrap solid cubes in foil and store in freezer. You will have instant beef stock when needed.

No bones about it
- Beef stock will obtain a rich brown color if bones are first browned under broiler about six inches from heat. Then add bones to stock and proceed to cook.
- When preparing soups or broths, remember that the gelatin in the bones gives body to the liquids and that veal bones, if available, give soup the most body.
- Don't throw away steak, roast, or chicken bones. Wrap and freeze until needed for soup stock.
- Always start cooking bones and meat in cold, salted water.

I want to make this perfectly clear
- Adding two or three eggshells to your soup stock and simmering it for ten minutes will help clarify the broth.
- Or strain stock through clean nylon hose or coffee filter.

Smoother soup—no scorching, clumping, or curdling

- To prevent scorching when cooking soup in a large stock pot, elevate the pot above the flame by putting two or three bricks on the burner. The platform permits long-term simmering over low heat without worries of boil-overs.
- When making split-pea soup, add a slice of bread when you start cooking the liquid and peas together. This will keep the peas from going to the bottom and burning or sticking.
- To prevent curdling of the milk or cream in tomato soup, add the tomato soup to the milk rather than vice versa.
- Or first add a little flour to the milk and beat well.
- Add minced clams to chowder at the very last moment. Otherwise they become mushy and tasteless.

Skimming off the fat

- If time allows, the best method is to refrigerate the soup until the fat hardens on the top.
- Eliminate fat from soup and stew by dropping ice cubes into the pot. As you stir, the fat will cling to the cubes. Discard the cubes before they melt.
- Or wrap ice cubes in a piece of cheesecloth or paper towel and skim over the top.
- Lettuce leaves also absorb fat. Place a few in the pot and remove them with the fat that clings to them.

To the Salad

Freshenin' up

- To remove the core from a head of lettuce, hit the core end once against the counter top sharply. The core will then twist out. This method also prevents the unsightly brown spots that result from cutting into lettuce.
- Fit the bottom of a colander with a nylon net and use as a receptacle for salad ingredients. When batch is washed, take the net out by the edges, squeeze out the water, and you've got everything handy for the salad bowl.
- Put cut-up salad greens or cole slaw in a metal bowl and place in freezer for a few minutes. The greens will arrive on the table in perky condition.
- To prevent soggy salads, place an inverted saucer in the bottom of the salad bowl. The excess liquid drains off under the saucer and the salad stays fresh and crisp.
- Do not add salt to a lettuce salad until just before serving—salt wilts and toughens lettuce.

Dressin' up

- Add a tablespoon of boiling water to an envelope of your favorite salad-dressing mix, cover, and let cool. The flavor is released immediately. Add other ingredients as usual.
- Make creamy dressings by pouring oil slowly into other ingredients in a slow-running blender.

Shakin' up
- Combine all ingredients for an oil-and-vinegar dressing in a screw-top jar. Add an ice cube and shake. Discard the ice cube and your dressing will be extra smooth and well mixed.
- Then put salad greens in a plastic bag, add dressing, and shake.

Storin' up
- Lettuce will not rust so quickly if you line the bottom of the refrigerator's vegetable compartment with paper towels or napkins. The paper absorbs the excess moisture, keeping vegetables and fruits fresher for a longer period of time.
- Or put a few dry sponges in the vegetable compartment to absorb moisture.

Toppin' up
- Slice leftover hot-dog buns into sticks, butter them, sprinkle with garlic powder and Parmesan cheese, then toast them in oven. Crumble them over salads.
- For a richer-looking potato salad, add some yellow food coloring to the mixed ingredients.

Do's
- Do add a touch of garlic by rubbing a crushed clove of garlic over the inside of the salad bowl before adding salad ingredients.
- Do keep packages of blue or Roquefort cheese in freezer. The cheese will crumble perfectly if scraped with a paring knife, and will be ready to serve with salad dressing by dinnertime.
- To keep a wooden salad bowl from becoming sticky, wash and dry it thoroughly, then rub bowl well, inside and out, with a piece of waxed paper.
- Or rub the inside of a wooden bowl with a piece of walnut meat. This also removes scratches.

And a don't
- Don't use a painted plate for serving salad with vinegar dressing. Vinegar corrodes the paint on the plate.

Vim, Vigor, and Vegetables

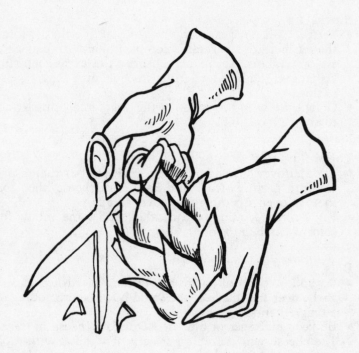

Artichokes
- Wear rubber gloves when handling artichokes and you won't prick your fingers while snipping off the ends of the leaves with scissors and removing the choke.
- Don't cook artichokes in an aluminum or iron pot. They turn the pot gray.
- To prevent their discoloring, stand artichokes in cold water with a tablespoon of vinegar an hour before cooking or dip the trimmed base in lemon juice.
- Wrap artichokes, unwashed, in a damp towel and store in a plastic bag in the refrigerator. This will prevent wilting for up to five days.

Asparagus
- Open asparagus cans from the bottom to avoid breaking the tips.
- Use a clean coffee percolator to cook fresh asparagus. The asparagus stand upright this way—stalk side down—and the tips steam perfectly while the stems cook to a tender finish.
- To revive limp, uncooked asparagus, stand them upright in a small amount of ice water in a deep pot and cover with a plastic bag. Let stand in the refrigerator for half an hour before cooking.
- To make thick asparagus stalks tender, peel the lower parts up to the tender part with a potato peeler. Stalks taste as good as the flowers this way.

Beans
- To improve their texture and prevent mushiness and cracking, add a pinch of baking soda to the water when cooking dry beans. Never salt until beans are tender.

Beets
- To keep beets red, cook them whole with two inches of stem. Also add a few tablespoons of vinegar to the cooking water to prevent fading.

Broccoli
- A slice or two of stale bread in cooking water minimizes the cooking odor of broccoli. Skim the bread from the surface after cooking. This works with cabbage, too.
- Broccoli stems can be cooked in the same length of time as the flowerets if you make "X" incisions from top to bottom through stems.

Cabbage
- To reduce odor while cooking cabbage, place a small cup of vinegar on the range.
- Or add a wedge of lemon to the pot.
- To remove cabbage leaves more easily for stuffed-cabbage recipes, place the entire cabbage in water and bring it to a boil. Remove head, drain, and then pull off the leaves that have softened. Return the rest of the cabbage head to the water and repeat until all the leaves are soft enough to peel off.

Carrots

- Drop carrots in boiling water, let stand for five minutes, then drop them in cold water. The skin slips right off.
- Remember, remove the tops of carrots before storing in the refrigerator. Tops drain the carrots of moisture, making them limp and dry.

Cauliflower

- To keep cauliflower a bright white, add a little milk during cooking.
- Cauliflower odor is almost eliminated if you drop a few unshelled walnuts into the pot. Also works for cabbage odors.

Celery

- To make celery curls: Cut celery into three- to four-inch pieces. Cut each piece into narrow strips, leaving about an inch at the end uncut to hold the piece together, then put them in ice water until they curl, about half an hour.
- Cook a stalk or two of celery with broccoli, cabbage, and sauerkraut to prevent strong odors.
- And don't discard celery leaves: Dry them, then rub the leaves through a sieve for powder that can be used to flavor soups, stews, and salad dressings.

Corn on the cob

- Tastes much better when the tender green leaves from the corn are removed and used to line the bottom of the pot while corn is cooking.
- The easiest way to remove corn from the cob is to use an ordinary shoehorn.
- To remove corn silk: Dampen a toothbrush and brush downward on the cob of corn. Every strand should come off.
- And don't waste butter: Use a pastry brush to spread melted butter on corn. A celery stalk also makes an instant pastry brush.

Eggplant

- To rid eggplant of bitterness, drop it into salted water as you peel it. Pat it dry with a paper towel and it's ready to cook.
- A good rule of thumb: If eggplant is to be cooked for a short time, peel off the skin. If it is to be cooked longer, peeling isn't necessary.

Lettuce
- To perk up soggy lettuce, soak it for an hour in the refrigerator in a bowl of cold water and lemon juice. Douse quickly in hot and then ice water with a little apple-cider vinegar added.
- Lettuce or celery will crisp up quickly if you place it in a pan of cold water, adding a few slices of raw potato.

Lima beans
- For quick shelling, with scissors cut a thin strip along the inner edge of the pod, where the beans are attached.

Mushrooms
- Never immerse mushrooms in water when cleaning them because they will absorb too much water.
- To be sure you get prime mushrooms, buy only those with closed caps. The gills should not be showing.
- Keep mushrooms white and firm when sautéing them by adding a teaspoon of lemon juice to each quarter pound of melted butter.
- If mushrooms are too wet when cooking, they release too much moisture and steam instead of browning. Stirring the mushrooms with a long-handled fork and keeping fat very hot keep steam from building up.
- Use an egg slicer to slice fresh mushrooms quickly and uniformly.

Onions

- Keep onions whole when cooking them by cutting a small cross, one-quarter inch deep, in the stem end.
- Once an onion has been cut in half, rub the leftover cut side with butter and it will keep fresh longer.
- To make onions less strong, slice and separate them into rings, then soak them in cold water for one hour. (Mild onions are great for salads.)
- Peel fresh white onions easily by plunging them into boiling water for two minutes.
- Shed fewer tears:
    - Cut the root end of the onion off last.
    - Refrigerate onions before chopping.
    - Peel them under cold, running water.
    - Rinse hands frequently under cold water while chopping.
    - Keep your mouth tightly closed while chopping.
    - Chop with the exhaust fan operating.

Peas

- Always cook peas in the pod. The peas separate from the pods when cooked and the pods float to the surface. It's less work and the peas taste better.

Potatoes

Baked

- Rub butter or bacon fat over potatoes before baking to prevent skins from cracking and to improve the taste.
- To reheat leftover baked potatoes, dip them in hot water, then bake in 350° oven about twenty minutes.
- In a hurry? Boil potatoes in salted water for about ten minutes before popping them into a very hot oven.
- Or cut a thin slice from each end before popping them into the oven.
- To cut baking time by as much as half, place potatoes on the oven rack and place an iron pot over them.
- Or insert a nail to shorten baking time by fifteen minutes.

French fries
- For the best French fries, first let cut potatoes stand in cold water an hour before frying. Dry thoroughly before cooking. The trick is to fry them twice. The first time, just fry them for a few minutes and drain off grease. The second time, fry them until golden brown. There's no better way.

Mashed
- A well-beaten egg white added to mashed potatoes improves appearance and taste.
- Overcooked potatoes can become soggy when milk is added. Sprinkle with powdered milk or instant potatoes for the fluffiest mashed potatoes ever.

Potato pancakes
- To prevent discoloration, grate potatoes directly into a bowl of ice water.
- Or add a little sour cream to grated potatoes.
- And to use leftover mashed potatoes, coat patties with flour and fry them.

Potato-skin chips
- Potato skins cut into strips, seasoned, and baked in a hot oven make a nutritious snack.

Rehardening potatoes
- If your raw potatoes become soft, put them in ice water for half an hour and they'll become hard again.

Red cabbage
- To keep it from turning purple, add a tablespoon of vinegar when cooking red cabbage.

Rice
- For the whitest rice, add a few drops of lemon juice to the cooking water.

Sweet potatoes
- For simple peeling, take sweet potatoes from boiling water and plunge them immediately into cold water. The skins fall off.

Tomatoes
- Always add a pinch of sugar to tomatoes when cooking them. It enhances flavor.
- Slice tomatoes vertically and the slices stay firmer.
- Baked tomatoes and peppers hold their shape when baked in a greased muffin tin.
- To peel many tomatoes at once, place them in an old pillow case or onion netting bag and plunge them into a pot of boiling water for a minute. The skins slip right off.

Two in the time of one
- By wrapping each batch of two different vegetables separately in aluminum foil, you can cook both at the same time in just one pot. Save time, fuel, and cleanup.

Prevent vegetable boilovers
- A toothpick inserted between lid and pot before cooking will let just enough steam escape later to prevent messy boilovers.

Keep vegetables colorful
- Add a pinch of baking soda to cooking water.

Evicting the bugs
- To chase insects from cabbage, cauliflower, and similar vegetables, soak the vegetables in cold water with a few tablespoons of either salt or vinegar for fifteen minutes.

Frozen vegetables
- To restore a fresh flavor to frozen vegetables, pour boiling water over them to rinse away all traces of the frozen water.

Perking up vegetables
- If fresh vegetables are wilted or blemished, pick off the brown edges. Sprinkle vegetables with cool water, wrap them in a towel, and refrigerate for an hour or so.
- Many vegetables can be freshened by soaking them for an hour in cold water to which the juice of a lemon or a few tablespoons of vinegar have been added.

Eggs–pert–ease

Seeing through the shell
- Add food coloring to water before hard-boiling eggs, then you can tell the boiled eggs from the raw ones in the refrigerator.
- Or mark hard-boiled eggs with a crayon or pencil before storing.

Yolklore
- Keep yolks centered in eggs by stirring the water while cooking hard-boiled eggs. Especially good for deviled eggs.
- Keep yolk intact when separating it from the white by breaking the eggshell and tipping the whole egg into the palm of your hand. The yolk will remain in your palm while the egg white runs between your fingers and into a small bowl.
- You can cook whole yolks without their shells. Slide yolks gently into water and cook for about ten minutes. You can use yolks in salads or in a spread for hors d'oeuvre.
- Prevent crumbling yolks by dipping your knife or egg slicer in cold water before slicing hard-boiled eggs.
- Do not pour raw eggs or egg yolks directly into a hot mixture at once. Begin by adding a little of the hot mixture to the yolks first. Moderating the yolks' temperature this way prevents them from curdling when they are combined with the total hot mixture.

This is all it's "cracked" up to be
- You won't drop the eggs if you moisten your fingers before removing them from the carton.
- Boil cracked eggs in aluminum foil twisted at both ends.
- Rub a cut lemon over eggshells to keep them from breaking while cooking.
- Rescue an egg that cracks while boiling by immediately pouring a generous quantity of salt on the crack. This tends to seal the crack and contain the egg white.

- To peel hard-boiled eggs easily, plunge them into cold water. Crack the shell, then roll the egg lightly between the palms of your hands and the shell will come right off.
- Crack the shell of a boiled egg all over. Insert a small wet spoon between shell membrane and egg, then turn with the egg. Keep the spoon wet while you go. Perfect peeled egg every time!

Whites made right

- Beaten egg whites will be more stable if you add one teaspoon of cream of tartar to each batch of seven or eight egg whites.
- Let egg whites warm to room temperature before you beat them. Then, as you beat them, add slightly less than one tablespoon of water for each egg white to increase the volume.
- Egg whites will not beat satisfactorily if the least bit of yolk is present. Remove specks of yolk with a Q-tip or dampened cotton cloth, to which they will stick. Also make sure the egg beater is free of oil.
- A tablespoon of vinegar added to water before poaching eggs allows whites to set without spreading.

Just omelets

- For a stick-proof omelet pan, treat your pan right: Wipe the pan with paper toweling and table salt after each session of omelet-making.
- For a more tender omelet, add a small amount of water to the beaten eggs instead of milk or cream. Water retards coagulation of the yolks; milk or cream tends to harden them.

"Egg-stensions"

- If poached eggs can't be served immediately, put them in cool water and when you're ready to serve, reheat them gently in hot, salted water.
- For silky-smooth scrambled eggs, start with a cool, buttered pan and cook eggs very slowly. At the very end, stir in one tablespoon of cream or evaporated milk per portion.
- Or mix with a white sauce when serving a large crowd.

Please with Cheese

Hard facts
- To keep cheese from hardening, butter the cut end.
- To soften hardened cheese, soak it in buttermilk.
- Wrapping in aluminum foil also prevents dryouts.
- Store cheese in a wine-vinegar–soaked cloth for extra flavor and freshness.
- To prevent mold, store cheese in a tightly covered container with some sugar cubes.
- Cottage cheese will remain fresher longer if stored upside down in the refrigerator.

Grate hints
- Brush a little oil on the grater before you start grating, and cheese will wash off the grater easily.
- Force a soft cheese through a colander with a potato masher instead of grating it.
- Use a potato peeler to cut cheese into strips for salads and other garnishings.

Edge-wise
- A dull knife works much better than a sharp one for slicing cheese.
- Warm the knife before cutting cheese, and the cheese will cut as easily as butter.

Feats with Meats

Bringing home the bacon
- To keep bacon slices from sticking together, roll the package into a tube shape and secure it with a rubber band before refrigerating.
- Bacon fries with less curling if soaked a few minutes in cold water before frying.
- To help reduce shrinkage, put bacon slices in a cold skillet and prick them thoroughly with a fork as they fry.
- To make bacon curls, fry only until cooked but not crisp. Then take bacon from the skillet and twist around the tines of a fork. Pierce with a wooden toothpick and broil under a low flame to complete crisping.

Sausage links and patties
- Make sausage broiling easy by pressing several links onto a meat skewer—one flip turns them all.
- To prevent sausages from breaking or shrinking, boil them about eight minutes before they are fried. Or roll them lightly in flour before frying.
- Flouring sausage patties on both sides gives them an appetizing, crunchy crust as they fry. This method also helps prevent splattering.

Rounder burgers
- To get perfectly round meat patties, press down on flat patties with closed end of a No. 2½ can, then trim around the patty.

Juicier burgers
- Form patties around chunks of cracked ice; once on the grill, the melting ice will prevent overcooking. For a very moist burger, also put a few drops of cold water on both sides of the patty as you grill.
- Or add one stiffly beaten egg white for each pound of hamburger.
- Or add one grated large raw onion to each one and a half pounds of ground beef.
- Or make patties with one tablespoon of cottage cheese in the center.

Faster burgers

- Make lots of hamburgers for a large crowd by cooking in stacks. First, line baking pan with foil and arrange bottom tier of patties. Place another piece of foil over this layer and arrange the second tier. Stack them four deep. In a 350° oven, the patties will be thoroughly done in about thirty-five minutes. Do the same for frankfurters, but cook for only fifteen minutes.
- Or partially cook the meat, using the above method, and finish off on the outdoor grill.

For "loafers" only

- To keep hands clean, place all meat-loaf ingredients in a plastic bag, manipulate to mix and shape into a loaf, then slide loaf into pan.
- Meat loaf won't crack while baking if you rub cold water across the top of the meat before popping it into the oven.
- Instant potato flakes will bind and stretch your meat-loaf mixture.
- Make an "icing" of mashed potatoes to cover your meat loaf. Spread the mashed potatoes over the surface and lightly glaze with melted butter about fifteen minutes before the meat loaf is done. Then return meat to oven so the potato gets a light-brown crust.
- Baking meat loaf in a muffin tin rather than in a loaf pan reduces cooking time by as much as half.

Ham session

- Have your canned ham sliced by the butcher, then tie it back together, garnish with pineapple, and bake. No messy job of slicing it hot.
- Ham will be more tender and juicy if allowed to cool in the water in which it has been boiled.
- Ham will be deliciously moist if you empty a bottle of cola into the baking pan and bake the ham wrapped in aluminum foil. Remove the foil about half an hour before the ham is done, allowing the drippings to combine with the cola for a tasty brown gravy.
- For a too-salty ham, partially bake it and drain all the juices. Pour a small bottle of ginger ale over it and let it bake until done.

Roasts and steaks

- A shallow pan is better than a deep one for roasting because it allows heat to circulate around the roast.
- Instead of using a metal roasting rack, make a grid of carrot and celery sticks and place meat or poultry on it. The additional advantage: Vegetables flavor the pan drippings.
- To prevent meat from scorching when roasting, place a pan of cold water in the oven.
- For easier slicing, let a roast stand for ten to fifteen minutes after removing it from the oven.
- And when broiling a steak, add a cup of water to the bottom portion of the pan before sliding it into the oven. The water helps absorb smoke and grease.

Lick your chops

- For tasty, greaseless pork chops, line a loaf pan with sliced bread and add browned chops, standing them up in the pan so that they lean against the bread. Cover with foil and bake. Grease is absorbed by bread.

Lamb glamour

- With toothpicks, fasten a piece of garlic bread, butter side down, to the meat. Sprinkle with water and roast. Garlic butter gives the meat a snappy flavor, and the bread makes an appetizing dressing.
- Or baste the roasting lamb with a cup of hot coffee containing cream and sugar.

For high livers

- Liver will be especially tender if first soaked in milk. Refrigerate meat about two hours, remove, dry thoroughly, bread and sauté.
- Or try soaking it in tomato juice for two to three hours before broiling or frying.

Tough meats

- Tenderize tough meat by rubbing all sides with a mixture of vinegar and olive oil. Let it stand two hours before cooking.
- For a very tough piece of meat, rub it well with baking soda, let stand a few hours, then wash it thoroughly before cooking.
- When pounding to tenderize meat, pound flour into it to prevent the juices from escaping.

Stop the splattering

- To keep hot fat from splattering, first sprinkle a little salt in the frying pan.

Gravy training

- Mix cold water and flour or cornstarch into a smooth paste. Cover the jar and shake it until the paste is smooth. Add mixture gradually to the pan, stirring the gravy constantly while bringing it to a boil.
- A quick way to darken gravy: Mix one tablespoon of sugar and one tablespoon of water and heat the mixture in a heavy pan until the water evaporates and the sugar starts to brown. Then pour the pale gravy into the sugared pan.
- Or add dark, percolated coffee to pale gravy. It will add color but won't affect the taste.
- For greaseless gravy: Pour pan drippings into a tall glass; the grease will rise to the top in minutes. Remove it and prepare grease-free gravy.
- Add one-quarter teaspoon of baking soda to greasy gravy.
- Buzz lumpy gravy in your blender.

Birds of a Feather

Freshness
- Never buy chicken on Monday. It is likely you'll get one that wasn't bought by the weekend.
- To keep fresh chicken fresher, immediately remove polyethylene wrap, loosely wrap chicken in waxed paper, and refrigerate. Fresh chicken should be used within three days.

No more fowl play
- Defrost a frozen chicken by soaking it in cold water that's been heavily salted. This draws out blood, and the breast meat will be pure white.
- An unpleasant poultry odor can be neutralized if you wash the bird with the juice of half a lemon, then rub it with salt and lemon.

A time saver
- Debone chicken with a pair of kitchen scissors. It is easier than hacking and whacking with a knife.

Chicken scoops
- After flouring chicken, chill for one hour. The coating will adhere better during frying.
- Marinate chicken breasts in milk, cream, or buttermilk for three hours in the refrigerator before frying or baking to ensure tenderness.
- For an especially light and delicate crust on coated fried foods, add about three-quarters of a teaspoon of baking powder to the batter and use club soda for the liquid.
- Chicken bastes itself when you roast it covered with bacon slices. Do not butter.

Deep frying
- To test whether hot oil is still usable, drop a piece of white bread into the pan. If the bread develops dark specks, the oil is deteriorating.
- When reusing frying oil, eliminate odors and unwanted taste by first frying a dozen sprigs of parsley or a raw potato in the oil for about fifteen minutes.

Dumplings
- Slice a stack of flour tortillas into one-inch strips and add to a simmering stew ten minutes before the stew is done. This is cheap, easy, and good enough to fool dumpling experts.
- To resist the "sneak peak" temptation when making real dumplings, cover pot with a glass pie plate while dumplings are cooking.

Talking turkey
- Buy a large turkey when it's on sale and have butcher cut it in half. Each part still has white and dark meat and a cavity for stuffing.
- Instead of one large turkey, buy two small ones. They will roast in much less time and you'll have a larger portion of the better cuts of meats.
- Unwaxed dental floss is good for trussing because it does not burn and is very strong.
- Or, instead of sewing a stuffed turkey, close the cavity with two heels of dampened bread. Push each into an opening with crust facing out and overlapping to hold the stuffing in.
- Or close the cavity with one or two raw potatoes.

- Instead of stuffing a bird, try steaming it by pouring one cup of water mixed with one-quarter cup of pineapple juice into the body cavity. The meat will be more flavorful and juicy.
- Always roast turkey in roasting pan with breast side down to prevent the white meat from getting dry. Turn breast up during the last hour of cooking.

"I've got juice under my skin"
- For a juicier bird, fill a basting needle with one-quarter pound of melted margarine. Inject into raw turkey around breast and thigh in six to eight places.

When the Dish Is Fish

From fin to finish
- You can tell a fresh fish by checking to see if the eyes are bright, clear, and slightly protruding. A stale fish has sunken, cloudy, or pink eyes. Make sure the scales are shiny and tight against the skin. Examine the gills: They should be red or pink, never gray.
- If in doubt about the freshness of a fish, place it in cold water. If it floats, it's probably just been caught.
- Make your own fish scaler by nailing several bottle caps to the end of a piece of wood, three bottle caps wide and eight inches long. The serrated edges will provide a fine scaling surface.
- Before scaling, rub the entire fish with vinegar and the scales will come off in a snap.
- Sprinkle some salt on a board when cleaning fish to keep it from slipping.
- After cleaning a fish, bend and roll it at each section and the bones will pierce through. Be careful not to tear fish when pulling the bones out.
- And to remove the bones easily after cooking, first rub melted butter down the back of the fish to be cooked.

More fish tips

- A dash of lemon juice and milk added to the seasoned liquid in which halibut or another white fish is cooked makes flesh white.
- Baking fish on a bed of chopped onion, celery, and parsley not only makes the fish taste better but also keeps it from sticking to the pan.
- Thaw frozen fish in milk. The milk draws out the frozen taste and provides a fresh-caught flavor.
- Try soaking fish in one-quarter cup of vinegar, wine, or lemon juice and water before cooking to make it sweet and tender.
- Use a piece of foil that's been crumpled and then smoothed out to bake fish sticks. Turn them over as required. They will brown equally on bottom and top and won't stick, either.
- Soak saltwater fish in vinegar to eliminate some of the salty taste. Then rinse fish under cold water.

Odor eaters

- To remove fish odor from hands, rub them with vinegar or salt.
- To reduce fish smell, put a dash of vinegar in the poaching liquid. Adding sesame oil before cooking also works.
- To rid frying pans of fish odor, sprinkle salt in the pan, add hot water, and let stand awhile before rinsing.

Shrimp primping

- After shelling and deveining shrimp, put them in a bowl and wash gently under cold, running water for half a minute. Next, rinse them in a colander under briskly running cold water for about three minutes. When cooked, they will almost crunch.
- Never boil shrimp, it makes them rubbery. Instead, after running them under cold water, put shrimp in pot with a dash of salt and cover with boiling water. Stir a few minutes, then put lid on tightly over pot. Very large shrimp are ready to eat in six minutes, average size in four, and small in three. The secret of perfection is that the pot is never set over the heat.
- Canned shrimp lose their "canned taste" if you soak them for fifteen minutes in two tablespoons of vinegar and a teaspoon of sherry.

Open-and-shut oyster case

- If you soak oysters in club soda for about five minutes, they are usually more easily removed from their shells.
- Clams and oysters are simple to open if first washed with cold water, then put into a plastic bag and kept in the freezer for half an hour.
- Or drop them into boiling water and let them stand for a few minutes. This relaxes their muscles and makes them easy to open with a knife or beer-can opener.

Using Your Noodle

Preventing boilovers

- Lay a large spoon or spatula across the top of the pot to reduce boilovers and splashing while cooking.
- Or first rub shortening around the top of the pot.
- Or add a pat of butter or a few teaspoons of cooking oil to the water. This method also prevents pasta from sticking together.

Perfect pasta

- Bring salted water to a boil, stir in pasta, cover pot, and turn off heat. Let sit for fifteen minutes or until done.
- When done, run cooked spaghetti under hot—not cold—water before draining to prevent stickiness.
- If pasta is to be used in a dish that requires further cooking, such as lasagna, reduce pasta cooking time by one-third.
- If you're not going to serve spaghetti immediately, you can leave it in hot water if you add enough ice cubes or cold water to stop the cooking process. Reheat spaghetti by running it under hot tap water in the strainer while shaking it vigorously.

Three steps in one
- Use your French-fry basket or a large strainer when cooking pasta. It is so easy to lift the basket out of the water before rinsing the pasta and transferring it to the serving bowl.

The best way to store
- After opening a box of any pasta product, store unused portion in a tightly covered glass container to preserve freshness.

Are you a noodle maker?
- If you make your own noodles, drape the noodles over an old-fashioned wooden collapsible clothes hanger to dry.

Pizza with pizzazz
- Try hard-wheat flour or pasta flour (available at health-food stores) for the best golden-brown pizza crust.
- Slice or grate the cheese and put it directly on the dough, under the sauce. Your pizza crust will get crispy without the cheese burning. Also keeps the crust from getting soggy.
- Pizza cuts more easily with scissors.

In Your Cups: Beverages

Ground rules for cutting coffee costs
- Grind beans until coffee is very fine, or use a food processor. You'll need about one-third less coffee than you ordinarily would.
- Use half as much ground coffee as you usually use, and pour water through grounds an extra time.
- Reuse old coffee grounds by placing them in the oven on a flat pan for half an hour at 350°. Then combine with half the usual amount of fresh-ground coffee.
- Coffee too weak? Add a little instant coffee to the pot.

Café mocha for half the cost
- Add one-half envelope of instant cocoa mix to one cup of strong black coffee.
- Put a piece of chocolate or a vanilla bean in the coffee filter before you add the coffee for a special flavor.

Filter tips
- Paper towels cut to size make inexpensive filters for percolators or drip pots.
- Remove some of the acid taste of coffee by adding a small pinch of salt before pouring in the boiling water. Works for hot chocolate, too!
- For clear coffee, put unwashed egg shells in after percolating coffee. Remember, always start with cold water.

Cream scheme
- When out of cream, try the beaten white of an egg in your coffee.
- A tiny pinch of baking soda in cream keeps it from curdling in hot coffee.

Just your cup of tea
- Add delicious fragrance and flavor to tea by keeping a few pieces of dried orange rind or dried orange blossoms in the tea canister.
- Prevent tea from getting cloudy by adding a pinch of baking soda per pot.
- Flavor tea by using sugar cubes that have been dipped in orange or lemon juice.
- If you like sweet tea, add powdered lemonade mix or dissolve old-fashioned lemon drops in your tea.

Hot chocolate
- Skin won't form on the top of hot chocolate if you beat the drink until frothy immediately after preparation.
- Add, per pot, a pinch of salt and a teaspoon of cornstarch dissolved in a little water to improve the flavor and texture of hot chocolate. Try adding a marshmallow dipped in cinnamon to each cup.

Fizzlers

- To reduce foam when pouring carbonated drinks over ice cubes, rinse off ice cubes with water before filling glasses.
- Use club soda instead of water for a bubbly Kool-Aid drink.
- Prepare frozen juice concentrate as directed. Fill glass half full and mix with club soda for a nutritious soda pop.

Juice spruce-ups

- Improve the taste of an ordinary large can of tomato juice by pouring it into a glass bottle and adding one green onion and one stalk of celery cut into small pieces. After it stands for a while, it tastes like the more expensive, already seasoned juice.
- Keep juice cold without watering it down by putting a tightly closed plastic bag of ice into the pitcher.
- Frozen orange juice will have a fresh-squeezed flavor if you add the juice of two fresh oranges to the reconstituted frozen juice.
- To thaw frozen juice in a hurry, spin concentrate with water in a blender for a few seconds.

An Ounce of Prevention

Safety "firsts"

- Keep cold water running in the sink while you pour hot water from a pot of vegetables. It prevents the steam from scalding your hands.
- Don't let oil heat to the smoking point. It may ignite. (It also makes food taste bitter and irritates your eyes.)
- Sharp knives should be kept in plain view in wooden holders—but out of the reach of young children—instead of among other utensils in drawer.
- When broiling meat, place a few pieces of dry bread in the broiler pan to soak up dripping fat. This not only eliminates smoking fat but also reduces the chance that the fat will catch fire.

Quick help for burns
- To help relieve pain from minor burns and reduce swelling of minor bumps and bruises, keep clean, damp sponges in your freezer. When you burn or bruise yourself, apply a frozen sponge to the affected area.
- Soothe a minor kitchen burn by rubbing it gently with the cut surface of a cold raw potato.
- Or dissolve baking powder in cold water to make a paste. Apply to burn and cover with clean gauze.
- To relieve painful burns on hands, dissolve a few aspirin tablets in a bowl of cool water and soak.

In case of fire
- Sprinkle bicarbonate of soda over grease flare-up or blazing broiler. If fire is snuffed out quickly, a partially burned steak may still be edible after the soda is rinsed off.
- NOTE: Never use flour as an extinguisher.
- If fire is in oven, immediately turn off heat and close the oven door. Shutting off the air supply will smother the fire.

The Best
of Helpful
Kitchen Hints
for Baking

Breadtime Story

When you knead a lot of dough
- Oil hands a little, and hard-to-knead dough, such as pumpernickel, whole wheat, and rye, will be easier to handle.
- To keep the bowl from slipping and sliding while mixing ingredients, place it on a folded damp towel.
- The tenderness and flakiness of biscuit dough and pie pastry depend on finely cut cold lard mixed with flour. To keep the fat from melting, handle biscuit dough as little as possible.
- Dough won't stick to hands if it is kneaded inside a large plastic bag. Neither will it stick to the bag or dry out.

Or care about the upper crust
- Press dough into a greased bowl, turn to bring it greased side up, and cover; then the dough won't form a crust while rising in the bowl.
- To brown the sides of a loaf almost as well as the top, use a dull-finish aluminum, dark metal, or glass pan for baking.
- To get the dull finish on a shiny new pan, first use it for something other than baking bread, or bake it empty in a 350° oven.
- Your bread will be crusty if the top and sides are brushed with an egg white diluted with one tablespoon of water.
- A small pan of water in the oven keeps crusts from getting too hard when baking. Spread warm crust with soft butter for a soft crust on freshly baked bread.

Or like it hot
- Place aluminum foil under the napkin in your roll basket and the rolls will stay hot longer.

Or cool
- Let baked bread cool on rack rather than in the pan. Cooling in the pan makes sides and bottom soggy.

Rise to the occasion
- Use water in which potatoes have been boiled to make yeast breads moister. The texture may be coarser, but the bread lasts longer and is slightly larger.

- Add half a teaspoon of sugar to the yeast when stirring it into the water to dissolve. If in ten minutes the mixture bubbles and foams, the yeast is alive and kicking. Or test by putting one teaspoon into a cup of hot water. If it fizzles actively, use it.
- In a cool room: Set the pan of dough in an unheated oven over smaller pan of hot water.
- Or, before baking, put the dough in a container on a heating pad set on medium. The heating pad makes dough rise perfectly.

- If the TV is in use, let the dough rise on top of the set. It's a good source of warmth—and if you're watching a program, you won't forget about the dough.
- Speed up slow-rising dough by putting the bowl with the dough in a large plastic bag; fold the ends of plastic under the bowl.

Put on a shiny face
- Brush a mixture of one tablespoon of sugar and one-quarter cup of milk on rolls before popping them into the oven for a really tip-top glaze.
- For a shiny crust, before putting the bread in the oven, brush the top of the loaf with a mixture of one egg beaten with one tablespoon of milk.

Smooth away wrinkles
- For wrinkled buns, moisten them slightly and heat in 350° oven for a few minutes. No more wrinkles.

Let Them Eat Cake

Better batters
- A beaten egg added slowly to batter prevents the batter from becoming too stiff.
- If you must use all-purpose flour for cake, use seven-eighths of a cup for every cup of cake flour called for. Sift twice to make it lighter.
- To cut down on cholesterol, for each whole egg called for in a recipe, substitute two egg whites stiffly beaten and folded into the cake batter.
- A little flour mixed into the remains of melted chocolate in the pan will get the last bit of chocolate out of the pan and into the cake batter.
- Two tablespoons of salad oil added to cake mix keeps the mix moist and less crumbly.
- Heat nuts, fruits, and raisins in the oven before adding them to cake and pudding batter. That way, they won't be as likely to sink to the bottom of the cake. Fruits and raisins may also be rolled in butter before being added; or put them in hot water for a few minutes. Sprinkle frozen berries, such as raspberries, in cinnamon sugar before adding them to cake batter for a great taste and an even distribution of berries throughout the cake.

Watch my dust
- Use cocoa to dust baking tins so cookies and cakes won't have that floury look.
- Or dust your prepared cake pans with some of the dry cake mix when making a box cake.

Pan plans
- Trace the outline of the baking-pan bottom on waxed paper and cut it out. Grease and flour the sides of the pan only and place the waxed-paper cutout on the bottom of the pan. Pour in the batter. After baking, when you remove the cake from the pan, it won't stick. Gently peel off waxed paper while the cake is still warm.
- Grease pans with a smooth mixture of oil, shortening, and flour to keep cakes from sticking to the tins.

- New tins should be greased and put in a moderate oven for fifteen minutes to prevent burned cake bottoms.
- Take cake out of the oven and set it briefly on a damp cloth to make the cake come loose from the pan.
- If the cake sticks to the pan and seems about to split, hold the pan over a low flame for five to eight seconds and the cake will come out nice and firm.

Done right by me

- If the top of your cake is browning too quickly, place a pan of warm water on the rack above the cake while it is baking in the oven.
- If toothpicks are too short to test a cake for "doneness," a piece of uncooked spaghetti does the job.
- A freshly baked cake that's too high in the center may be flattened to the right shape by pressing the bottom of a slightly smaller pan down onto it. It won't hurt the cake.
- A cake rack covered by a paper towel lets the cake "breathe" as it cools. The cake won't stick to the paper towel, either.
- To keep cake from cracking when baked, avoid overbeating. Too much air in the batter causes cracking.

Serving you right

- If a cake is to be cut while hot, use unwaxed dental floss instead of a knife.
- To cut cake without breaking the icing, wet your knife in boiling water before beginning the job.
- To eliminate mess, freeze your unfrosted cake before cutting it into decorative party shapes. Your cake will slice evenly, too.
- Before adding bananas to cake or pie, dip them in fruit juice and they won't burn.
- Freeze, then thaw an angel-food cake for neat slices and no crumbs.

Flavor savors

- For a moist and fluffy chocolate cake, try adding a spoonful of vinegar to the baking soda.
- When a recipe calls for chocolate slivers, you can make the finest shavings of chocolate yourself. A chocolate bar and a potato peeler will do the trick cheaply and conveniently.
- By adding a pinch of salt to dishes containing chocolate you enhance the flavor.
- To melt chocolate without scorching, always melt it in the top of a double boiler. If it starts to harden after melting, add enough vegetable oil to liquefy.
- Use orange juice instead of water to make a sponge cake more flavorful.

Re-fresher course

- Wrap cake tightly in transparent plastic wrap and let it stand about a day before serving for that extra tenderness.
- To preserve the creamy texture, thaw frozen cheesecake in the refrigerator for twelve hours.
- When storing cake, place half an apple in the container along with the cake to retain freshness.
- Or fasten a slice of fresh bread with toothpicks to the cut edge of a cake to keep the cake from drying out and getting stale.
- Dip stale cake quickly in cold milk and heat in a moderate oven.

Tips to top it off

- To prevent hardening and cracking, add a pinch of baking powder when making a powdered-sugar icing. It will stay moist.
- To prevent icings from becoming granular, add a pinch of salt to the sugar.
- Icing a many-layered cake is easier when you secure the layers by inserting a few sticks of dry spaghetti through them as you go. No more sliding before the icing sets.
- To make your own cake decorator, roll a piece of paper into a cone shape so that one end has a smaller opening than the other. Snip the small end with scissors to make a good point. Put icing in and squeeze it out through the pointed end. A plastic bag will also work well.
- Powdered sugar sprinkled on top of each cake layer before frosting or filling prevents filling from soaking through the cake.
- Try using devil's-food cake mix instead of cocoa in frostings.
- For a delicious frosting, top each cupcake with a marshmallow two minutes before removing pan from the oven.
- If frosting becomes too hard or stiff as you are beating it, beat in some lemon juice.
- To light birthday candles, use a lit piece of uncooked spaghetti as a punk.

Smooth, soft, and so good

- To make a smooth-looking frosting, first frost cake with a thin layer of icing. When this "base coat" sets, apply a second, final coat. It goes on easily and looks superb.
- To keep fudge frosting soft and workable, keep frosting in a bowl in a pan of hot water. Add one teaspoon of cornstarch for the smoothest frosting yet.
- An instant and delicious frosting for cakes and other desserts is made by adding a little chocolate syrup to a prepared whipped topping.

Hello, doily

- For a fast topping for cakes, place a paper doily with a large design on top of the cake, then dust powdered sugar over it lightly. Lift doily off gently.

Doughnut do's

- The more egg yolk you use in doughnuts, the less grease the doughnuts will absorb.
- Or let the doughnuts stand for fifteen minutes or so before frying them; they'll absorb less fat.
- Dip doughnuts quickly in boiling water after removing them from oil. Drain as usual. They'll be less greasy.
- A few slices of potato added to the grease will keep doughnuts from burning.
- Stale doughnuts become breakfast treats when you split them, then dip them in French-toast batter and brown them in butter.
- Use a potato parer or a grater to remove burned crusts.
- For quick and easy doughnuts, use the cap from the cooking-oil bottle to make holes in the center of each biscuit roll from a tube of prepared refrigerator dough. Fry as you would homemade doughnuts, drain, cool, and roll in sugar or frost.

Flaky ideas
- For the flakiest upper pie crust, just brush the top crust lightly with cold water before baking. The crust will melt in your mouth.
- Use ice water in making pie and pastry crust. The cold keeps the shortening intact and makes the pastry flakier.
- Another good way to keep pie crust from becoming soggy is to sprinkle it with equal parts of sugar and flour before adding filling.
- A "nuttier" method is to spread finely ground nuts over the bottom crust. This keeps the crust from becoming soggy and adds a delicious flavor.
- Lard is better than vegetable shortening for making pie dough. While butter imparts a better flavor, it also melts easily when the dough is handled and makes the crust less flaky.
- Brush the unbaked bottom crust of your pie with well-beaten egg white before filling. This keeps berries and other fruits from making pie bottoms mushy.
- Before filling, place pies in a very hot oven for the first ten minutes to firm the lower crust.
- Brush your pie lightly with milk before baking to give it a rich brown glaze.
- Brush your frozen pies with melted butter before baking. The butter eliminates the dryness that freezing causes.
- Rolling pins or pastry boards should be scraped with a knife or scraper—never washed. This prevents dough from sticking the next time around.

Facts about fillings
- When fresh fruit is plentiful and you don't have the time to make the whole pie, try this: Mix the fruit as you would in preparing a pie. Put the pie filling in several pie pans lined with waxed paper or aluminum foil. Cover and freeze. When you have time to prepare crusts or if you want to fill a frozen pie crust, just pop your pie-shaped fillings into the crust and bake.
- Add a spoonful of tapioca to pie fillings that contain especially juicy fruits. The tapioca absorbs the excess juice and keeps the filling in the crust.

- Moisten a narrow strip of cloth with cold water and fit it around the edge of a juicy pie to keep the juice from overflowing.
- Add a beaten egg white to sugar used for juicy fruit pies to prevent juice from spreading when pie is served, or lightly beat a whole egg and add a little flour to the fruit for pies.

Vent-sures
- Before baking, insert tube-type macaroni in the center of the top of your pie so that juice can bubble out.
- Or cut a paper drinking straw into three pieces and place them in the center of the pie for the same effect.

Mile-high meringues
- For the highest meringue, the secret is to add some baking powder to room-temperature egg whites before beating them.
- For a meringue that won't stick when it's cut, sift a little sugar over the top of the pie just before it browns.
- Or butter the knife first.
- Or dip the knife in boiling water before cutting the pie and the meringue won't crumble.
- For a higher, more stable meringue, add one teaspoon of lemon juice for every three egg whites.
- Always spread meringue all the way to the edge of the pie crust. This prevents shrinking and watery edges.
- If you turn off your oven and open the door slightly when the meringue is just perfectly brown, the pie cools slowly and prevents the meringue from cracking or splitting.

Here's the Way the Cookie Crumbles

Coping with cookie sheets

- If you have no cookie sheet or you need extras, turn a baking pan upside down and drop the dough on the bottom.
- To keep cookies from burning on the bottom, cool the cookie sheet before reusing. Run cold water over the back of sheet only, then dry and bake the next batch.
- When cookies stick to the cookie sheet, run the sheet over a gas burner. If this doesn't work, return cookies to the oven for a few minutes.
- Or remove soft and sticky cookies from the cookie sheet with a greased spatula.
- Or rub a piece of crumpled waxed paper over warm cookie sheet and repeat after each batch.

Breaking up is hard to do

- To break up lumpy brown sugar and make it easier to cream into butter or margarine for cookie dough, run it in blender until it becomes soft and fluffy.
- Or grate it.

Dealing with cookie dough

- To make rolled cookies thinner and crisper, roll the dough directly on the bottom of a greased and floured cookie sheet. Cut the dough into shapes and remove the extra dough from between them.
- Or put cookies by teaspoonful on baking sheet. Press with the bottom of a water glass that's first been dipped in sugar each time.

Cookie coating

- To add a crispy coating to cookies, sprinkle a mixture of flour and sugar on the pastry board before rolling out the dough.
- Or add a nuttier flavor by toasting oatmeal topping first. Sprinkle it over a pan and place in the oven, at low temperature, for ten to fifteen minutes.
- Brush the surface with slightly beaten egg yolk thinned with water. Once the coating dries, you can leave as is or paint on some designs.
- To keep molasses cookies soft, add a little cream cheese to the frosting. Not too much, or the frosting tastes cheesy.
- Take cookies out two minutes before baking time is up and they'll continue baking right on the hot sheet pan— and will never overbake.
- Crumble stale, hard cookies, save them in a jar, and use for toppings for coffee cakes or for a pie crust instead of graham crackers.
- To keep cookies moist, keep bread or an apple in the cookie jar.

Cookie cutting

- By dipping the cookie cutter in slightly warm salad oil you get a much cleaner cut. This works especially well with plastic cutters.
- Pack homemade refrigerator cookie dough into large juice cans and freeze. Thaw fifteen minutes, open the bottom, and push up. Use the edge as a cutting guide.

Sweet send-offs

- The best way to cushion cookies for mailing is with popcorn.
- Stale angel-food cake can be turned into delicious cookies. Shape half-inch slices with a cookie cutter, toast the "cookies," and frost with glaze or icing.

Just Desserts

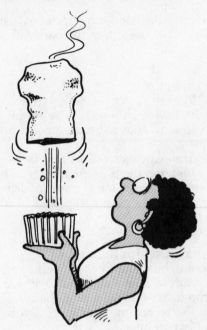

Keep it light

- For a lighter soufflé, fashion a collar from brown or waxed paper or aluminum foil, butter it well, and wrap it about five inches high around soufflé mold. Tie with twine, then pour soufflé mixture into dish. Uncollar before serving.
- To bake a soufflé with a soft center, cook it in a slightly hotter oven and for a shorter time than the recipe recommends. When the top is brown, remove the soufflé from the oven.
- For a lighter steamed pudding, substitute bread crumbs for half the flour.
- Skin won't form on puddings if you place plastic wrap directly on its surface.
- To keep baked custards and puddings from becoming watery, place the baking dish in a pan of water in the oven during baking. The water should be halfway up the dish.
- Spread a thin layer of melted butter or cream over jellies, puddings, and sauces right after cooking. Stir—all the skin and foam will disappear.

- For lighter crêpes, use three parts skim milk and one part water. Using just milk or light cream for the liquid makes a heavier crêpe.
- For perfectly thin and tender crêpes, use just enough batter to cover the bottom of the pan. A thin, thin layer is the secret.

Pancake makeup
- For the lightest pancakes ever, replace liquid in pancakes and waffles with club soda. Use up all the batter; do not store. Close windows before cooking or pancakes may float out!
- Store extra pancakes or waffles in plastic bags in your freezer. Just pop them in the toaster to heat.
- Add several tablespoons of your favorite jam or preserves to one cup of light corn syrup. Heat and serve as pancake topping.

For wonderful whipping cream
- Chill cream, bowl, and beater well.
- Whip cream in a double boiler over ice cubes and salt. It will whip faster and have more body.
- For stubborn cream, gradually whip in three or four drops of lemon juice.
- Add the white of an egg. Chill, then whip.
- Preserve the firm shape of whipped cream by using powdered sugar instead of granulated sugar. The whipped cream won't get watery.
- Cream whipped ahead of time will not separate if you add a touch of unflavored gelatin (one-quarter teaspoon per cup of cream).
- Cover the top of the bowl with a piece of waxed paper in which a hole has been cut for the beater.

Tiptop toppings
- Just as you remove hot baked apples from the oven, top with honey. The honey will be absorbed fully by the apple and won't burn during baking.
- To make a strawberry glaze, mix two tablespoons of strawberry juice, one-quarter cup of sugar, one tablespoon of lemon juice, and stir until sugar is dissolved.

The Best
of Helpful
Kitchen Hints
for Fruits

The Fruits of Success

Peels off pronto
- Place *thin-skinned* fruits in a bowl, cover with boiling water, and let sit for one minute. Peel with a paring knife.
- Or spear the fruit on a long-handled fork and hold over.a gas flame until the skin cracks. Then peel it.
- To peel *thick-skinned fruits,* cut a sliver of peel from the top and bottom. Then set fruit on a cutting board, cut end down. Using a knife, cut off the peel in strips from top to bottom.

Preparing cut fruit ahead of time
- Keep fruit from turning brown by dissolving two crushed vitamin-C tablets in a bowl of cool water before adding fruit.
- Toss freshly cut fruit in lemon juice and it won't darken. The juice of half a lemon is enough for a quart or two of cut fruits.
- For fruits cut in two, brush surfaces with lemon juice to prevent discoloration.

Apples
- Apples keep longer if you make sure they don't touch one another.
- When baking apples, remove a horizontal slice of peel from around the middle. Apples won't shrink while baking.
- Wrinkled skins can be avoided by cutting slits in a few places before baking.
- Soak cut apple pieces in salted water for ten minutes. They'll remain crispy and won't turn brown.
- Dried-out apples will regain their flavor if you cut them up and sprinkle the pieces with apple cider.
- For winter storage, wipe apples dry and pack in dry sand or sawdust. Keep in cool, dry place.

Avocados
- Avocados ripen quickly when put in a brown paper bag and set in a warm place.
- Test for ripeness by sticking a toothpick in the fruit at the stem end. If it goes in and out easily, the fruit is ripe and ready to eat.
- If ripe, store avocados in the refrigerator.

Bananas
- Ripen green bananas more quickly by placing them near an overripe banana.
- Or wrap green bananas in a wet dish towel and put them in a paper sack.
- Store bananas in the refrigerator after they have ripened. The cold, although it turns the skin dark brown, does no damage to the fruit inside and helps slow down further ripening.
- And bananas will keep much longer if stored in the refrigerator in a tightly closed jar. Do *not* peel the skin.

Berries
- Before purchasing, check the bottom of the berry container to make sure it is not badly stained from mushy or moldy fruit. If stained badly, forget it; the berries aren't fresh.
- When you get home, separate the bruised and spoiled berries from the good ones because mold spreads quickly from berry to berry.
- Do not wash or hull any berries until you're ready to eat them.

Cranberries
- Add one teaspoon of butter to each pound of cranberries when cooking them to eliminate foam and overboiling.
- If you add one-quarter teaspoon of soda to cranberries while cooking them, they'll need less sugar.
- Cook cranberries just until they pop. Further cooking makes them taste bitter.

Strawberries
- Strawberries can be kept firm for several days if you store them in a colander in the refrigerator, which allows the cold air to circulate around them.
- Never hull strawberries until they have been washed or they will absorb too much water and become mushy.

Cantaloupe
- *Study it!* The skin color should be yellow-green to creamy yellow—not green.
- *Shake it!* If it's really ripe, you can hear the seeds rattling inside.
- *Smell it!* It should give off a fragrance.
- *Feel it!* The "belly button" should be somewhat soft. If the melon is soft all over, it is probably overripe.

Grapefruit
- The thickness—not the color—of the skin tells you a lot about the quality of the fruit. Thin-skinned fruits are probably juicier than thick-skinned ones. Thick-skinned fruits are usually pointed at the stem end and look rough and wrinkled.
- Let grapefruit stand in boiling water for a few minutes and see how much more easily they'll peel.

Lemons
- Look for lemons with the smoothest skin and the smallest points on each end. They have more juice and a better flavor.
- Submerging a lemon in hot water for fifteen minutes before squeezing it will yield almost twice the amount of juice.

- Or warm lemons in your oven for a few minutes before squeezing them.
- Or roll a lemon on a hard surface, pressing with your hand.
- If you need only a few drops of juice, prick one end with a fork and squeeze the desired amount. Return the lemon to refrigerator and it will be good as new.

Oranges
- The color of an orange is no indication of its quality because oranges are usually dyed to improve their appearance.
- Brown spots on the skin indicate a good-quality orange.
- Pick a sweet orange by examining the navel. Choose the ones with the biggest holes.
- If you put oranges in a hot oven before peeling them, no white fibers will be left on them.
- To increase juice yield, follow hints for lemons (above).

Peaches
- Peaches ripen quickly if you put them in a box covered with newspaper. Gases are sealed in.
- Skins come off smoothly if peach is peeled with a potato peeler.
- Remember when peaches had a fuzzy topcoat? What happened to all that peach fuzz? Today, peaches are defuzzed by a mechanical brushing process before shipment.

Pears
- Ripen pears quickly by placing them in a brown paper bag along with a ripe apple. Set in a cool, shady spot and make sure a few holes are punched into the bag. The ripe apple gives off a gas, ethylene, which stimulates the other fruit to ripen. The ripe-apple trick has the same effect on peaches and tomatoes.

Pineapple

- Don't use fresh pineapple in gelatin desserts. It contains an enzyme that prevents gelatin from setting. In gelatin, use either the canned product or fresh pineapple that has been parboiled for five minutes.
- When pineapple isn't quite ripe, remove top and skin, slice, and place in pot. Cover with water and add sugar to taste. Boil a few minutes, cool, and refrigerate. Fruit tastes fresh and crunchy.

Raisins

- Chopping raisins is easier to do if you put a thin film of butter on both sides of the chopping knife.
- Raisins won't stick to food chopper if they are soaked in cold water for a short time before grinding.

Watermelon

- To test for ripeness, snap thumb and third finger against the melon. If it says *pink* in a high, shrill tone, the melon isn't ripe. If you hear *punk* in a deep, low voice, the melon is ready to eat.

The Best
of Helpful
Kitchen Hints
for Spices

Come Let Us Season Together

Bay leaves
- Place bay leaves in a tea ball for easy removal from a stew before serving.
- Or skewer with a toothpick, making it easy to spot them. The same applies for any other herbs, such as garlic cloves, that don't dissolve as they cook.

Capsicum
- Spices from the Capsicum genus include paprika, red pepper (cayenne), and chili powder. During hot summer months store these in dark containers on the refrigerator-door compartments; they deteriorate in heat and high humidity.
- The best way to store hot chilies is in the refrigerator in a porous brown paper bag, loosely sealed. They will retain their potency for days.

Chives
- To chop chives, a chopping board isn't necessary. Take chives from the freezer and grate only enough for use, returning the remainder to the freezer. That way chives taste the same as when freshly chopped. Do the same with parsley.

Cinnamon
- Add one teaspoon of cinnamon as a "secret ingredient" for deep-fried beer-batter chicken.

Cloves
- Hang an orange stuck with whole cloves in your closet to keep the air fresh and fragrant.

Fresh herbs
- Keep fresh herbs flavorful by soaking them in olive oil; then refrigerate.
- Triple the amount of fresh herbs used in place of dry herbs.

- To release flavor oils from dried or fresh herbs, rub them briskly between fingers.

Garlic

- To get the skins off garlic before chopping, pound each clove with the side of a heavy knife, meat pounder, or a bottle. The skin pops right off.
- Or soak garlic in warm water and the skin will peel off easily.
- To make fresh garlic salt: Cut or mash garlic on a board sprinkled with salt. The salt absorbs the juices. It also reduces the garlic odor. And garlic won't stick to the knife if you chop it with a little salt.

Ginger

- After cleaning fresh ginger root with a scouring pad, cut or chop it up, place in a screw-top jar, then immerse in dry sherry or vodka. This will keep for months in your refrigerator.
- Store ginger by burying it in moist soil or sand. It lasts for months and may even grow into a plant!

Herbs

- Make up herbed and other flavored butters (such as garlic and butter) for a quick sauce to add to a hot vegetable.
- A good idea for seasoning soups, stews, and sauces is to bundle herbs together in a small cheesecloth bag that can be easily removed before serving.

Mint

- When chopping mint, sprinkle a pinch of sugar over it. This will draw out the juices and make chopping easier.

Onion salt

- Make fresh onion salt instantly: Cut a slice from the top of the onion, sprinkle salt on its juice, and scrape with a knife.

Parsley

- You can grow parsley in your own kitchen by cutting a small sponge in half and sprinkling a few parsley seeds over the halves. Put the sponges on dishes on windowsill, making sure to keep them moist.

- Did you know that parsley lends its freshness to other herbs? Try mincing equal amounts of fresh parsley with such spices as dried dill, basil, marjoram, or rosemary. You'll taste the difference.
- Put fresh parsley on a cookie sheet in the oven and leave it with only a pilot light on for a few days to dry it out. Store in jars in a cool dry place.

Pepper
- A few peppercorns in your pepper shaker will keep holes from clogging and give ground pepper a fresh taste.

Rosemary
- As rosemary is a rather splintery spice, you may want to put it in a pepper grinder for grinding over foods.

Salt
- A salt shaker that delivers salt too fast can be easily remedied by plugging up some of the holes. Wash shaker to remove all salt, dry thoroughly, and use colorless fingernail polish to stop up the desired number of holes.
- To prevent clogging, keep five to ten grains of rice inside your shaker.
- Since most recipes call for both salt and pepper, keep a large shaker filled with a mixture of both. A good combination is three-quarters salt and one-quarter pepper.

When to add salt
- Soups and stews: Add early.
- Meats: Sprinkle just before taking off the stove.
- Vegetables: Cook in salted water.

Whole spices
- In slow-cooking dishes use whole spices, as they take longer to impart their flavor.

A common error
- Never keep spices close to a kitchen range—they lose their flavor and color. For best results, store in refrigerator or any other cool dry place.

The Best of Helpful Kitchen Hints for Entertaining and Holidays

Let Me Entertain You

Faking baking
- Before guests arrive, give your home that "What's bakin'?" fragrance. Sprinkle cinnamon and sugar in a tin pie pan and burn it slowly on the stove.

Candle tips
- Make candles drip-proof by soaking them in salt water (two tablespoons of salt per candle and just enough water to submerge).
- Candles burn more slowly and evenly with minimal dripping if you place them in the refrigerator for several hours before using.

Nature's own cups
- Use a large green pepper as a cup for dips. Cut off top, scrape pepper clean of ribs and seeds, then fill with sour cream or other dip.
- Slice cucumber in half lengthwise, scoop out seeds, salt, and drain. Then fill.
- Use halved and hollowed-out melon or orange as a cup to fill with cut fruit.

Keep it on ice
- Fill a large bowl with crushed ice and place a bowl of potato, shrimp, or fruit salad in the ice up to the rim. Add a little kosher or ice-cream salt to the ice to make it colder.
- Your ice bucket is insulated so it will keep foods either hot or cold. Use it as a serving dish.
- Keep ice from melting by putting dry ice underneath a container of regular ice.
- Freeze red and green maraschino cherries in ice cubes. Or cocktail onions, mint leaves, or green olives for martinis on the rocks.
- To keep a salad, dip, or beverage really chilled, first weight your salad bowl down inside a larger bowl filled with water and freeze. Then remove from freezer and fill empty center bowl. Your dish will keep its cool throughout the meal. NOTE: Use only temperature-resistant bowls in the freezer.

Serve without spillovers
- To prevent dishes and tumblers from sliding on a serving tray, place them on damp napkins.
- Or, for silver trays, use a sheet of plastic wrap.

It's fun to flambé
- Any dessert wine can be used to flambé. First heat the wine over a low flame until it starts to boil. Reserving a tablespoonful, pour the rest of the heated wine over the food. Then carefully ignite the tablespoon of hot wine and pour over the food to flambé it. If the original liquor in a flambé pan refuses to light, heat fresh liquor in a spoon, pour over food, and ignite.

The party's over
- Treat a red-wine spill on the rug with ordinary shaving cream from an aerosol can. Then sponge off with cold water. Always test on an out-of-sight area first.
- Or immediately cover the stain with a liberal amount of salt or baking soda. Leave until the stain is completely absorbed, then vacuum.
- Or remove with club soda.

- Remove white water rings from furniture with a soft, damp cloth and a dab of white toothpaste, then polish as usual. Make sure you always rub along the grain of the wood.
- Candle-wax drippings on cloth and carpets can be removed by placing a brown paper bag over the spot and running a hot iron over it.
- To repair a burn, remove some fuzz from the carpet, either by shaving or pulling out with a tweezer. Roll into the shape of the burn. Apply a good cement glue to the backing of the rug and press the fuzz down into the burned spot. Cover with a piece of cleansing tissue and place a heavy book on top. The fluff will dry very slowly and you'll get the best results.
- Smoke smells will quickly disappear when a cold wet towel (wrung out) is swished around the room.

Keep Up
the Holiday Spirit

A "cover-up" for New Year's Eve
- For an elegant New Year's Eve dinner party, use refrigerated Crescent dinner rolls as a quick and easy pastry to prepare a beef Wellington.

Have heart-shaped cake

- Make a heart for *your* Valentine: First bake both a round and a square cake. Cut round cake in half, then turn the square cake so the corners face you in a diamond shape. Place each half of the round cake on the two uppermost sides of the diamond. Now you have a perfect heart-shaped cake. Frost and serve.

The egg hunt is on

- Make your own Easter-egg dyes. Boil the eggs with grass for green, onion skins for yellow, and beets for red.

For April showers

- Color cream cheese with powdered or liquid vegetable coloring as a filling for dainty rolled sandwiches. Try a different color for each layer and slice as you would a jelly roll.
- For attractive individual butter servings, squeeze softened butter through a pastry bag or plastic bag onto a cookie sheet; set in refrigerator to harden.

Gobs of cobs

- For Fourth of July cookouts or other large parties you can grill corn, husk and all. First let cobs soak in water for an hour or so, then secure the ends with wire-twist ties, and place on grill, turning every ten minutes until done (about thirty to forty-five minutes).
- For hot, buttered corn, fill a large quart jar with hot water and sticks of butter. When butter melts and floats to top, dip in the cobs and pull out slowly. The butter covers the corn perfectly.

Keeping pumpkins very well

- To preserve Halloween pumpkins, just spray inside and outside surfaces with a spray-on antiseptic to kill bacteria and keep the pumpkin in shape.

A good measure of blessings

- To be sure your turkey's done, test your thermometer by placing it in boiling water. It should read 212°. If it doesn't, just add or subtract the difference from your reading while cooking. Remember to warm the thermometer in water before plunging it into poultry or meat, and for a more accurate reading keep it away from fat or bone.
- Keep your mashed potatoes hot simply by covering them with cotton or linen napkins and putting the cover back on the pot.

All the trimmings

- Sift a little cornstarch over hard Christmas candy when you put it in the dish. Stir. Candy will not stick together or to the dish.
- To restore a dried-out fruitcake, turn it upside down, poke a few holes, and drop in some frozen orange juice. The juice will melt slowly and spread throughout the cake instead of running right through. After the juice has melted, turn the cake over and the holes won't show.
- Keep fruitcakes fresh indefinitely by wrapping them in a damp towel. Dampen the towel with wine for a special flavor.

It is better to give

- For wrapping an extra-large gift, try a Christmas table-cloth made of paper. It's easy to handle and less expensive than several sheets of wrapping paper.
- For a last-minute gift, keep a best-selling cookbook available and quickly add an inscription.
- Wrap a current issue of a popular magazine and add a tag saying that a subscription is on the way.

Keeping and reusing cards

- Want to save special cards? Giving each card a coating of hair spray prevents the colors from fading.
- Reuse cards you receive for any occasion by putting a little household bleach on a cloth and rubbing gently over any handwriting.

"Choc" it up

- After holidays, shop for the half- and 1-pound solid chocolate bunnies, Santas, Valentines, etc., when they go on sale for half price. Cut up for excellent chocolate-chip cookies or a multitude of other chocolate uses and save more than double your money.

A bowl with punch

- Mix a wine punch in advance so ingredients blend better. To serve the punch fresh and bubbly, add well-chilled club soda just before serving.
- Melting ice cubes won't affect your party punch if you use cubes made by freezing a moderate amount of punch in ice-cube trays. Or fill small rubber balloons with water and freeze them. The colorful ice balloons will float. (Wash balloons well first.)
- For huge cubes to keep punch cold, fill washed milk cartons or salad molds with water and freeze them. When ice is partially frozen add fruit for a colorful touch. Remember, the larger the ice cube, the more slowly it melts.
- Poke peppermint sticks through the centers of orange or lemon slices and float them in your Christmas punch for a beautiful garnish.

Swizzle sticks you can eat

- Use long, thin slices of peeled cucumber for Bloody Marys.

- Make your own "dilly" beans by marinating fresh green beans in leftover pickle juice for martinis on the rocks.
- Use candy canes for eggnog drinks.

Vodka

- Vodka kept in the refrigerator is more flavorful. Pour over ice cubes of frozen tomato juice for a Bloody Mary on the rocks.
- To pour gin or vodka over vermouth-tinged ice cubes, first swirl ice in a few drops of dry vermouth, then empty all liquid from glass for the hard stuff.

Champagne

- Chill champagne bottle in ice bucket only up to the neck, or removing cork may be troublesome.
- If removing plastic cork is difficult, run hot water on the neck of the bottle. Heat expands the glass, causing the cork to pop out.
- Do not chill champagne in refrigerator for hours. Its flavor is more delicate if chilled for only a short while on ice.

Keeping wine well

- Wine from jugs that have been opened can be rebottled and its life extended by being poured into smaller wine bottles, but be sure to leave very little air space between wine and cork.

The Best of Helpful Kitchen Hints for Outdoor Barbecuing

Grill Work

Light my fire
- Pour enough briquettes into a grocery bag for one barbe-cue and fold it down. When you have a quantity of bags filled, pile one on top of the other until ready to barbecue. Then simply place one paper bag of briquettes in the bar-becue and light. The charcoal will catch very quickly and you will have clean hands.
- Pack charcoal briquettes in egg cartons and tie shut. There's no mess and you can light them right in the car-ton in the barbecue.
- To get a quick blaze when you build a wood fire, soak an unglazed brick in kerosene for a day. The brick will start your fire immediately. It will ignite damp logs without kindling and burn for quite a while on the kerosene fuel alone.
- Add a delicious flavor to barbecuing by sprinkling the coals with fresh herbs that have been soaked in water first.

Fast action for flareups
- When flareups from fat drippings start to burn the meat, place lettuce leaves over the hot coals.
- Or keep a pan of water and a turkey baster next to the barbecue, and squirt water to put out flare-ups.
- Or, when flare-ups occur, simply space the coals farther apart and raise the grill.

On and off the grill
- Put the burger fresh from the grill into the bun and place the whole thing in a plastic bag for about a minute. The warmed bag becomes a wonderful steamer.
- Put on a few extra steaks and broil them over charcoal until partly done. Then freeze. At a later date, finish broil-ing them indoors for that outdoor taste.

Marination sensations
- To marinate meats easily, place in a plastic bag with sauce and seal tightly. Turning the bag just once coats all the pieces at the same time.

- To tenderize chicken or pork chops, boil them in a saucepan for fifteen minutes. Then drain and let marinate in barbecue sauce for thirty minutes. Now meat is ready to barbecue.

Fire tending
- To prevent burns when roasting hot dogs and marshmallows on a stick, cut a hole in the center of an old pie tin and slip the stick through. The pie tin shields the hand.
- Or, for other work near the fire, a canvas work glove soaked in water protects hands. NOTE: Never touch extremely hot objects with wet gloves.

Cut the cleanup
- Coat the bottoms of pots and pans with shaving cream or bar soap before cooking on open fire. The black marks come off without much scouring.
- Coat the grill with vegetable oil before cooking. Begin cleaning as soon as the grill is cool to the touch.
- Or wipe the grill with a piece of crumpled aluminum foil while it's still warm.
- Or spray a greasy grill while it's still warm with window cleaner.
- Or, using a thick kitchen mitt, wrap the grill in several layers of wet newspaper while it's still hot. It steams itself clean.

Blow-away insurance
- To prevent picnic tablecloths from blowing in the wind, sew pockets into the corners, putting old keys in each one to weight them down.

- Or put two-sided adhesive tape here and there on the table, especially the corners.
- Or try a fitted sheet for a junior-size bed. Most are the same size as the standard picnic table and fit the tabletop as they do a bed.
- Paper plates won't blow away if you use thumbtacks.

Cool ideas
- Melted paraffin wax, applied to the inside and outside of a cooler leak, will seal it.
- Use a sugar bag instead of a plastic bag for storing ice cubes because it's thicker and insulates better.
- Wrap a watermelon as soon as you take it from the refrigerator in burlap or dry newspaper. It should stay cool until ready to eat.

The Best
of Helpful
Kitchen Hints
for Freezing

The Cold Facts

On your mark
- If you need a label in a hurry when freezing an item in aluminum foil, write food description on a plastic bandage, then peel off the backing and apply to foil.

Get set
- To freeze food in plastic bags, remove as much air as possible. Gather the tip of the bag around an inserted straw, suck out the air, then remove the straw and close the bag tightly.
- Freezing expands food and liquids, so always allow at least one-half inch of space at the top of the container before putting it in freezer.
- Most foods stick together when frozen, so flash-freeze them to eliminate this problem. Spread food on cookie sheet, freeze it, then remove and wrap in airtight containers before returning food to the freezer.
- Always scald or steam vegetables before freezing, as this prevents loss of color, texture, and flavor.

Everybody Freeze!

Bananas
- Run overripe bananas through a sieve or mash them, add a little lemon juice, and freeze. Perfect for later use in cakes and breads.
- Or freeze whole bananas that are on the verge of going bad. They make delicious popsicles.

Bacon

- Lay strips side by side on a piece of aluminum foil or waxed paper. Roll them up lengthwise so they don't touch each other and put the roll in the freezer in a plastic bag. The bacon can be cooked as soon as it is thawed out enough to unroll.
- Crumble those extra pieces of cooked bacon and freeze them. Use as toppings for baked potatoes.

Blueberries

- Freeze them in the basket they come in, unwashed. Wrap container in aluminum foil or plastic wrap. They will keep their color and shape.

Bread (stale)

- Cut into tiny cubes. Brush with melted butter and toast them in the oven for later use as croutons. Then pop them into the freezer.

Brown sugar

- It won't harden if stored in the freezer.

Butter

- Save wrappings from sticks of butter or margarine. Keep in the refrigerator in a plastic bag for future use in greasing baking utensils.
- Unsalted butter can be stored in the freezer indefinitely if it's wrapped and sealed airtight. Salted butter can be stored for a shorter period in its orginal container with no wrapping.

Cabbage

- Wash and dry a head of cabbage with paper toweling, then wrap in a plastic bag and freeze. When defrosted, the leaves are limp and easy to remove and handle. Perfect for stuffed cabbage—and you won't have the odor of boiled cabbage throughout the house.

Cheese
- Cheese that can be frozen includes processed, Swiss, Greek cheese, Cheddar, and even cream-cheese dips. If, after defrosting, the cream cheese appears grainy, whip it well.
- Parmesan and Romano grate quite easily when frozen.
- And fifteen minutes in the freezer makes soft cheese easier to grate.

Coffee
- Coffee beans and ground coffee stay fresh longer when kept in the refrigerator or freezer.

Cream
- Freeze in original cartons if there is a half-inch space at the top of the container.
- Heavy cream whips well if a few ice crystals remain after defrosting.
- Leftover whipped cream: Drop dollops of whipped cream on a cookie sheet, then flash-freeze before storing in plastic bags.

Crêpes
- Stack with waxed paper between them. Let cool and wrap in aluminum foil to freeze.

English muffins
- Separate muffin halves before freezing. Later they'll be easier to toast.

Eggs
- Freeze them whole or separated.
- Freeze whole eggs in ice-cube trays that have been sprayed with vegetable oil. Freeze as many eggs as there are sections in the tray. Beat eggs gently in a bowl and add three-quarters teaspoon of sugar and one-quarter teaspoon of salt for every six eggs. Set a divider in the tray and pour the eggs into it. When eggs are frozen, place them in plastic bags. Each cube will equal one egg.
- Egg whites freeze perfectly for up to one year. Two tablespoons of white equal one egg white.
- Before freezing egg yolks, mix them with a pinch of salt and sugar to prevent coagulation.

Fish
- Freeze in clean milk cartons full of water. When thawing fish, don't forget that the water makes a good fertilizer for your houseplants.

Flour
- Flour can be frozen. Stock up when it's on sale.

Green pepper, garlic, and onions
- Chop and freeze in plastic containers. Keep adding to or use as needed for soups, stews, sauces, etc.

Ginger root
- Peel and freeze whole. When needed, grate the frozen piece.

Hamburger patties
- Flash-freeze individually and stack in aluminum foil.

Herbs
- They're not going to look too attractive when defrosted, but their flavor will still be great.

Honey
- Flash-freeze in ice-cube trays. If the honey becomes granular, simply place cubes in a jar in boiling water.

Ice cream
- Sometimes ice cream that has been opened and returned to the freezer forms a waxlike film on the top. To prevent this, press a piece of waxed paper against the surface of the remaining ice cream and reseal the carton.

Lemon and orange rinds
- Freeze. Grate rinds when needed.

Marshmallows
- Flash-freeze—and no more stale marshmallows!

Pancakes, French toast, waffles
- Too many? Flash-freeze and, when needed, toast in toaster or heat in 375° oven and serve.

Pickles, pimentos, olives
- Condiments in partially filled jars freeze well in their own liquid.

Popcorn
- It should always be kept in the freezer. It stays fresh, and freezing helps eliminate "old maids" when you pop it.

Potatoes
- Leftover mashed potatoes: Make patties and coat with flour for potato pancakes. Flash-freeze, then store in plastic bags. Don't bother defrosting before frying them in oil.
- Leftover baked potatoes: Cut in half; scoop out and mash potato. Mix in sour cream, grated Cheddar cheese, chives, salt, and pepper. Return to shells, then freeze.

Potato chips
- Freshest when wrapped and stored in the freezer. They don't get soggy.

Prunes, raisins, dates
- Dried fruit in partially filled boxes maintains freshness if frozen.

Sauerkraut
- Ready-to-use "kraut" freezes well in its own juice.

Tomatoes
- Freeze leftovers for use in soups and stews. They'll be mushy, but that won't affect the taste.

The thaw
- To defrost meats fast and safely, place meat in its original wrap or foil in bowl of cool water to cover. Pour salt in water and on wrap. Cover with lid and let stand about one hour.
- To defrost frozen ground beef quickly, sprinkle it with the amount of salt you plan to use in cooking. Salt greatly speeds thawing.
- Or try defrosting in your dishwasher, set on the drying cycle.
- Thaw a turkey quickly in an ice chest or picnic cooler placed in the bathtub. Fill the cooler with cold water and change the water frequently.

Freezer-failure emergencies
- To be sure that refrigerator or freezer hasn't defrosted and refrozen while you're on vacation, put a few ice cubes in a plastic bag in the freezer before you leave. On your return, if you find the ice in any other shape but cubes, you'll know you've got problems.

You put these in the refrigerator?
- Keep plastic wrap in the refrigerator to prevent it from sticking to itself when handled.
- Batteries and film stay fresh longer when kept in the refrigerator.
- Hydrogen peroxide won't lose its fizzle if kept in the refrigerator.
- Put your damp ironables in the refrigerator. They won't mildew and will be ready to iron when you are.
- Keep Band-Aids in the refrigerator and their backing will peel off in a snap.

The Best of Helpful Kitchen Hints for Children

All My Children

On the bottle

- Keep the bottom of an electric coffeepot filled with a few inches of water in baby's room and use as a bottle warmer for early-morning feedings.
- Keep extra formula on hand in the refrigerator to add to a bottle of too-hot formula. It's faster than trying to cool a bottle under a faucet.
- Instead of traveling with bottles of milk, which will spoil, carry powdered milk in the bottles in the right amount. Later, just add water and shake bottle.

For crying out loud

- Remove peel and seeds from an orange, divide it into sections, and wrap and put them in the freezer. Baby will be soothed by the coolness when teething and get vitamin C as well.
- Use brown sugar instead of honey in making teething cookies. Honey keeps the cookies too moist.
- Stale bagels and other kinds of hardened bread make perfect teething foods.

Going off the bottle

- If you have trouble weaning your tot, take the nipple off the baby bottle and start him drinking directly from his familiar container—the old bottle.
- Or put a straw in the bottle.

Get a grip on the problem

- If you have trouble unscrewing the lids on baby-food jars, punch a small hole in the top of the lid. The hole lets air out of the jar, and it can be easily opened. If any food is left over, cover the lid with aluminum foil and refrigerate jar.
- A couple of wide, colorful rubber bands wrapped around children's drinking glasses provide a steadier grip for tiny hands. A strip of adhesive tape can also help.

Cleanups

- Get rid of baby-food stains with this solution: one cup of bleach, one cup of dishwasher detergent, and two to three gallons of water. Let material soak a few hours before washing it.
- Also, try rubbing a paste of unflavored meat tenderizer on formula stains. Roll the clothes up and wait a few hours before washing them in the machine.
- To remove odor instantly from spit-ups, apply a paste of baking soda and water to the fabric.

Avoiding falls

- Attach to the back or side of baby's highchair a small-sized towel rack to hold all the things needed at mealtime (bib, washcloth, and towel).
- Prevent baby's highchair from tipping over by screwing a screen-door fastener to the wall. Attach the hook to the back of the highchair and latch the chair to the wall.
- Put a small rubber mat you would use in the sink on the seat of the highchair to keep baby from sliding out.

It's partytime

- Write the invitation on blown-up balloons with felt markers. Let them dry, then deflate. Then mail them to the children, who must blow up the balloon to read the invitation.
- Prepare your favorite cake mix according to directions. Fill ice-cream cones, the kind with flat bottoms, half full with cake batter and arrange on a cookie sheet. Bake at 350° for twenty minutes, cool, and add a scoop of ice cream.

- Use small marshmallows as candleholders for a birthday cake. They prevent the wax drippings from running into the frosting.
- To keep ice cream from leaking through the bottom of a cone, put a marshmallow in the bottom.

Painting the town

- Make fingerpaints in your kitchen by mixing two cups of cold water and one-quarter cup of cornstarch, then boil liquid until thick. Pour into smaller containers and color with various food colorings.
- For a great playdough for your children, mix one cup of salt and two cups of flour and add enough water to make a soft dough. Add any food coloring desired. Keep tightly sealed.
- Make colorful beads from cut macaroni by dunking them into assorted food colors. Drain and dry completely. Pour the beads into individual paper cups and let older children make their own necklaces.

These little kiddies went out to lunch

- Most sandwiches can be stored in the freezer for two weeks. Make them once every two weeks and save yourself a lot of time.
- To keep sandwiches from becoming limp and soggy, spread butter or margarine all the way to the crusts of the bread before adding filling.
- Here are a few suggestions for fillings that can be frozen: cold cuts, peanut butter (jelly does not freeze well), cheese, meat loaf and catsup, chicken, turkey, beef, and tuna-fish salad. (Mayonnaise can be frozen if the filling is no more than one-third of the sandwich volume.)
- To prevent frostbite, wrap sandwiches very securely in freezer paper or aluminum foil.
- Pack sandwiches in the lunchbox right from the freezer. They will thaw in time for lunch.
- Save small plastic pill containers with snap-on lids. They're great for holding salad dressings, catsup, or mustard.
- Make portable salt and pepper shakers by cutting straws, filling with salt and pepper, and twisting ends up.

This little kiddie stayed home

- Turn a Sloppy Joe into a "Tidy Joseph" by slicing a thin layer from the top of an unsliced hamburger bun. Scoop out enough bread to make a bowl. Fill with Sloppy Joe mixture. Replace the top slice and you now have a "Tidy Joseph."

Thermos thoughts

- Wrap a cooked hot dog in plastic and put it in a Thermos of hot soup or water. At lunchtime, the hot dog can be served in a bun. No more soggy buns!
- For a shrunken Thermos cork, boil the cork in a covered pot until it expands to fit the bottle again.
- To prevent the cork from souring in a Thermos, place a small piece of plastic wrap over the cork.
- To protect a Thermos bottle from breakage, cut the foot off a large old sock and slip it over the Thermos.

Choice "kid-bits"

- Sandy bottom: Bring along a playpen minus the floor. Set it on the beach or grass so young tots can play safely while you picnic.

- Brushups: Keep a minuteglass in the bathroom. Following meals, have your child brush until top of glass empties.
- On trays: Serve meals to a sick child in bed in a muffin tin. There are enough compartments for food and even a small drinking glass.
- Smooth sledding: A child's sled will go down the hill faster if you spray vegetable oil on the bottom. Works on inner tubes, too.

Getting gum off hair
- Rub on a dab of peanut butter. Massage the gum and peanut butter between your fingers until the gun is loosened. Remove it gently with a comb, then shampoo hair.

Making sharing easy
- If children argue over who gets the largest portion when sharing a treat, let one child divide the treat while the other selects his/her portion first.

Safety firsts
- Always turn the handles of pots and pans toward the inside of the stove to avoid their being knocked off by children.
- Keep your toddler out of kitchen cabinets by placing a yardstick through the handles of each cabinet drawer.
- Keep tablecloth edges folded up on top of the table so your toddler won't be able to pull them.
- Always keep dishware and utensils in the middle of the table or counter to keep them from falling on your child.
- Your tot will be able to tell the hot-water faucet from the cold one if you mark the hot with red tape.

The Best
of Helpful
Kitchen Hints
for Cleaning

Startin'
at the Bottom

Note: When using these hints, remember: Unplug any household appliance before cleaning it. Rinse and dry thoroughly any appliance, pot, or pan after cleaning and before using it again. Before using any of these hints on floors, carpets, fabrics, lineoleum, etc., always test first on a small corner or, if possible, on an out-of-sight area. Special care should always be taken in households with small children.

The kitchen carpet
- Instant spot removers:
    Prewash commercial sprays
    Glass cleaner
    Club soda
    Shaving cream
    Toothpaste
Apply one of the above to the stained area. Rub it in and wait a few minutes before sponging it off thoroughly. If the stain is still present, combine two tablespoons of detergent, four tablespoons of white distilled vinegar, and one quart of warm water. Work into stain and blot, blot, blot.

Carpet brighteners
- Combine two cups of cornmeal and one cup of borax for an excellent carpet cleaner and deodorizer. Just sprinkle on and leave for one hour before vacuuming.
- Or sprinkle a generous amount of baking soda on the carpet before vacuuming.

A static and shock remover
- Mix one part liquid fabric softener with five parts water in a spray bottle. Mist the carpet very lightly. Let dry and you'll have no more clinging pet hairs or unwanted carpet fuzz on clothing.

A step saver
- Make your vacuuming easier by adding a thirty-foot heavy-duty extension cord to your sweeper cord.

Touch-ups
- Dingy, discolored carpet spots will disappear if indelible ink of the same color is rubbed in.

Sliding rugs
- Throw rugs will stay in one place if rubber canning rings are glued to the bottom.

The Linoleum

The best floor care
- If a mopped floor dries with a film that dulls the luster, pour one cup of white vinegar into a pail of water and go over the floor again.
- Before putting your mop away, soften it by dunking it in a fresh pail of water and a capful of fabric softener.

When you're out of floor wax
- Add one-half cup of vinegar and two tablespoons of furniture polish to a pail of warm water.
- Or add a capful of baby oil to detergent and water.
- Or add some skim milk to the wash water.

It's time to strip the old wax
- Try this solution: one cup of Tide laundry detergent, six ounces of ammonia, and one gallon of warm water.

Nonsticking tiles?
- No linoleum cement available and tiles won't stick to the floor? Apply a layer of denture cream to the back of the tiles. Put a few heavy books over the area and let dry for twenty-four hours.

Heel and crayon marks?
- Black heel marks and crayon marks can be removed by rubbing with a damp cloth and a dab of toothpaste.

Cleaning hard-to-reach places
- Slip a sock or two over the end of a yardstick and secure with a rubber band.
- Or staple a small sponge to the end of a yardstick to reach under the refrigerator and radiators.

Smooth move
- Glue pieces of old carpeting to the bottom of chair legs. The chair will slide more easily and won't leave marks on the floor.

Broken glass?
- To pick up shards of broken glass, mop the area with a piece of soft bread or damp paper toweling.

Movin' on Up

The best wall cleaner
- Combine one-half cup of ammonia, one-quarter cup of white vinegar, one-fourth cup of washing soda, and one gallon of warm water.

Start from the bottom
- Always begin washing walls at the bottom instead of the top and wash upward. Why? If dirty water runs down over soiled areas it leaves streaks that are harder to remove.

To remove everyday smudges
- Erase light marks with gum erasers (avilable at stationery and art-supply stores).
- Or rub the soiled areas with chunks of fresh bread.

Grease spots?
- Sprinkle white talcum on a clean powder puff. Rub the puff over the spot, repeating the process until the grease disappears.
- Or make a paste of cornstarch or fuller's earth and water. Let it remain on the spot for a few hours, then brush it off. If the stain is still present, try, try again.

Filling nail holes
- On wallpapered walls: All you need is a box of crayons. Soften the crayon tip over a match for a few seconds. Wipe it off with paper toweling before rubbing it into the hole. Two or more colors may have to be used to match unusual shades. Wait several minutes, then remove the excess color by rubbing gently with paper towels.
- On white walls: Patch with equal parts salt and starch. Add enough water for a smooth surface.
- Or fill hole with white toothpaste.
- On colored walls: Use one of the above methods but add food coloring to match wall color.
- On woodwork: Mix a little dry instant coffee with spackling paste or starch and water. Smooth with a damp cloth.

Is your screw loose?
- Instead of replacing the paper-towel holder because the screw hole in the wall has been stripped, saturate a cotton ball with Elmer's glue. Gently push the entire cotton ball into the hole. Allow it to dry at least twenty-four hours, then insert the screw gently with a screwdriver.

Disappearing paste-ups
- Hang posters and lightweight pictures on your kitchen walls with toothpaste. It's easy to clean off when you take the picture down, and you won't have unnecessary nail holes.

High-gloss paneling
- Add one cup of any type of time-saving floor wax to one gallon of water. Wash with a soft cloth. This solution helps guard against finger marks, too.

The Windows

The best window cleaner
- Add one-half cup of ammonia, one-half cup of white distilled vinegar, and two tablespoons of cornstarch to a bucket of warm water for a perfect window-washing solution.
- For fast cleanups, wash with a cloth soaked in white vinegar. Dry with crumpled newspapers.

More cleaners
- For stubborn spots, spray glass with oven cleaner. Leave it there for a few minutes before wiping grime away.
- Your windows will sparkle when washed with one quart of cold water and two capfuls of Woolite Cold Wash.
- During the winter, add denatured alcohol to water you use for cleaning windows to prevent freeze-ups.

Curtains

- Kitchen curtains will hold their body and require less ironing if one-half cup of Epsom salts is added to the final rinse water when washing.
- Preventing curtain ripoffs: Cut off the finger of an old glove to cover your curtain-rod end before slipping it through delicate curtains. Plastic bags work well, too.
- A foolproof way to get tiebacks straight across from each other when hanging curtains is to use your window shade as a measuring guide.

Round 'n' Round the Kitchen

The cupboards

- Cold tea is a good cleaning agent for woodwork of any kind.
- Renovate cupboards that have become faded in spots by rubbing and buffing shoe polish of the same color into the stained areas. Two or three different colors may be needed to accomplish the job.

To remove old contact paper

- Run a warm iron over the contact paper and it should peel right off.
- Instead of contact paper, try using floor tiles to line pantry shelves. They clean easily and last forever.

The counters

- To remove juice, coffee, or tea stains, scrub them vigorously with a paste of baking soda and water. Let set for half an hour, then wipe paste up with a wet sponge.
- Nicked Formica counter tops can be touched up with matching crayon or paint.

The oven
- An inexpensive oven cleaner: Set oven on warm for about twenty minutes, then turn it off. Place a small dish of full-strength ammonia on the top shelf. Put a large pan of boiling water on the bottom shelf and let it sit overnight. In the morning, stand back and open the oven. Let it air awhile before you wash it with soap and water. Even the hard, baked-on grease will wash off easily. For a badly stained oven, repeat the operation the next night. (Ammonia fumes are dangerous, so open the outside kitchen door before opening oven door. Do not use this hint in kitchens with inadequate ventilation.
- Put all the removable parts of your stove into a plastic garbage bag and pour in a couple of cups of ammonia. Seal the bag with a tie and leave outdoors for several hours. Rinse clean with the garden hose. No mess and no scrubbing. Try this trick to keep the chrome rings on electric ranges clean.
- Following an oven spill, sprinkle the area with salt immediately. When the oven is cool, brush off burned food and wipe with a damp sponge. Or sprinkle the oven bottom with automatic-dishwasher soap and cover with wet paper towels. Let this stand for a few hours.

Badly stained broiler pan
- Sprinkle the hot pan heavily with dishwasher detergent or dry laundry detergent. Cover with a dampened paper towel and let the burned food stand for a while.
- Or spray with oven cleaner.

The refrigerator
- Add a little baking soda to the soapy wash water to deodorize the inside of the refrigerator.
- To prevent mildew from forming, wipe refrigerator with vinegar. The acid effectively kills mildew fungi.

The freezer
- After the freezer has been defrosted, spray it with alcohol or vegetable-oil spray. The next time you defrost, it will take less work.
- Place a piece of waxed paper under your ice-cube trays and they will never stick to the bottom.

Automatic ice maker not working?

- When ice cubes freeze together and jam up ice maker, hold hair-dryer blower about eight inches from frozen mass until melted.

Butcher blocks

- To clean butcher blocks, cutting boards, and wooden rolling pins, wash, then dry with cloth, then cover with salt to draw moisture out of the wood. Treat with mineral oil to maintain surface.
- To remove gummy dough, sprinkle salt on a wet sponge and start rubbing.
- Scrape butcher blocks and pastry boards with a plastic windshield scraper. It's easier to use than a knife, and it won't mar the wood.

Everything and the Kitchen Sink

All-purpose kitchen cleaners

- Try trisodium phosphate (TSP), available at paint and hardware stores. It's a fantastic cleaning agent. Follow directions carefully: If the mixture is too strong, it can remove paint.

The sink

- When water corrosion or mineral-deposit buildup is a problem, try Chrome-R-Tile, by Santeen Products. It's available at hardware stores.
- Or lay strips of paper toweling around faucets where lime has accumulated. Pour vinegar on the toweling and leave it alone for one hour. Lime deposits will soften and be easy to remove.
- For a sparkling-white porcelain sink, place paper towels across the bottom of sink and saturate with household bleach. Let sit for half an hour or so.
- Sprinkle cream of tartar on a damp cloth to clean porcelain surfaces. This method also removes rust.

- Sprinkle automatic-dishwasher crystals on a wet sponge and scrub. This also works well on bathtub rings.
- Use a cloth dampened with rubbing alcohol or white vinegar to remove water spots from stainless steel.
- Rub stainless-steel sinks with lighter fluid if rust marks appear. Wash sink and hands thoroughly.

Chrome
- To keep chrome gleaming, polish with a soft cloth saturated with rubbing alcohol.
- Or ammonia and hot water—this is terrific.
- Or rub with dry baking soda and a dry cloth.
- Nail-polish remover is excellent for cleaning chrome decorations and knobs, especially on stoves. Be sure that all units are off and rinse well with water.

Stained dish drainers and trays
- Clean by soaking in bleach and water.
- Coat rubber drainboard trays with a light film of furniture polish to prevent staining. It makes the tray easier to clean, too.

Dishes
- Save time and money by using the cheapest brand of dishwashing detergent available and add a few tablespoons of vinegar to the dishwater. The vinegar cuts the grease and leaves dishes sparkling clean.
- When out of liquid dishwashing detergent, use a mild shampoo.
- A large cup hook hung in the kitchen by the sink makes a very handy holder for rings, watches, and bracelets while you're doing dishes.

Rust-free soap pads
- Stop a partially used steel-wool soap pad from rusting by wrapping it very tightly in aluminum foil and stashing it in the freezer.

Want a clean sponge and dish towel every day?
- To add freshness to old sponges, soak them overnight in a bowl of bleach and rinse well in the morning.
- Or wash them in the dishwasher.
- You'll have a clean towel every day if you wrap your dirty towel around one of the wires on the top shelf of your dishwasher and run it through a cycle.

Cookware and Appliances

Blender
- If it cannot be taken apart to wash, fill part way with hot water and add a drop of detergent. Cover and turn it on for a few seconds. Rinse and drain dry.
- To lubricate blenders, egg beaters, and any other kitchen appliances with movable parts, use mineral oil. Salad oil may corrode the metal. Mineral oil is noncorrosive and, like salad oil, it doesn't harm food.

Grater
- When you have two or more things to grate for one dish, grate the softest one first. Then the firmer foods "clean" the openings in the grater.
- After grating cheese, clean the grater by rubbing it with a raw potato.
- Use a toothbrush to brush lemon rind, cheese, onion, or other particles out of the grater before washing it.

Meat grinder
- Before washing the grinder, run a piece of bread or a raw potato through it.

Percolator
- Fill the percolator with water, add five tablespoons of salt, insert the tube, and let perk for fifteen minutes. Restore luster to a percolator by boiling vinegar in it.
- Sprinkle some salt into the strainer and pour hot water over it. This procedure removes the coffee grounds that clog the strainer basket.

- To clean the vertical tube of a percolator, run a pipe cleaner through it.
- To clean glass coffeepots: Drop in five or six ice cubes and sprinkle with salt. Swish around until pot is clean.

Pot holders
- If sprayed heavily with spray starch, pot holders will stay clean longer.

Pots and pans
- Sprinkle burned pots liberally with baking soda, adding a few cups of water. Simmer on stove awhile and then let stand for a few hours. You can usually lift the burned portion right out of the pan.
- Stubborn black burn marks: Heat pan and spray with oven cleaner. Wait half an hour before scouring.
- Stubborn stains on no-stick cookware can be removed by boiling two tablespoons of baking soda, one-half cup of vinegar, and one cup of water in stained pan for fifteen minutes. Reseason pan with salad oil.
- Enamel-pot stains can be easily removed. When a dark brown stain develops, mix bleach with water and boil in the pot until the stain disappears.
- To make your stainless-steel pots shine like a mirror, add one-quarter cup of bleach to the bottom of your dishwasher at the beginning of the cycle.
- To clean the inside of an aluminum pot that has turned black, boil a solution of two teaspoons of cream of tartar and one quart of water in it for a few minutes.
- Or cook tomatoes. The acid in tomatoes will bring back the old sparkle.
- Never use strong soap or alkaline scouring powders. These products darken and discolor aluminum.

A hint that takes the caking— off!
- Drop used fabric-softener pads (the kind you use in your dryer) into cooking utensils caked with baked-on food. Fill with water and let stand for one hour.

Cast-iron skillets

- Boil a little vinegar and salt in an iron skillet and watch the black spots and charred food disappear.
- Clean the outside of the pan with oven cleaner. Let it stand for an hour; the accumulated black stains can then be removed with vinegar and water.
- After washing and towel-drying, place the skillet in a warm oven to complete drying. Moisture is a skillet's worst enemy.
- Or, when it is clean, rub a small amount of oil on the inside of the pan to keep it seasoned.
- If rust spots appear, apply salad oil and allow to stand before wiping thoroughly. If rust spots do not disappear, try the same procedure again.
- Always place paper towels between cast-iron pans when stacking them.

Stainless-steel knives

- To get rid of black spots on steel knives, sprinkle some cleanser on the blade and wet an old wine-bottle cork. Scrub both sides of the knife with the flat end of the cork until the metal is clean.
- To keep stainless steel shiny and bright, rub with a piece of lemon peel, then wash in sudsy water.
- Or use rubbing alcohol.

Teakettle

- To remove lime deposits, fill the kettle with equal parts of vinegar and water. Bring to a boil and allow to stand overnight.
- Or fill with water and refrigerate for about half a day. The lime is worked free by the cold and will come out when the kettle is emptied.
- For Corningware teapots, fill with water and drop in two denture-cleaning tablets. Let stand thirty minutes and rinse well.
- Or pour one-quarter cup of vinegar or lemon juice in the pot and fill with hot water. Let stand a couple of hours and rinse.

Toasters
- Shine up with club soda or a little ammonia and lots of water.
- Use lighter fluid or nail-polish remover to remove plastic that has burned on the toaster and any other electrical appliance.

Waffle iron
- Use a toothbrush to spread oil around waffle iron. When you're finished using the iron, use the same brush to scrub between the rows with soapy water.

Pampering the Valuables

Brass
- Mix equal parts of salt and flour and add a little vinegar to make a paste. Spread a thick layer on the brass and let it dry. Rinse and wipe off paste.
- Or use toothpaste or very fine steel wool dipped in furniture polish.

China
- Before washing fine china and crystal, place a towel on the bottom of the sink to act as a cushion.
- To remove coffee or tea stains and cigarette burns, rub spot with a damp cloth dipped in baking soda.
- Wash plate in warm water, a mild detergent, and one-quarter cup of ammonia. Rinse it very thoroughly.

Copper
- Fill a spray bottle with hot vinegar and add three tablespoons of salt. Spray solution liberally on copper pots. Let sit for a while, then rub it clean.
- Or try lemon juice and salt.

Glass

- Never use your dishwasher or hot water for washing fine glass, especially when it is gold-rimmed.
- Never put a delicate glass in water bottom side first; it can crack from sudden expansion. The most delicate glassware is safe if slipped in edgewise.
- Keep crystal shining by washing in a sinkful of warm water and one-quarter cup of ammonia.
- White distilled vinegar is a must for rinsing crystal. Add one cup of vinegar to a sinkful of warm water.
- Dry with completely dry towels.
- Or try a chamois. It eliminates all lime and water spots, and polishes windows and mirrors, too.

Glass troubles

- When fine crystal stains or discolors, fill glasses with water and drop a denture tablet in. Let stand until discoloration disappears.
- Or mix sand with denatured alcohol and swish it around the glass until the cloudiness is gone.
- Clean vases with narrow necks by dampening the inside of the vase with water and adding toilet-bowl cleanser. Let stand for ten minutes and stains will disappear.
- Or fill with hot water and add two teaspoons of vinegar plus some rice and shake well.
- Or, to clean a glass decanter, chop and dice a large potato into small pieces, put it into the decanter with some warm water, and shake rapidly.

Pewter

- To clean *old pewter*, use a mild kitchen scouring powder moistened with olive oil. For a very stubborn stain, dip very fine steel wool in water or kerosene and rub gently. Rinse with soap and water.
- Today's *new pewter* requires a minimum of cleaning because it is made from a tarnish-proof alloy. It can be cleaned by washing with soap and water.
- Or try a homemade mixture of wood ashes moistened with water on both new and old pewter.

Silver

- Here's an amazing time saver for polishing tarnished silver: Line the bottom of a pan with a sheet of aluminum foil or use an aluminum pan. Add three tablespoons of baking soda or Spic and Span or Soilax to each quart of water used. Heat the water to almost boiling. Dip the silver into the water and let it remain until the tarnish disappears. The silver must touch the aluminum.
- When using silver polish, add a few drops of ammonia and watch the results.
- If polishing only a few pieces, try toothpaste.
- Make sure silver is dry before putting it away. It's best to leave out for several hours after polishing or washing. Dampness can cause silver to rust, which appears as black spots.

Do's

- Do wash silver as soon as possible after it's had contact with eggs, olives, salad dressings, vinegar, and foods heavily seasoned with salt. These foods, especially eggs and salt, cause silver to tarnish rapidly.
- Do place a piece of chalk in silver chest to absorb moisture and prevent tarnishing.
- Do buy silvercloth, the tarnish-retardant flannel, available at better fabric stores, and make your own bags for storing silver. You'll save those extra dollars.

Don'ts

- Don't store plated silver in newspaper. Printer's ink can remove the plating.
- Don't use rubber gloves when polishing silver or fasten silver with rubber bands or place near rubber—rubber darkens silver.

Nose Encounters of the Worst Kind

Refrigerator and freezer odors

- Pour one of the following "odor eaters" into a saucer and place it in your refrigerator: charcoal, dried coffee grounds, vanilla bean or extract on a piece of cotton, baking soda, or crumpled newspaper.

For odors that won't go away

- When all else fails, place a coffee can full of charcoal on the refrigerator shelf and leave it for a few days. Repeat until odor is gone.
- Also make a paste of baking soda and water and spread it all over the inside of the refrigerator. Use cotton swabs to ensure that you get every corner and crevice. Wait a few days before sponging off.
- And make sure the drain pan on the bottom of the refrigerator is clean.

Drain away odors

- Once a week, pour one-quarter of a mixture of one cup of baking soda, one cup of salt, and one-quarter cup of cream of tartar down the drain. Follow with a pot of boiling water, then flush with cold water. This helps keep drains open and free of odors.

Cats and dogs on the go

- To get rid of odors from pet accidents, blot the area with paper towels, getting up as much of the mess as possible. Then shampoo the kitchen carpet or mop the floor with a strong solution of Massengill douche liquid. Carpets may need a few applications.

The nose "no's"

- Eliminate odor in shoes by shaking a little baking soda in them.
- Use baking soda as an odorless deodorant.
- For sweet breath, chew parsley.

Cover-ups

- When the trash compactor is running to full capacity, a few drops of oil of wintergreen will reduce odors.
- Before vacuuming, saturate a cotton ball with lemon juice or oil of wintergreen and place it in vacuum-cleaner bag or canister to deodorize air as you go.
- Add a drop of cologne or air freshener to the wheel of your humidifier. The fragrance will spread throughout the house.
- After cleaning an oven, eliminate the lingering smell by baking orange peels in a 350° oven.
- Lighted candles will help keep rooms free of cigarette smoke.

The Best
of Helpful
Kitchen Hints
for Trash/Pests

Getting the Bugs Out

Bugging off
- Throw a few mothballs in the garbage can to neutralize odors and keep out insects.
- Or sprinkle ammonia around trash cans to keep dogs and pests away.

Downright upright
- Place outdoor garbage can inside an old car tire for a firm anchor.

Roaches take a powder
NOTE: These hints are not for use in homes with small children and/or pets.
- Sprinkle boric-acid powder or borax along baseboards in closets, under sink, refrigerator, stove, etc. Repeat every six months.
- Mix four tablespoons of borax, four tablespoons of flour, and one tablespoon of cocoa. Put mixture in jar lids or bottle caps and place them wherever roaches run.
- Fill a large bowl with cheap wine and set it under the sink. The roaches will drink it, get drunk, fall in it, then drown. This is not a joke. Its been known to have great results.
- Or place a bowl of dry cement and a bowl of water next to each other . . . and guess what happens.

Don't Mickey Mouse around
- Mice can't stand the smell of fresh peppermint. Put the sprigs in mouse-haunted places or saturate a piece of cardboard with oil of peppermint, available at most drugstores.
- If mint is hard to obtain, try trapping mice with a piece of cotton soaked in lard or bacon grease. Mice like to eat lard, and they like the cotton for their nests. Tack the cotton to the bait pan of the trap.
- Another good mousetrap bait is peanut butter. It usually works better than cheese.

Keep insects at bay

- Several bay leaves in a cupboard that has been thoroughly scrubbed are particularly effective against pests of all kinds. The leaves last about a year.
- Or sprinkle insect powder on a slice of raw potato and put it in a spot frequented by pests.

Worm squirms

- A few sticks of *wrapped* spearmint chewing gum placed on the shelf near open packages of noodles, macaroni, or spaghetti keep mealworms at a distance.
- A slice of raw potato in soil surface of potted plants draws out worms that could damage them.

Ant agonizers

- To keep ants out of the house, place whole cloves where they enter. And tuck a few in the corners of your kitchen cupboards and under the kitchen sink.
- Ants are never supposed to cross a chalk line. Draw a chalk line on the floor or wherever ants tend to march and see for yourself.
- Ants are also deterred by dried coffee grounds sprinkled around outside doors leading to the kitchen.
- For a lethal ant concoction, mix two cups of borax and one cup of sugar in a quart jar. Punch holes in the lid and sprinkle around the outside foundation of the house.

The sting

- Treat insect bites with a poultice of cornstarch or baking soda mixed with vinegar, fresh lemon juice, or witch hazel.
- Or try the white of an egg to relieve itching.
- Or rub the area with the juice from a broken rhubarb stalk.

The Best of Helpful Kitchen Hints for Making Do

Using
Something Else

Basting syringe
- Use to water small terrariums.

Cutting board
- For a good cutting board that can be taken anywhere, cover a thick magazine or several layers of cardboard with heavy-duty aluminum foil. It can also double as a hot pad.

Eyeglass case from the kitchen
- Make an inexpensive glasses case from a square pot holder. Just fold it in half and sew the bottom side. If you leave the loop on, you can keep reading glasses on a hook near where you cook.

Flour duster
- Keep a powder puff in your flour container. It's excellent for dusting flour on rolling pins, pastry boards, and other surfaces.

Funnel
- Make an instant funnel for dry substances such as sugar, salt, or flour by clipping the corner from an envelope or paper bag.
- For liquids: Clip the corners from a plastic bag or the fingertip of a rubber glove.
- Or use your gravy boat.
- Or cut a detergent bottle in half and clean it thoroughly.

Ice scraper
- Scrape ice from car windows with a Teflon spatula. It won't scratch the windows.

Measuring cup
- Use an ice-cream scoop; the average one holds exactly one-third cup.

Oyster and clam opener
- Use a beer-can opener to open oysters. Insert the point under the hinge at the top of the oyster and push down hard.

Rack or counter space
- Slide out a refrigerator shelf and use it as a cooling rack if you're baking a lot of cakes or bread.
- Or cool a pie or cake on a gas-burner grate.
- Create extra counter space when doing a lot of baking. Pull out a drawer or two and place a cookie sheet or tray across the top.

Rolling pin
- Use a wine bottle, filled with cold water and recorked, as a quick and efficient rolling pin.
- Or a cold bottle of soda pop wrapped in a stocking.

A ruler
- A dollar bill (or any other U.S. paper money) makes a handy measuring guide. Every bill is six and a quarter inches long.

Steamer
- If you don't have a steamer, improvise: Set a round strainer into a pan deep enough to hold several inches of water. The water level should be just below the strainer so that it doesn't touch or boil into it. You're ready to steam.

New twists for old problems
- Keep bread twist closures in your purse to attach buttons that might come off. Push through button's holes and twist closed on inside.
- Or temporarily repair with a twist eyeglasses from which the small screw is lost.

Using It All

...BUT WATCH WHERE YOU'RE SWINGING!

Last drops of catsup
- To get the last drops out of almost any catsup bottle, grab the bottom of the bottle and start swinging in a circular motion from your side. Just make sure you have the cap on tightly. The remaining drops will be forced to the top of the bottle.

Left with crumbs
- Keep a jar handy to store the leftover crumbs from empty boxes of cereals, crackers, or bread.

Sour wine
- Use it in place of vinegar, especially in marinades.

Flat club soda
- Don't throw away your fizzless club soda. It has just the right chemicals to add vigor and color to your plants.

Milk cartons
- They are free kindling. Start your fires with them. The same goes for candle stubs.

Egg cartons
- These serve as excellent storage containers for jewelry.

Eggshells
- Dry them in the oven and pulverize in the blender to make bonemeal, which is a good plant fertilizer.

Dried-out coconut
- Sprinkle with milk and let it stand until it regains its freshness.

Dried-out dates, figs, and raisins
- Steam in a strainer over hot water.
- Or place in a jar and sprinkle a little water over them. Set in refrigerator for a short time.
- Or heat in a 350° oven for a few minutes.

Crystallized jelly, honey, and syrups
- Set the bottle in a pan of hot water. Heat on stove until crystals disappear.

The last of the jelly
- Heat the jar in a pan of hot water and use the jelly to top waffles or pancakes.

Cardboard tubes
- Extension cords can be conveniently stored without tangling if you wind the cord loosely and slip it into a cardboard tube (from paper toweling or toilet tissue).

The energy crisis

- Use your pilot light in a gas range as a home food dehydrator. Lay chopped food you want to dry (celery, apples, onions, etc.) on foil and put in broiler oven on rack for about twenty-four hours. Store dry food in tightly closed containers. Buzz dried onions or garlic in blender to powder.
- Place small amounts of leftovers wrapped in aluminum foil in a large frying pan in one inch of boiling water. Cover and heat. Only one burner is used, and there are no extra pots to wash.

Teach
an
Old Bag
New Tricks

For shaking

- Place freshly made French-fried potatoes in a paper bag, add salt, and shake. In one easy motion the excess grease is absorbed and the potatoes are salted.

For keeping fresh

- To keep mushrooms from becoming slimy, always refrigerate them in a brown paper bag—never plastic. Paper lets the mushrooms breathe while holding in the humidity that keeps them fresh.

For storing

- Lettuce and celery will keep longer if you store them in the refrigerator in paper bags instead of cellophane. Do not remove the outside leaves until ready to use.

For draining
- To drain fat from foods, cover two paper bags with one sheet of paper toweling. Newspaper works also.

For baking
- When baking a pie, put it in an oven browning bag or a plain paper bag. Cut four or five slits in the bag and twist shut. Place on a cookie sheet and bake ten minutes longer than required time. Crust will turn a beautiful golden brown, and oven spills are eliminated.

Re–news for Nylons

For cleaning
- To clean kitchen drawers without removing the contents, cover your vacuum-cleaner nozzle with panty hose or cheesecloth and fasten with a rubber band.
- Cut the foot off an old nylon stocking, roll it up, and use it with cleansers for cleaning sinks without scratching.

For straining
- Use a clean, discarded nylon instead of cheesecloth for any straining jobs.
- Attach a used nylon stocking to the drain hose leading from your washing machine to shortstop lint that can clog the drain.

For finding
- Covering the vacuum-cleaner nozzle with panty hose and fastening with a rubber band is also a great way to pick up a contact lens lost in the carpeting.

For storing
- Store onions or potatoes in old nylon stockings so air can circulate around them and they'll last longer. Hang inside the kitchen closet.

For tying
- Use old nylons to tie up garbage bags, trees, plants, and shrubs, as well as old newspapers.

For dying
- Two similar stockings of different shades can easily be made into a matching pair. Drop them into boiling water and add a couple of tea bags. Remove them when the water has cooled and they will match perfectly. The more tea bags you use, the darker the shade will be.

Speedy Res–cubes

For household help
- To raise the nap of carpeting after heavy furniture has crushed it, place one or two ice cubes on the area. The next day, the cubes will have melted and the nap will be high.
- Ice cubes help to sharpen garbage-disposal blades.

For aches and pains
- Apply an ice cube immediately to lessen swelling and discoloration of a bruise.
- Or use to numb the area where a splinter has to be removed. This reduces pain.
- Make an instant ice bag by filling a zip-lock plastic bag with ice, placing a towel over bag, and beating ice with a hammer to crush.
- Hold an ice cube in your mouth to desensitize your taste buds before swallowing bitter medicine.

For ice-cube trays
- Ice-cube trays won't stick to the freezer compartment when a rubber fruit-jar ring or waxed paper is placed under the tray.
- Ice cubes won't stick to metal trays as much if the trays are oiled as you would a new frying pan. Coat them, wait a day, then wash with mild soap and warm water.

For crystal-clear cubes
- Boil water first, then chill in refrigerator and freeze. Did you know that boiling water makes ice cubes faster than cold because there is less oxygen in the water?

For cool-downs
- Use an ice cube to cool off children's soup so they don't burn their tongue. Tell them to stir it through the hot soup and that when it is melted, the soup is ready to eat.

The Best
of Helpful
Kitchen Hints for
When Something
Goes Wrong

Too Much

Too salty
- To soup or stew, add cut raw potatoes and discard once they've cooked and absorbed the salt.
- Or add sugar.
- Desalt anchovies by soaking them in cool water for fifteen minutes. Remove and pat dry with a paper towel.

Too sweet
- Add salt.
- Or add a teaspoon of cider vinegar.

Too much garlic
- Place parsley flakes in a tea ball and set it in the stew or soup pot until it soaks up the excess garlic.

Too sour-kraut
- When sauerkraut is too sour, drain and soak it in a large pot of cold water for ten minutes. Stir a little and drain.

Too much mayo
- If you slip and put in too much mayonnaise when making tuna salad and don't have another can of tuna to add to it, add some bread crumbs.

It's a Scorcher

Burned food
- Remove the pan from the stove immediately and set it in cold water for fifteen minutes to stop the cooking process. Then, with a wooden spoon, carefully remove the unburned food to another pan. Don't scrape, and don't include any pieces with burned spots unless they have been trimmed.

Meats
- Soak a towel in hot water and wring it out. Cover meat with it and let stand for five minutes before scraping off burned crust with a knife.

Milk
- Remove the burned taste from scorched milk by putting the pan in cold water and adding a pinch (one-eighth teaspoon) of salt.
- A small amount of sugar added but not stirred will help prevent milk from scorching.
- For easier cleaning, always rinse a pan in cold water before scalding milk in it.

Cake
- Let it cool before scraping off the burned layer with a knife. Frost with a thin coating of very soft frosting to set crumbs. Then cover with another thicker layer.

Biscuits
- Use a grater rather than a knife to scrape the bottom of burned biscuits. If you use a knife, you may end up holding a handful of crumbs.

Rice
- To remove the burned flavor from rice, place a piece of fresh white bread, preferably the heel, on top of the rice and cover the pot. In minutes the bad taste should disappear.

Gravy
- Add a teaspoon of peanut butter to cover up the burned flavor.

Butter or margarine
- Pour it over vegetables the way the French do, or use it for frying eggs.

It's Sticking

Unmolding the gelatin
- Soak a towel in hot water, wring it out, and wrap it around the mold for about fifteen seconds. Then, with both hands, unmold with a quick downward snap of the wrists.

Pasta
- If drained pasta is glued together, reboil it another minute or so.

Fried foods
- When fried foods such as hash browns stick, place the pan on the cold surface of the bottom of the sink or in a large pan of cold water. Slide a spatula under the contents of the pan and everything slides right out. You even save the crusty bottoms this way.

Pastry dough
- If it sticks to the rolling pin, slip a child's sock (with the foot cut off) over it and sprinkle with flour.
- Or place the rolling pin in the freezer until chilled before flouring.

Cakes and cookies
- When a cake has cooled and is stuck to the pan, reheat cake in oven briefly. Still not loose? Place a damp towel on pan and let stand awhile.

It's Curdling

Mayonnaise
- Start over with another egg yolk and add the curdled mayonnaise drop by drop.

Hollandaise
- Remove sauce from heat and beat in one teaspoon of hot water, a few drops at a time. Do not return to heat. Serve warm or at room temperature.
- Or put hollandaise in saucepan over hot water in a double boiler. Add sour cream by the teaspoonful until the sauce is smooth.

Egg custard
- Slightly curdled egg custard can be restored by putting it into a jar and shaking hard.

Butter sauce
- If butter sauce is ruined by curdled yolks, keep heating it until the yolks release most of the butter. Strain out the butter and start over with fresh yolks, using the same butter.

The Best
of Helpful
Kitchen Hints
for . . .
Believe It or Not

Look What Things from the Kitchen Can Do!

Ammonia

- To remove a cork from the inside of a beautiful empty wine bottle, pour some ammonia into the bottle and set in a well-ventilated spot. The cork will disintegrate in a few days.

Bread

- A slice of bread will often remove makeup smudges from dark clothes.

Chili sauce

- Cats hate the smell of chili sauce! If your cat is climbing and scratching woodwork, just rub the area with chili sauce, buff off thoroughly, and your cat will stay clear! (Use this hint only for dark woodwork.)

Coke

- Along with detergent, add a bottle of Coke to a load of greasy work clothes. It will help loosen serious grease stains.
- Battery-terminal corrosion can be prevented by saturating each terminal with a carbonated drink.
- Instead of throwing leftover Coke down the kitchen drain, dump it down the toilet bowl and watch what happens. After it has soaked awhile, the toilet bowl should be sparkling clean.

Flour

- Clean white kid gloves by rubbing plain flour into the leather and brushing the dirt away.
- To clean plastic playing cards, drop the deck into a paper bag and add a few tablespoons of flour. Shake briskly, then wipe completely clean.

Karo syrup
- Grass stains can be removed from clothing by pouring a little Karo syrup on the stain. Rub fabric lightly, toss it into the washing machine, and the grass stain should wash away.

Kool-Aid and Tang
- Clean an electric coffeepot with Kool-Aid. Run it through entire cycle, then rinse and dry it thoroughly.
- Clean the inside of your dishwasher by filling the dishwasher cup with Tang (the orange drink) instead of detergent. Wash without dirty dishes and run it through a complete cycle.

Lard
- If nothing else has worked to remove a grease spot from a solid-colored dress, try this—but only if you feel you have nothing to lose. Work lard through the material, covering every part of the spot evenly. Wash the garment thoroughly in hot suds and rinse well. The spot should have disappeared.

Lemon extract
- Will remove black scuff marks from luggage.

Milk

- Stains from ballpoint pens can be removed by sponging the area with milk until stain disappears.
- Red-wine stains on linen can be removed by immediately putting the material into a pot containing enough milk to cover the stained area. Bring to a boil and remove from burner. Let stand until the stain has completely disappeared. This method should also work on older wine stains.
- A simple way to remove cracks in china cups is to simmer the cup in milk for thirty to forty-five minutes, depending on the size of the crack. If the crack is not too wide, the protein in the milk will seal it.

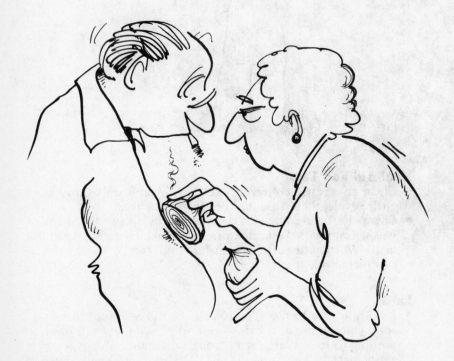

Onions

- Light scorch stains on linen can sometimes be removed by rubbing the cut side of an onion over the stain. Then soak material in cold water.

Oven
- Have your tennis balls lost their bounce? If so, place the can of balls with the lid off overnight in a closed oven. The heat from the pilot light will get them back into shape.

Rice
- When postage stamps won't stick to the envelope, apply a few grains of cooked rice or some evaporated milk as a good emergency substitute for glue.

Salt
- A handful of salt in the washday rinse water will help keep clothes from sticking or freezing to the clothesline on damp, cold days.

Spoons
- To banish onion, garlic, and bleach odors from hands, put all five fingers on the handle of a stainless-steel spoon and run cold water over fingers.

Spaghetti
- To light candles in tall, deep containers, use a lit uncooked piece of spaghetti.

Tomato juice
- Help banish the odor from a new hair permanent. Apply enough juice to saturate dry, unwashed hair. Cover hair with a plastic bag and wait fifteen minutes. Rinse hair a few times before shampooing thoroughly.

Vegetable-oil spray
- Before cutting tall, damp grass, spray the cutting blade of the lawn mower with vegetable-oil spray and wet grass won't stick.

And Two More Amazing Hints

- If you have a cast-iron skillet without wooden handles that is encrusted with hard, baked-on outside grease, clean it by putting the pan in the fire in your fireplace. Let it get red for an hour or so. When it has cooled off, wash off soot with soapy water, then dry and oil it. It'll come out clean as a whistle.
- To prevent drinking glasses from cracking when filled with hot liquids (coffee, hot chocolate, etc.), place new glasses in a large pot. Fill the pot with cold water so the water covers the glasses entirely. *Slowly* bring the water to a boil. Turn the heat off and let the water cool. The glasses will never crack from hot beverages.

Index

A

B

C

E

Furniture Care (cont.)
*pots on, 187; dusting, 161;
cornstarch for high-gloss, 161;
polishing tools, 161; wax buildup,
161; tables and sunlight, 162;
wrought iron, 162. (See Also Chairs;
Sofas; Tables; Upholstery)*

Furniture Polish Uses: *ashtray
cleaning 138; for brooms, 166; as
coating for stove wall, 143*

Furniture Stains, 320

Furs: *care of, 150–151; storage, 159*

Fuse Box Switches, 173

Fuzz Balls on Clothing, 69

Fuzz (Carpets), 343

G

Garage: *security clamps on doors, 203;
floor cleaning, 241; peephole viewer
for, 203; tight space and car
protection, 241*

Garage Floors, 65

Garage Sale and Prices, 252

Garbage Disposal, 28

**Garbage Disposal Blade
Sharpening,** 370

Garbage and Trash Cans, 361

Garden Tools, 65; *carrier for, 185;
handles painted, 185; avoiding rust,
185; trowel marks when planting,
185*

Gardens. *(See Plants)*

Gardening and Gardens, 185–187;
*aluminum foil as light reflector, 187;
homemade compost, 186; mulch,
186; outside faucet tips, 187;
planting of trees, 185. (See Also
Flowers; Garden Tools; Lawns;
Planting; Plants; Shrubbery; Trees)*

Garlic, 33; *bread for lamb roast, 281;
dried, powdered in blender, 368;
freezing of, 333; hand odors, 381; for
salad bowls, 267; salt, made fresh,
315; skinning of, 315; too much of,
373*

Garnishes: *for cocktails, 318; for*

*eggnog, 324; for punch, 323; and
pineapple, 312*

Gas Leaks, 84

Gelatin: *unmolding, 20, 375; for
fingernails, 210; for plants, 187*

Gems, *cleaning of, 152*

Geraniums, 106

Get-Well Greeting Cards, 207

Gifts, 323; *and airline security
inspection, 246; from new baby,
192; balloons, 229; for bride, 230;
for expectant mother and father,
229; inexpensive, 229; duplicate
receipts for returns, 228; recipe
combined with ingredient, 229; for
good report card, 198; telephone gift
certificates, 230; thank-you photos,
228; original wrappings, 228;
wrapped for mailing, 228. (See Also
Birthdays; Parties)*

Gift Wrapping, 117

Gin and Vermouth, 324

Ginger Ale for Salty Ham, 280

Ginger Root: *cleaning and storing,
315; freezing of, 333*

Glass, 78

Glass Coffeepots, 353

Glass Replacement, 125

Glasses. *(See Eyeglasses)*

Glass-Top Tables, *cleaning of, 163*

Glassware: *cracks in, 382; washing of,
356. (See Also Broken Glass)*

Glove Compartment Items, 240

Gloves, 378; *for car, 115; darning of,
224; wet, for barbecuing, 327;
cleaning white kid, 378. (See Also
Mittens)*

Glue Removal, 54, 79

Glue Substitutes, 381

Gluing Tips, 171

Golf Balls and Clubs, *cleaning of, 139*

Grapefruit, 310

Grass, 107; *cutting of, 381; stains,
379. (See Also Lawns)*

Graters, 29

Grating Cleaning, 352

Grating Tips: *cheese, 278, 332, 352;
chives, 314; potatoes for pancakes,
274; soft foods first, 352*

I

J

K

W

More Helpful Hints
to Remember